Praise from entrepreneurs for *Feed the Startup Beast*

"Williams and Verney have written the operating manual for driving market share and revenue in the twenty-first century. They simplify a number of deeply complex marketing concepts and practices in a way that anyone can quickly put them into practice with tangible results. Most refreshing is that they put the customer in the center of every chapter and discussion. Drawing on personal and client experience, they lay out and explain the 7 Steps to identifying your target market, setting revenue targets, leveraging digital marketing, nurturing leads and customer relationships, and measuring the progress being made along the way. Well written and fun to read, there is something in this book for everyone—startups as well as established companies."

CHRISTINE CRANDELL, chief experience innovator,
New Business Strategies;
Forbes and Huffington Post blogger

"You're an entrepreneur, not a marketer, right? Wrong! Every startup's growth requires people eager to buy its products and services. But customer enthusiasm doesn't magically happen. In this important book, you'll learn how to create the fuel that flies your business like a rocket ship to success."

DAVID MEERMAN SCOTT, bestselling author of
The New Rules of Marketing and PR,
now in over 25 languages from Bulgarian to Vietnamese

"There are a lot of great marketing ideas in this book. If you use just a few of them, you'll be way out ahead of your competitors. If you use all of them, your competitors had better dive for cover."

LOIS GELLER, author of *Customers for Keeps* and *Response!*
and contributor at Forbes.com

"*Beast* is indispensable for the ambitious entrepreneur looking to successfully navigate the treacherous waters of growing a business while running it. Its 7 Steps provide a trusty compass, leaving you with a plan that is executable, measurable, and repeatable. As I work on building Guide, my third company after Bradshaw Vineyards and JESS3, I am finally reaching a level of wisdom that *Beast* already contains."

LESLIE BRADSHAW, serial entrepreneur and contributor at Forbes.com

A 7-Step Guide to
BIG, HAIRY, OUTRAGEOUS
Sales Growth

FEED THE
STARTUP
BEAST

DREW WILLIAMS AND **JONATHAN VERNEY**

Mc
Graw
Hill
Education

New York   Chicago   San Francisco   Athens   London   Madrid
Mexico City   Milan   New Delhi   Singapore   Sydney   Toronto

1 2 3 4 5 6 7 8 9 0   DOC/DOC   1 9 8 7 6 5 4 3

ISBN   978-0-07-180905-4
MHID   0-07-180905-8

e-ISBN   978-0-07-180906-1
e-MHID   0-07-180906-6

Library of Congress Cataloging-in-Publication Data

Williams, Drew.
  Feed the startup beast : a 7-step guide to big, hairy, outrageous sales growth / by Drew Williams and Jonathan Verney.
      pages cm.
  ISBN-13: 978-0-07-180905-4 (alk. paper)
  ISBN-10: 0-07-180905-8 (alk. paper)
  1. Small business marketing. 2. Marketing—Management. 3. Small business—Growth. I. Verney, Jonathan. II. Title.
  HF5415.13.W535 2013
  658.8'02—dc23
                                                                                          2013004770

McGraw-Hill Education books are available at special quantity discounts to use as premiums and sales promotions or for use in corporate training programs. To contact a representative, please visit the Contact Us pages at www.mhprofessional .com.

This book is printed on acid-free paper.

A Note

Within this book we make reference to several third party, web-based software tools that we think are worth your considering. We do not receive any compensation for these mentions. We highlight them only because we think they have the potential to make your life easier. As well, given the breakneck pace of the web, it's possible that by the time you read this, some of these software tools may no longer exist. For an updated list of active and alternative tools, please visit our website at http://tools.FeedTheBeast.biz.

To access our tool site on your mobile device, use this QR Code.

QR Code
tools.FeedTheBeast.biz

CONTENTS

A Beastly Foreword

I believe that startups are at the core of everything we do. Every company, institution, and city begins as a startup. It's likely that our country was the ultimate startup. And now, faced with a world economy that's determined to go sideways for a while, the startup has a more important role to play in our future than at any time in history. The creativity, innovation, and drive that produced such forces as Zipcar, Salesforce.com, and LinkedIn need to be encouraged and unleashed so we can bootstrap ourselves into this twenty-first century on our terms. So how do we do that? I'd like to suggest that one of the most important things we can do as entrepreneurs is to learn.

Most startups struggle with the idea and the practice of marketing. If you started a business, it was probably to write software, produce exciting creative content, build great buildings, or make chocolate. It wasn't to become a marketer. In fact, marketing may well be the necessary evil that you grudgingly haul out every year or two, when your business threatens to stall. This is the first thing that we, as entrepreneurs, have to unlearn. To succeed, you must become a marketer.

It isn't a fluke that Steve Jobs, one of the greatest technology entrepreneurs of the last century, wasn't even a technologist. He was a marketer.

We live in a time of hyper-competition driven by technologies that make it easier to start a business, easier to create comparable products, and harder to get the attention of intensely informed buyers. To succeed as an entrepreneur today, you need to understand your prospects' needs with laser precision. You need to know how they think and speak about their needs. You need to understand how their needs affect what they do. You need to know where to find these prospects and how to break through to them so that you can earn their consideration. You need to develop meaningful relationships with these prospects on their terms. You need to be a marketer.

I first met Drew Williams, marketer, at the turn of the century during a time that may one day be called "the revenge of the entrepreneurs." This was the dot-com era, filled with irrational exuberance, when suddenly anything was possible, and everyone wanted to be an entrepreneur. We fast-forward to today, and while we've mostly left the irrational part behind, the exuberance is still with us. Many of us today want to be entrepreneurs because being an entrepreneur feels meaningful and exhilarating.

Drew is an exuberant entrepreneur who actually wanted to be a marketer. He's poured 30 years of his marketing passion into this book, which is designed to help you, the entrepreneur, become an effective marketer. With his cowriter, Jonathan Verney, they've created a unique idea in *Feed the Startup Beast*, which I'll call marketing leverage: doing only the stuff that matters, to get the biggest possible return on your effort. There just aren't many marketing books out there that do that. *Beast* gives you a seven-step marketing system that you can use, that actually works, and that lets you get back to the work that made you become an entrepreneur in the first place.

If you are an entrepreneur who's out to change our future for the better, I suggest that one of the guides you carry around in your back pocket is *Feed the Startup Beast*. When the beast is fed, the world becomes a less uncertain place.

Brad Feld
Managing Director, Foundry Group
February 2013

Preface

Businesses are Beasts. When the Beast is happy, there's lots of back-slapping and everyone gets to go on cruises. But when the Beast gets hungry, things change. Suddenly heads start disappearing and bodies start flying. It's not a pretty thing.

Keeping your Beast happy is hard. In fact, it's so hard that 80 percent of entrepreneurs fail at it. But it doesn't have to be that way. The fact is, the ingredients for growth are well known: Patience, Persistence, and a Plan. The first two *P*s are up to you. This book will help you with the third *P*—the Plan.

But not just any plan, mind you. If you want to achieve success beyond your wildest dreams, you need an intensive action plan, a roadmap with a clear focus and a compelling purpose. You need something concrete that will *transform* your marketing and help turn it into the most powerful weapon your business has ever had. That's what this book is all about. *Feed the Startup Beast* is for every entrepreneur who dreams of building something special but struggles with how to make it happen.

What you'll find inside this book is a roadmap unlike any other. Each of the 7 Steps along the road is designed to help your Beast unleash its underutilized power. To help you absorb the process quickly, you'll follow three entrepreneurs—fictional composites of real-world businesses—as they follow the Steps and find success. The 7 Steps are easy and affordable to execute because each makes use of readily available, street-tested marketing tools and techniques that any business that depends on sales leads can use.

How do I know all of this? Over the last 30 years, I've marketed everything from television to high-tech to financial services to chocolate as head of marketing for a $10 billion company, a $100 million company, and a $10 million company. Along the way, I started and ran six businesses and was lucky enough to sell business number four for eight figures to a Boston-based software firm. I've also practiced digital marketing since 1993, when I started one of the earliest blogs out there on GE's GEnie online service.

Through all of it, here's what I found out: *the smallest marketing efforts can produce outsized sales results if you focus on the right things.* Believe me, there's a world of wrong things you can focus on. I know because I've worked my way through most of them. So here, in this book, I'd like to share with you what works.

One more thing. This book isn't mine alone. I couldn't have completed it without the invaluable insight, creativity, and dogged persistence of my writing partner, Jonathan Verney. This book springs from both our minds.

Drew Williams

Introduction: Out of the Wilderness

*I haven't had a full night's sleep in weeks. Holding onto customers
is tough enough, but getting new ones is incredibly expensive. Remind me
one more time why I decided to become an entrepreneur.*

Does this sound familiar? Do you lie awake at night trying to make sense of things that don't make sense, wondering if tomorrow will be your breakthrough or your breakdown? Do you feel like you're operating in a marketing wilderness filled with bigger and more aggressive competitors who seem to know where they're going, have deeper resources, and are way more marketing savvy?

Well, appearances can be deceiving. Thanks to the web, there's never been a better time to be a growth-oriented entrepreneur—provided you're willing to embrace the digital world in innovative new ways. The truth is, the Internet has leveled the playing field. Today, more than ever before, marketing success is no longer about having the deepest pockets. Rather, it's about having great information, great tools, and a great pair of ears.

Why the ears? Because great ideas come from listening. And great ideas, systematically applied, are the foundation of marketing success and sales growth.

ABOUT THIS BOOK

This is no book of theory. Inside these pages is a real-world program designed for business-to-business entrepreneurs just like you. Whether you're wondering how to get your startup off the ground or searching for answers as to why your business has stalled, you've come to the right place. But understand this: if you're good with just letting things roll along, if you're more comfortable walking your business than running it, you might want to find another book to read. Seriously. Life's too short.

On the other hand, if you're a hardworking, driven, ambitious, energetic, open-minded, impatient, left-brained, right-brained, or whole-brained entrepreneur looking to kick-start your business or start a new one, *Feed the Startup Beast* is perfect for you.

LISTEN TO YOUR BEAST

Every business is a Beast. When you hear rumblings in its belly, your Beast is trying to tell you something, and if your Beast could talk, this is the very first thing you'd hear:

They say armies march on their stomachs. So do Beasts. And what separates the biggest, baddest, boldest Beasts from the rest of the herd isn't genetics or money or luck or good timing (although these can help). It's the quality of what's inside their stomachs. Beasts that enjoy Big, Hairy, Outrageous Sales Growth are fueled by a steady diet of high-quality sales prospects who are primed to be converted into customers.

If your Beast is struggling or has lost a bit of its mojo, the first thing you need to do is listen to the rumblings.

Intuit's founder did.

Scott Cook grew his accounting software firm into a multi-billion-dollar business by successfully exploiting two trends—the rise of the personal computer and the growing need for people to manage their personal finances electronically. For years, Intuit made its name selling personal finance software, but then one day Cook discovered something extraordinary. He learned that a substantial percentage of his customers were using his software for *business* purposes.

Cook listened to the rumblings in his Beast, changed course, and made Intuit into one of the world's leading providers of personal *and* small business accounting software. Cook's story reminds us that no matter how innovative our products or services may be, our customers drive the bus, not us. That is one of the organizing themes of this book.

HOW THIS BOOK IS ORGANIZED

Feed the Startup Beast is divided into two parts.

Part One (Steps 1–3) shows you how to breathe new life into your slumbering Beast by focusing your marketing strategy. (*Strategy* is one of those "big" words, but really it's just about listening better.)

Part Two (Steps 4–7) leads your Beast into the land of Big, Hairy, Outrageous Sales Growth by building a Beast-enriching marketing and sales funnel.

Part One: Focus

In Part One, you'll discover how a single question can reveal your business's growth potential and help predict whether it's going to be a Beast or a bust. You'll identify your most profitable best customers, discover your business's true value proposition, and learn who your "Beast" prospects are. You'll learn why the Laws of Engagement lie at the core of your marketing success and how your Engagement Spreadsheet lays the foundation for growth.

Figure I.1 The Beast Cave

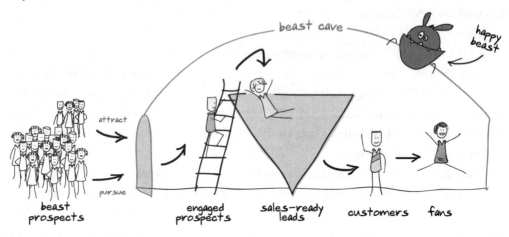

Part Two: Grow

Part Two of the book is all about unleashing your Beast and growing it outrageously fast, using a variety of powerful tools that no successful entrepreneur should be without. You'll learn specific tactics to get more prospects into your Beast Cave, tactics to nurture them up your Engagement Ladder, and then useful approaches to close the gap between the marketing ladder and the sales funnel—making sure that whoever sells for you is fully engaged through the whole process and is better able to close the new Sales-Ready Leads you're now delivering (see Figure I.1).

HOW TO GET THE MOST OUT OF THIS BOOK

If your goal is to give your business a swift kick in the pants, read and implement the three Steps in Part One. However, if your goal is Big, Hairy, Outrageous Sales Growth, you need to go further and read and implement all 7 Steps. The choice is yours, of course. But whatever route you choose, our hope is that you'll make *Feed the Startup Beast* your constant companion, because it will equip you with a marketing system that will help you succeed and arm you with the tools and shortcuts you need to do so, *even on the tightest budget.*

　　A quick note: This book is geared toward growth-oriented businesses that sell a complex product or service (a "considered purchase" from the buyer's point of view)—typically involving a higher selling price, the need for sales leads, a sales team, and a longer sales cycle. The 7 Steps work particularly well for small- and medium-sized businesses with limited budgets. But all businesses that depend on *sales leads* can benefit from developing a better repeatable marketing system that works, which is what *Feed the Startup Beast* offers.

The 7 Steps

Marketing doesn't have to be complicated, no matter what you've heard. In a world of shiny objects (the latest technology innovation goes here) and hyper competition (good ideas travel faster than ever), the basics still apply: buyers have pains, and if those pains are big enough, buyers will pay to have those pains resolved. A retailer suffering from the pricing practices of Amazon.com will pay to get real-time visibility into Amazon's pricing movements. A real estate agent who needs to turn homes more quickly by sprucing them up prior to sale will engage a trusted design partner to sell the homeowner on the idea and then execute the transformation. A retail buyer looking for creative ways to enhance gross margins will gladly work with a supplier who adds resources to her team so she can find new margins in unexplored areas. *Your job is to earn the right to be considered as the solution to a potential buyer's pain.*

Successful marketing is all about the 80-20 rule. Of all the marketing things you can do in the world, only 20 percent of them probably count for anything. That 20 percent will vary from company to company, so the question becomes, *how do you figure out which 20 percent to focus on for your business?*

That's what *Feed the Startup Beast* will help you do. *Feed the Startup Beast* is a simple, easy-to-follow marketing system for growth-oriented and profit-minded entrepreneurs. Through a series of seven discrete but interrelated Steps that build in sequence, *Feed the Startup Beast* shows you that it *is* possible to substitute finesse (the right tactics) for brute force (big budgets). You're going to get to know these seven Steps quite well. They're not only the core around which this entire book is structured; they're going to be your future traveling companions. So let's introduce them:

Ask

If you ask the right question, your customers will tell you whether your business is likely to be a Beast (a great success) or a bust (Yikes!). Isn't that worth finding out before you spend any (more) of your scarce capital on marketing? This first and most important of the 7 Steps is about understanding what your customers are really saying about you. (No customers yet? Don't worry, we have some thoughts for you, too.)

Listen

The next step is to listen to the rumblings inside the belly of your Beast. These are your customers talking. If you want to make sense of their rumblings (and you really do), you have to listen as if your future depends on it—because it pretty well does.

Focus

Getting ready is the secret to success, said Henry Ford. That's why Step 3 is about laying the groundwork and focusing your marketing resources with the help of your new best friends: your website, your Engagement Spreadsheet, your Engagement Pages, and your sales team.

Attract

Today, the majority of business buyers begin their decision-making process by researching online. If you're not being picked up by search engines and social media sites (and it's quite possible you aren't), you're not only invisible, your Beast is limping around with one arm and one leg tied behind its back. Step 4 introduces you to the secrets of "being found" by your prospective buyers.

Pursue

Getting found is great, but it's not enough. You have to pursue prospects as well. Step 5 is going to focus your marketing efforts like never before, showing you the secrets of proactively "finding" and engaging your Beast Prospects.

Nurture

Here's where your Attraction and Pursuit strategies (Steps 4 and 5) pay off. Using everything you've learned to this point, you'll start feeding your Beast by nurturing your prospects and converting them to Sales-Ready Leads for your sales team to close.

Grow!

Step 7 is what happens in the secret room inside your Beast Cave behind the big Oz mask. This is where all the measuring is taking place. Done right, a steady, predictable flow of your prospects will become customers and then later fans (and some of your best salespeople). Now's the time to manage the results and measure your success in dollars and cents as you build toward your ultimate goal: Big, Hairy, Outrageous Sales Growth.

The 7-Step Cycle

These 7 Steps form a repeatable cycle that brings together, in one concise marketing system, the most widely acknowledged best practices in marketing today (we call them Beast practices) with a few twists of our own thrown in. Underlying it all is this one idea: *the simpler we can keep it, the better you'll be able to use it.* So our motto is simplicity.

Jim Collins introduced the concept of the business flywheel in his book *Good to Great.* Think of the 7-Step Cycle (see Figure I.2) as your marketing flywheel, where each of the 7 Steps you complete causes the marketing flywheel to rotate with increasing speed, energy, and momentum. When you repeat the complete 7-Step Cycle, the effect is even greater. Before long you'll hear the unmistakable "whoosh" of Big, Hairy, Outrageous Sales Growth. You might want to dog-ear this page, because you'll want to refer back to this diagram as you go through the book.

Figure I.2 The 7-Step Beast Marketing System

A word of caution. The 7 Steps and the methodology behind them may not be for everyone. You must have the courage to hear the truth from your customers, and you must be willing to let them change your direction and maybe even let them drive the bus. If you're willing to do this, the sky's the limit. And the best part? You'll find that your customers are more than willing to help you out. All you have to do is ask.

So let's start asking.

PART ONE

Focus Your Beast

How a single question can reveal your future

Step 1 ASK

CHAPTER 1

Understanding
Your Beast

What you'll find in this chapter:
- Beast or bust?
- The one question you *must* ask
- Fans, Fence-sitters and Critics
- A home stager sees the light
- A chocolate manufacturer gets a sweet gift
- A software developer finds his calling

We want you to *stop* marketing.

Right now.

This very minute.

Until you've asked a question. In fact, it's probably the single most important question you'll ever ask if you want your business to grow *outrageously* fast. It may seem hard to believe at first, but by asking your customers this question, you can virtually predict your company's future growth.

This is The Question:

> *How likely are you to recommend my [product/service/company]*
> *to a colleague or business associate?*

Sounds innocuous enough, doesn't it? Well, looks can be deceiving. Remember those three *P*s we mentioned earlier—Patience, Persistence, and a Plan? Well, all the patience and persistence in the world won't matter if the third *P*—the Plan—isn't up to snuff. The Plan is the secret sauce that's going to make your Beast perk up, smack its lips, and become a winner. And before you can get your plan in motion, you must find out if your base—your customer base, that is—is stable enough to support it. Knowing how your customers really feel about you is essential, because they're the ones who'll tell you what the future holds and whether you're going to be a Beast (yeah!) or a bust (forget about it!). That's why you have to ask your customers the question: *How likely are you to recommend my [product/ service/company] to a colleague or business associate?*

It's a Big, Hairy, Outrageous Question to ask. The average entrepreneur doesn't want to know the answer because it may disappoint or because it'll just confirm what he or she already knows.

So why bother?

Because you're not the average entrepreneur. Because you're beginning to realize that how you *interpret* the answers may enlighten and guide you like nothing ever has before. The reality is, not all of your customers are the same. Some may like you very much. Some would switch to another vendor under the right circumstances. And some aren't overly fond of you at all and may be in the process of dumping you or worse—badmouthing your product or service all over the Internet. (This happens more often than you might think.)

SHOW ME THE LOVE

If you're like most entrepreneurs, you'll likely find three types of customers in your business: Fans, Fence-sitters, and Critics.

1. *Fans* are your most loyal and enthusiastic customers. They love you.
2. *Fence-sitters* have no particular loyalty to you one way or the other.
3. *Critics* aren't just disloyal, they cost you money. They're dissatisfied, demanding, and costly to service. And they're very capable of spreading negative word of mouth about you.

Critics can destroy your Beast if there are too many of them. You want to make sure you have as many Fans and as few Critics in your cave as possible because:

More Fans = faster growth
More Critics = slower growth

This may seem obvious, but what's not so obvious is the contribution each customer type makes to your revenues. Studies have shown that "totally satisfied customers" (Fans) contribute 2.6 times the revenue of "somewhat satisfied customers" and 14 times more revenue than "somewhat dissatisfied customers." At the same time, "totally dissatisfied customers" (Critics) were actually found to *decrease* revenue at twice the rate that Fans *contribute* revenue, because those Critics typically have much higher service costs, produce lower revenue, and can damage market growth through negative referrals.[1]

Fans Will Grow Your Beast
Fans generate 2.6 times the revenue of "somewhat satisfied customers."
Fans generate 14 times the revenue of "somewhat dissatisfied customers."

Critics Can Mortally Wound Your Beast
Critics decrease revenue at twice the rate that Fans contribute revenue.
Too many Critics and not enough Fans spells disaster.

The key takeaway is that you can have twice as many Fans as Critics and *still* be losing ground! That's why you need to know who's in your Beast Cave, and fast. And yet, most businesses don't. When Bain & Company surveyed 362 American companies in 2005, a whopping 80 percent of those who responded declared their companies were delivering a "superior experience" to their customers. But when Bain asked the customers themselves, only 8 percent agreed (see Figure 1.1). That's a huge, frighteningly hairy, 72-point gap![2]

Figure 1.1 Perceived Corporate Love

To make matters worse, the average U.S. business loses up to half of its customers every five years. In contrast, the most profitable companies lose less than 10 percent of their customers every five years.[3] This strongly suggests that the most profitable companies have a better customer mix (more Fans, fewer Critics) than average companies. If you want to grow, you can't do it without making sure that your customer mix is working *for* you.

So what has this got to do with your marketing? Everything! If you don't have enough Fans in your Beast Cave, there may be a problem with your business. No matter how great your need to boost short-term sales, running a marketing campaign with too few Fans in your fold will not likely be the best use of your time, people, and money. In fact, if your product or service is broken in some way, exposing more people to your "broken-ness" sure won't help. It's almost always better to address the problem first.

On the other hand, if you discover you have a Beast Cave full of Fans, congratulations! You'll want to ramp up your marketing programs. In this case, the next thing you'd want to do is profile your cave-guests so you can run smarter, more productive marketing programs. But before we get ahead of ourselves, we'd like to introduce you to a few people.

THE THREE ENTREPRENEURS

Say hello to Sophie Growmore, Paul Treadwater, and Karim Stardupta, our three entrepreneurs. Outsiders might say they're pretty successful since Sophie and Paul are over the $1 million mark in sales, and 23-year-old Karim runs a software startup. But revenue growth has stalled at Sophie's and Paul's companies, Karim is looking for customers, and none have a growth strategy that really passes the sniff test. That's where we come in. Throughout this book, you'll follow our three entrepreneurs as they guide their Beasts up the road to Big, Hairy, Outrageous Sales Growth. *A quick note:* Keep in mind, Sophie, Paul, and Karim are fictional composites of real-world clients (for confidentiality reasons), but their struggles and stories are absolutely real. Let's meet them and see how they found their way out of the marketing wilderness.

Sophie Growmore: *29, Home Stager, Entrepreneur*

Sophie's been an entrepreneur since she was six and began helping her interior decorator mom charm clients and pick up checks. After college, Sophie put her entrepreneurial talents to work building Staged2Go, a successful home staging and design business that prepares homes for sale within her local market.

The key to Sophie's business success to date has been a strong and loyal base of real estate agents who have come to know and trust her over time. She's always grown her business or-

ganically, so she's been able to pace her investment in her business with the growth of the business itself. But Sophie's sales peaked at $1 million annually and showed no signs of increasing. And Sophie wanted to grow big. In order to grow big, it appeared Sophie needed to expand her business into new markets, first locally, and then into new cities across the country—markets she knew nothing about. To do this, Sophie would have to make sizable up-front investments in local warehousing and inventory, as well as hire staff to manage those locations—all before supporting revenue was available.

When we were introduced to Sophie, she was uncertain how to rapidly attract new agents in the new markets. We asked her if she knew how many Fans she had in her customer base. She gave us a withering look, so we explained the importance of knowing her customer mix (percentage of Fans, Critics, and Fence-sitters) and its correlation to long-term growth.

She agreed to conduct a simple *one-question survey* to determine her Beast Potential score. Beast Potential is an extremely powerful predictor of a company's current and future sales growth determined by your customer mix.[4] This is the question she asked her real estate agent customers:

How likely are you to recommend Staged2Go's
home staging services to a colleague or business associate?

For the one-question, web-based survey, her customers were given a scale of 0 to 10 to express their support (10 being "extremely likely"). Any customers who indicated 9 or 10 were considered Fans. Customers who indicated 7 or 8 were Fence-sitters, and customers who scored 6 or less were considered Critics.

Sophie began to understand that this powerful little survey, originally devised by Frederick Reichheld of Bain Consulting Group, could prove invaluable in obtaining critical insights into her firm's marketing health and future growth potential. Because the survey had only one question and was targeted to her customers, Sophie elicited a 40 percent response. She was happy as a clam—that is, until she reviewed the responses. Our post-survey conversation went like this:

US: Only 33 percent of your customers love you.

SOPHIE: I don't get it. Our agents rave about the work we do. Almost every job!

US: But sales are slowing. The referrals are slowing.

SOPHIE: That's why we're going after new markets.

US: Or maybe there's something else going on.

The next step was to dig a little deeper and follow up with the other 67 percent—the 37 percent who gave her a firm 7 or 8 (the Fence-sitters) and the 30 percent who gave her 6 or less (the Critics). Our next conversation went like this:

US: It seems the majority of your customers love your staging work but really don't like your billing and collections. Apparently, there have been a lot of screw-ups. As a result, you received more 7s and 8s in the survey than your staging success would suggest.

SOPHIE: Accounting is really boring.

US: Clearly.

———

In the rush that is her business, it was easy for Sophie to get caught up in the success of her design work and overlook operational issues. If Sophie had charged ahead with a full-blown expansion of her business, there's every reason to believe that she would have found sales growth a lot slower than she expected. Sophie would have spent a lot of very dear money exposing her weakness to many more agents. That would have been the path to a saw-toothed sales curve, not a smooth, upward-to-the-right, hockey-stick sales curve that makes entrepreneurs so happy. Armed with fresh insight, Sophie took a step back, hired a better-qualified bookkeeper, and decided to get her operations in order before contemplating expansion.

Paul Treadwater: *44, Chocolate Maker, Entrepreneur*

Sophie's story is echoed by Paul Treadwater's. Paul manufactures and packages gourmet chocolates under his own Treadwater Chocolates brand, which he sells to thousands of small retailers and corporate gift basket companies across the country. Paul also has a profitable private label business going with large department stores and specialty food retailers. Like Sophie, his sales were stagnant, even though Paul himself was a whirling dervish who always seemed to be just one step ahead of a heart attack. What's more, Paul's contract sales force was aging, and new, younger salespeople weren't being attracted to the profession. His sales connection to his thousands of customers was on the wrong side of the growth curve.

Although Treadwater Chocolates generates approximately $5 million in annual sales, profits are continuously eroded by margin pressure from his retailers on one side and significant increases in ingredient costs on the other. Paul is chief product development officer, chief large-account salesperson, chief operations person, and chief cheerleader. Trapped working "in" the business, he has almost no time to stand back and work "on" the business. He seems to be stuck on a treadmill that he can't get off.

We had Paul do the one-question survey. Unlike Sophie, he was pleasantly surprised by the results. His Beast Potential was significantly higher than the average for his industry. What's more, the survey unearthed another compelling insight. His highest scores came from corporate gift basket companies.

Our post-survey conversation with Paul went like this:

US: So you have high Beast Potential, but you're struggling to be profitable. What do you think it means?

PAUL: It's the problem I've had from the beginning. Everyone loves our product, but the cost of selling to and servicing so many small retailers is really high. We do a good job, but we make no money. And yet small retailers are where most of our revenue comes from.

US: What about the gift basket companies?

PAUL: That one's interesting. Our cost of sales to gift basket companies is quite a bit lower. They don't require as many SKUs, and our product seems to be perfect for them—beautifully packaged but well-priced. As a group, they're far lower maintenance.

US: Makes sense. The perceived value of a gift basket is more important than the quality of any one component. The sale is less product-focused.

PAUL: There's something else. For whatever reason, gift basket companies are more Internet-savvy than our small retailers. They love our partner ecommerce site.

US: How big is the corporate gift basket market?

PAUL: Quite substantial—around $3 billion annually—although it is seasonal.

US: How big is your share of the gift basket business?

PAUL: I'd say minuscule.

US: Looks like you may have a market opportunity to test out.

PAUL: Looks like.

Karim Stardupta: *23, Software Developer, Entrepreneur*

Karim has five customers. He started his business in his bedroom when he was looking to buy a new camera online. He used several comparative pricing websites and was disappointed by the results. He knew he could do a better job. After a little investigation, he realized there was no money in a consumer price comparison site—there were too many, and they were all free. He decided he would rather eat his keyboard one letter at a time than develop yet another high-traffic, zero-revenue website. But speaking with his neighbor (and soon-to-be first customer), a retail merchandising manager, Karim discovered that retailers were getting crushed by the price transparency brought on by pricing apps on smartphones. A shopper could manhandle a product in-store, price-check it, and buy it cheaper elsewhere—all in a couple of clicks. Retailers needed to be able to see what their competitors were pricing like products at, so they could manage their pricing policies accordingly. Karim had a novel idea of how all that web-based pricing could be pulled together and presented to a retailer in a way that would allow the retailer to make better pricing decisions. And so BigFatData was born.

After nine months, Karim had signed five large retail customers, all on the back of his success at helping his neighbor deal with his price transparency issues. The sales had come quite organically, through referrals, word-of-mouth, and a bit of free press. He now had 10 employees and an office, but he had noticed that the sales weren't just walking through the door in the same way anymore. He had also noticed that several other firms had gotten wind of the same aching retail pain and had built their own companies, offering similar solutions. Karim decided it was time to ramp up his marketing. Before doing so, however, he wanted to step back and try to get a better understanding of what caused his initial success and what that might tell him about his future growth plans.

Karim started with a simple one-question survey, much like Sophie and Paul, to take the pulse of his customers. While he received a 100 percent response rate, his sample size—a grand total of five responses—was too small to assign a meaningful Beast Potential score. However, he did notice that the results from the two retail sectors he served, consumer electronics and mass merchandise, skewed in different directions. His mass merchandise customers seemed to huddle a little closer to a score of 8, while his consumer electronics customers veered closer to a score of 10. While the sample size was far too small to draw any conclusions from, the results did reinforce something Karim had suspected: he was better at providing price information for consumer electronics retailers than for mass merchandise retailers. He resolved to book face-to-face meetings with each of his customers to further his investigations.

———

By asking their customers a simple, pointed question, Sophie, Paul, and Karim learned more about their businesses and took the first step on their journeys to growing their businesses into Big, Hairy Beasts. Not bad for one question.

CAVE SCRATCHES
- To recommend, or not
- More Fans = more growth
- More Critics = slower growth
- The three entrepreneurs:
  Sophie, Paul, and Karim

NEXT UP

So what about *your* Beast? What kind of customers do you think are in your Beast Cave? Lots of higher-margin Fans? Lots of lower-margin Fence-sitters? Maybe a surprising number of costly Critics? The best way to find out is to perform your own one-question survey.

Step 1   ASK

CHAPTER 2

How to Discover Your Beast Potential

What you'll find in this chapter:
- Putting your survey together
- Scoring your customers' answers
- Six simple tips

Now that you realize how important it is to understand just who's in your Beast Cave, it's time to assemble your survey. Remember, you're going to ask your customers a single question:

How likely are you to recommend [my product or service]
to a colleague or business associate?

The wording here is critical. You're not asking them how much they like your product, or how likely they are to buy more, or how likely they are to switch. You're asking each customer to put his or her reputation on the line and (if asked) make a commitment to promote your product or service to people who presumably trust them. The question works because your customers can't be sure if you intend to take them up on their referral or not. Since they don't know, they're inclined to consider their answers *very* carefully.

Figure 2.1 shows how the survey form might look (customized with your logo).

Notice the "submit" button at the bottom of the form. This form is web-based, making it simple and interactive, not to mention a big timesaver. We recommend going this route

Figure 2.1 Example of a Web-based One-question Survey

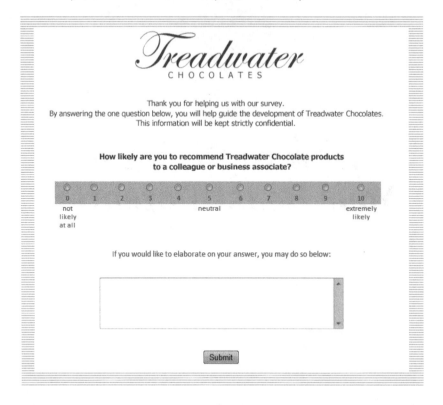

for cost reasons as well. You can find a wide range of inexpensive, web-based survey tools online, all of them designed for nontechnical users. Examples include snapsurveys.com, surveymonkey.com, and questionpro.com. Simply follow the instructions the web survey tools provide, and when you get to "question type," select "rating scale" or "multi-point scale" so your survey looks like Figure 2.2.

Lastly, include an open text box below your 0 to 10 scale with the heading: "If you would like to elaborate on your answer, you may do so below." Many customers add comments here that will provide you with great insights.

What if you don't have email addresses for your customers?
You can print out your one-question survey and mail it, fax it, or include it with other material you send to your customers, like your billing or catalogs. Just make sure that you send it to as many decision influencers as you can. The more input, the better.

Figure 2.2 Recommended Survey Style

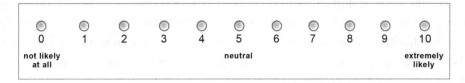

The online survey tools will allow you to send an invitation email to all your survey respondents, who should include as many decision influencers as you can identify (Deciders, Influencers, and Users). Figure 2.3 shows how your invitation email might read.

You'll find that the online survey tools will force you to include an opt-out option on your email (the removal link noted in the sample email message in Figure 2.3), *even though you're emailing your own customers*. Don't sweat it. Including an opt-out is good practice anyway, and if your customers are opting out of your email, you might take that as

Figure 2.3 Survey Cover Note

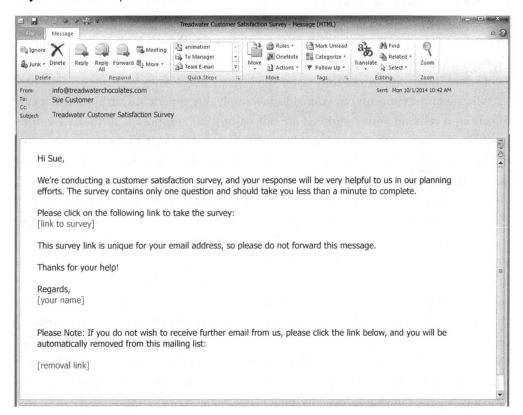

a bad sign regarding your relationship. If you're concerned (okay, anxious) about putting your customers on the spot with this survey, don't be. Buyers actually like to feel that their vendors care about them. In fact, research shows that surveyed customers are more likely to buy, less likely to defect, and tend to be more profitable than nonsurveyed customers. And the benefits aren't short-lived. Many surveyed buyers were measured as much as a year after the survey had been conducted.[1]

Because you're surveying your own customers and already have a relationship with them, chances are you'll be very successful conducting the research yourself rather than engaging a research firm.

SCORING YOUR ANSWERS

To measure the responses from your one-question survey, have a look at the diagram in Figure 2.4. Customers who give you a score of 9 or 10 should be recorded as "Fans." Any 7s or 8s are "Fence-sitters," and any responses below 7 are "Critics."

Why are only 9s and 10s considered Fans? Simply put, experience has shown that customers who respond with 7s and 8s are not enthusiastic supporters. If they were, they would have indicated they were "extremely likely" (9 or 10) to refer your company. Eliminating 7s and 8s removes the "grade inflation" bias common to many customer satisfaction surveys where a customer, just one tick above neutral, is considered "satisfied." Overall, this approach isn't perfect, but what it lacks in robustness from a research point of view, it more than makes up in ease of execution, ease of response, and directional insight.

It's not enough to identify your Fans, however. You also need to find out how many Critics you have because of their potential to form a very destructive, negative, word-of-mouth network. McKinsey & Company notes that positive and negative word-of-mouth (or word-of-mouse) is the primary factor behind 20 to 50 percent of all consumer purchasing decisions today.[2] Marketo, a marketing software company, reports that 93 percent of B2B buyers use search to begin the buying process,[3] while DemandGen reports that 59 percent of B2B buyers engage with their peers who may have addressed similar challenges—much of that engagement being online.[4] Word-of-mouse is a reality, so if you have lots of Critics in your midst, this math is not going to work in your favor.

Figure 2.4 One-Question Survey Scale

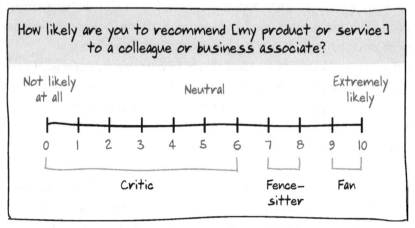

WHAT YOUR FINAL SCORE MEANS

In the next chapter, we'll do a deep dive into the details of your final score, but for now let's get a high-level sense of what your Beast Potential score means. To do this, take the Fence-sitters right out of the equation. The results will be more predictive of your future growth potential if you consider only your Fans and Critics. While you may not think of customers who score you a 6 (or less) as Critics, consider that whatever else you want to call them, they're not your Fans. So what you're left with are a group of Fans (best customers) and a group of Critics. To find out what the customers milling about in your Beast Cave really think about you, simply subtract the percentage of one from the percentage of the other to determine your Beast Potential score.

% Fans – % Critics = Beast Potential

If you do get an overrepresentation of Fence-sitters in your results, this points to another type of problem, even if your Beast Potential score looks acceptable. In general, if Fence-sitters total 40 percent or more of your respondents, too many customers just aren't sure about you, indicating there may be a gap between what you promise and how you're actually delivering it–the problem that Sophie's company had in our earlier example.

You can compare your Beast Potential score to other companies like yours and, more important, against yourself over time. (More on this in the next chapter.) High Beast Potential relative to other companies in your category bodes well for your growth prospects. As you might expect, low Beast Potential bodes poorly.

If you don't have a healthy proportion of Fans in your cave, you may want to reconsider spending your scarce cash or, worse, your borrowed capital, on marketing at this moment. Having too few Fans suggests that something is awry in your business, and it needs to be fixed before you go throwing good money after bad. To paraphrase an old advertising saying: "Nothing kills a bad company faster than good marketing."

As you can see in Figure 2.5, Company A's Fans vastly outnumber its Critics, which helps it achieve a very healthy Beast Potential score of 50. Meanwhile, Company B has an "average" Beast Potential score of 20. Company C has a very large percentage of Fence-sitters, which creates a deceptively high score of 20. However, because so many customers are Fence-sitters, this is a warning flag that should be investigated. Finally, Company D's boat is threatening to capsize because it has a bunch of Critics who have all congregated over in the stern. This is every marketer's worst nightmare.

A negative Beast Potential score almost certainly suggests a substantial amount of negative word-of-mouth is swirling in and around the company. It *is* possible for profitable companies to have a large number of disloyal customers. Insurance companies, telecoms, and financial firms frequently have negative scores because the average customer satisfaction level in the industry is so low. For companies in industries with negative scores, market leadership is often a matter of who has the least bad score. Low Beast Potential scores across an industry often point to an industry that is ripe for disruption by a smart competitor.

After your survey results are in and you've tabulated the scores, you may find your Beast Potential to be a pleasant surprise, or it may reveal a darker side that needs dealing with. This is a tough pill for some to swallow, but if you happen to score low, you can save yourself a lot of future pain by asking this question: *Where should I spend my next dollar— on marketing or on righting my listing boat?*

SIX BEAST PRACTICES TO A BETTER SURVEY

Beast Practice 1: Your sales team matters. Involve your sales team and/ or customer service team (if you have one). Most often, the customer belongs to them, so let them know what you're doing, why you're doing it, and enlist their help. As you can imagine, they'll be *very* interested in the results.

Figure 2.5 Sample of One-Question Survey Results

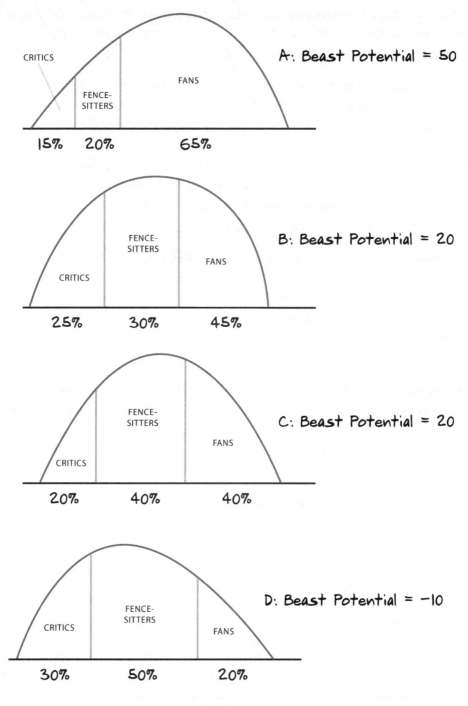

A: Beast Potential = 50

CRITICS

FENCE-SITTERS

FANS

15%   20%   65%

B: Beast Potential = 20

FENCE-SITTERS

CRITICS

FANS

25%   30%   45%

C: Beast Potential = 20

FENCE-SITTERS

CRITICS

FANS

20%   40%   40%

D: Beast Potential = -10

FENCE-SITTERS

CRITICS

FANS

30%   50%   20%

Beast Practice 2: Keep it short and sweet. You'll only be asking a grand total of *one* question. Since you have your customers' attention, you'll probably be tempted to ask more questions. Don't. Keep it simple and you'll (a) get more responses and (b) get the only response you need at this point.

Beast Practice 3: Make hay with your network. You (and your sales and customer service team) already have contacts within each of your customer companies. Use them to identify and confirm as many of the key decision makers/influencers as you can, and make sure to include as many of these individuals as possible in your survey for each customer company. You can find upwards of 20 decision makers in larger companies, so if any of your customers have multiple decision makers/influencers, average the score from their responses. If you're able to, weight each score by the estimated importance of each decision maker/influencer.

Beast Practice 4: Track your email. Most of the web-based survey tools enable you to send and track email messages to the customers you've elected to survey. Take advantage of the system's real-time reporting so that you can see who among your customers has opened the email, clicked on the survey link, and completed the survey. You can also automatically send out follow-ups to those customers who haven't yet responded.

Beast Practice 5: Best times to call. After conducting thousands of business email campaigns, we've discovered that the best times to send this type of survey are either *8 a.m. Tuesday* or *8 a.m. Friday*. Surprisingly, Saturday morning is coming on as a strong mailing alternative as well. Just remember to pay attention to the time zones your customers are in.

Beast Practice 6: Tick tock, mind the clock. Let three full business days pass before you analyze your results. By then, you'll have captured the majority of those who are going to respond. If you haven't received responses from at least 30 percent of your customers, use your web-based survey tool to resend the survey to those who did not respond. It's quite possible that the first mailing was missed by some of your customers due to work pressures or travel schedules. If you do resend, tack on an additional three days before you sit down and tally your scores.

When you resend the survey, you'll increase the overall response rate to your program, but if you're not able to scare up responses from at least 30 percent of the customers you mailed, you should get in touch with them and find out if there's an issue.

NEXT UP

That's it! The entire process shouldn't take you more than a couple of hours to execute, and the total turnaround is about three to six business days. Not a bad investment of your time, considering the potential payback. Now it's time to take a big breath, compare your Beast Potential to others in your industry, and get the answer to the burning question: *What color is your Beast?*

CAVE SCRATCHES

2
- Survey reveals your Fans (9s, 10s)
- Fans – Critics = Beast Potential
- Track by email
- Include sales
- Low Beast Potential score?
    Time to reassess

Step 1   ASK

CHAPTER 3

What Color Is Your Beast?

What you'll find in this chapter:
- Green means *go*—time to amp things up
- Yellow means *caution*—careful, there are bumps in the road
- Red means *stop*—Beast-threatening danger ahead

Now that you've got your survey results back, tallied your scores, and worked out your Beast Potential, what's next? First, if your score seems low, *don't panic*. You might be interested to know that the average Beast Potential for B2B companies is usually between 20 and 25. Only the best and rarified few have scores over 50.[1]

SELECT COMPANY BP SCORES

Company	Beast Potential Score
AMEX	41
Siemens	43
Rackspace	50
Google	53
Apple	72

WHAT YOUR SCORE MEANS

Your Beast Potential Score tells you who's in your Beast Cave and how they feel about being there. As mentioned earlier, your Beast Potential score is based on Reichheld's Net Promoter Score™, which, over the last decade, has been pretty consistent in linking high scores with future revenue growth.[2] Research and case studies aside, it just makes sense that if you have a significant base of Fans and a manageable number of Critics, then you're doing something right, and you're well positioned for growth.

At a very high level, here are some recommendations we've developed over time. Keep in mind that this should be used as directional information only. Because different industries are perceived differently by their customers, the green, yellow, and red indicators can vary by industry.

DIRECTIONAL BP SCORE INDICATORS

Beast Potential Score	What Color Is Your Beast?
Over 30	**Green light:** Your business is a Beast. Step on the marketing gas pedal (provided your Fence-sitters don't total above 40 percent).
10-30	**Yellow light:** Proceed with caution. Move forward, but you may want to take the opportunity to improve your product, service, or business model.
Under 10	**Red light:** There's a good chance that you need to reassess your business before going any further. Your Beast appears to be gnawing on one of its own limbs.

It's very important to balance your score findings with what your customers tell you in the open text box beneath the 1-to-10 scale on your survey. You'll find that many (if not most) of your customers will take the time to write something in this box. Usually, you'll see patterns emerging pretty quickly from the comments, and these can be added to your Beast Potential assessment.

Okay. So let's say you get a score of 12. What do you do? Keep in mind that the important thing is your score *relative* to others in your industry. If you have a BP score of 12, and your industry average is an anemic 1, then you're actually looking pretty good, and you might consider spending money on marketing. You should keep in mind, however, that industries with low customer satisfaction levels across the board are ripe for disruption by a smart competitor. You might want to think about how you could be that competitor. Just ask all the sales force automation software vendors whose lunch was handed to them

Figure 3.1 Directional BP Score Indicators[3]

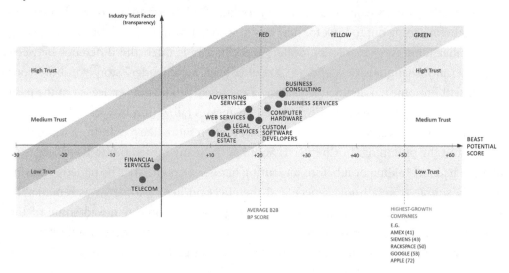

by Salesforce.com—a cloud-based solution that didn't require you to load any software on your computer, and whose data could be accessed from any computing device at any time.

What are relative scores for different industries? Refer to Figure 3.1 if you wish to add a little more context to your Beast Potential score. The horizontal bands represent industry trust, while the diagonal bands represent green, yellow, and red Beast Potential scores. The X-axis is the Beast Potential score. A "green" score in a low-trust industry like financial services could be close to zero, while a "green" score in a higher-trust industry like business consulting would be between 20 and 30. Once again, this information should be used directionally. The most important Beast Potential score will be your own, over time. If you don't see your industry in Figure 3.1, you may be able to estimate its position based on other industries on the chart and your perceived level of customer trust in your industry. Regardless, you'll get a sense of the relative strength of your Beast Potential score.

A CONFEDERACY OF YELLOWISH BEASTS

The unfortunate reality is that the majority of B2B companies are Beast-yellow, which suggests that there's a lot of opportunity out there for you to be better than your competitors. Not surprisingly, when you think about it, most companies *are* mediocre, meaning they're neither red nor green but simply average. That doesn't mean that these companies (or perhaps you) should stop marketing. However, it does suggest that they could make their marketing dollars work a lot harder by looking for opportunities to tweak their yellowness before going out to look for new business. When you're a small business, making every dollar (and every marketing dollar) work harder is often the difference between a long-term, thriving business and an "I coulda been a contender" story you bore your friends with in some bar. Remember: selling a mediocre product or service is not the path to success. It's why the vast majority of small businesses fail within five years.

Addressing your yellowness (should it exist) is often more like repainting a room than pulling out the plumbing. In Chapter 1, Sophie's company turned out to be yellow (not that she had any inkling of it before measuring her Beast Potential). The remedy was surprisingly simple (hire a bookkeeper), and the effect on her customers was remarkable. Within weeks, her real estate agents were taking notice. Sophie removed some of the unnecessary friction in her business and discovered that new business growth flowed a lot easier than before. The last thing you need as an entrepreneur is a handicap. We have enough of those. As you'll see in later chapters, it's wise to let your customers help you identify your handicaps so you can quickly remove them. *Then* reach out to your market for more business.

No matter if your Beast is green or yellow or red, it's critical to follow up and find out the reasons for your score. Why did your customers answer the way they did? What can you do to improve the situation, if necessary? These are the types of questions you want to ask a select number of your customers, and you'll want to do it in person, if possible. Some entrepreneurs find the process too painful and avoid it. Don't. Think about it from the customer's point of view. She'll likely be happy that a vendor or business owner took the time to contact her to get her opinion. And don't take the responses personally. Remember to check your ego at the door.

What if you're a startup with few or no customers?

Ahh. Thought we'd forgotten you? If you have even one or two customers, you should run the one-question survey by them. You're sure to learn something of value. That said, there are many startups that have no customers, so it's tough to ask them even one question. If "customerless" or "prerevenue" (sounds cooler) defines you right now, here's what you should do. Go out and get your first customer. It's what every entrepreneur does. You can skip right to Steps 4 through 6 to get some marketing ideas you can use right away, or you can swing whatever connections you have to get your Beast on the road. Whatever you elect to do, once you get your first customer, go to Step 2, learn about the three Laws of Engagement, and interview your customer using the Engagement Questionnaire you'll find there. The insights you gain will focus your subsequent marketing efforts and help you train your Beast's sights on the ultimate goal: Big, Hairy, Outrageous Sales Growth.

CAVE SCRATCHES

3

~ Who's in your Cave?
~ GREEN means GO
~ YELLOW means CAUTION
~ RED means STOP
~ Most companies are Yellow
~ Yellow can be fixed

NEXT UP

Okay. You've now completed the first of the 7 Steps. The results of your one-question survey have been tallied and your Beast Potential established. If your Beast is red, don't despair. It's time to make some positive changes. Enlist your Fans to help you. On the other hand, if your Beast is yellow or green, you're ready to move ahead with an eye to improving any yellowness that threatens to handicap your potential. So now it's time to take the next step toward Big, Hairy, Outrageous Sales Growth and discover the secret to finding and engaging new customers. But first you need to understand something. You're not in the "selling" business; you're in the "engagement" business. Business buyers need to be engaged before they'll even consider buying from you. How do you engage and then transform this engagement into Big, Hairy, Outrageous Sales Growth?

You lure prospects to your Beast Cave (your website or your landing page) by offering tangible, relevant rewards that match their buying needs and purchase process, and you build relationships by helping them expedite their journey through their Decision Cycle.

That's what the Laws of Engagement are all about.

Step 2

1: ASK
the right
question

2: LISTEN
to your best
customers

3: FOCUS
your resources

4: ATTRACT
your best prospects

5: PURSUE
your best prospects

6: NURTURE
your engaged
prospects

7: GROW!
measure your
success

7 Step Beast Marketing System

Let your customers drive the bus

The Laws of Engagement

> ### What you'll find in this chapter:
> - The tools of engagement
> - The art of listening
> - Questions, questions
> - Inside the customer's mind
> - Putting your engagement strategy to work

Engage first, sell later. That should be every B2B entrepreneur's motto. Why engage? Because business buyers tend to be risk averse, and they'll need to get to know you before buying—especially if you're a smaller, less established company. Here's what makes them willing to engage:

1. They have a *business pain* that needs remedying.
2. They are actively looking for information to help them solve their pain.
3. They are willing to trust people who can help take the thorn out of their paw (that's you).

So how do you engage buyers so you can earn their trust? You'll have to do the heavy lifting on this one, because the odds of them looking you up and giving you a call are pretty slim. To help you with some of the lifting, we've distilled the engagement job you need to do down to three very important principles:

1. Target
2. Value
3. Offer

These principles—Target, Value, Offer—aren't new. In fact, millions of marketers have made good use of them over the decades. What we've done in *Feed the Startup Beast* is to simplify and codify them into a sequential, three-pronged engagement strategy that will power the Beast Marketing System you'll be learning all about. We call these elements (and the strategy that builds around them) the Laws of Engagement.

THE LAWS OF ENGAGEMENT

The Laws of Engagement are a set of rules, principles, and best practices that concentrate your marketing efforts so you can more effectively engage your Beast Prospects—leading to a mutually rewarding relationship that significantly increases your likelihood of a sale.

1. The Law of Targeting

If you find more customers like your best customers, you will sell more.

The Law of Targeting states that in order to engage your prospects, you must be talking to the ones who will buy. Well, how obvious is that? Apparently not very. Most companies violate this law every day by targeting too widely. The secret is to identify those prospects who share the same pain and the same need to remedy that pain as your best customers, then *target* them.

2. The Law of Value

Your value proposition must be presented in terms of your prospect's pain and viewpoint.

The Law of Value states that in order to engage your prospects, you must talk to them in *their* language about *their* pain. What is their pain? A problem *that you appear able to solve.*

These prospects need a solution, but if you want them to buy the solution from you and not someone else, they need to *understand how your product or service can solve it better than the next guy's.* What's the secret? Frame your message in their terms, not yours. Not "Here's how great my product is," but rather "Here's how your problem can be solved." They want to know WIIFM—"What's in it for me?" And that leads us to the third law.

3. The Law of the Offer

Your offer must be valuable, timely, and relevant.

The Law of the Offer states that in order to engage your prospects, you must offer them information and insight that will help them better understand their problem or a potential solution to their problem. Your offer, be it information or a webinar or a white paper, must fit where they are in their Decision Cycle. If it doesn't, you must refine your offer until it does fit.

WHO, WHAT, AND HOW

OK. That's a lot of information to absorb. But don't worry, we're going to spend the next three chapters fleshing out how it all fits into a strategy that will work for your company. To make it easier for you to remember the laws, you might want to think of them as simply *who*, *what*, and *how*.

1. **Target.** *Who* you'll be talking to
2. **Value.** *What* you'll be saying
3. **Offer.** *How* you'll be saying it

> **Who.** *You need to know exactly* who *you'll be talking to because you don't have any time or money to waste, so your message must be focused on, and entirely relevant to, your prospects' situation, problem, and pain.*
>
> **What.** *You need to know exactly* what *you'll be saying because you have only a few seconds to get your prospect's attention. You have to make your value story as relevant and compelling as humanly possible.*
>
> **How.** *You need to know exactly* how *to bundle your value story so that once you've got your prospect's attention, you get them to respond to your offer.*

With the Laws of Target, Value, and Offer as the critical elements of your engagement strategy, it's now time for you to create a plan that makes them work as one.

YOU DON'T HAVE TO DO IT ALONE

The Big, Hairy, Outrageously Smart entrepreneur sees marketing as a team effort. Even if you think you're too small to have a team, you do. Who are the other players on your marketing team? Your customers, of course. And it's not just because they're a potential source of referrals (we'll discuss referral marketing in Chapter 18). It's because they're a huge source of (too often overlooked) market intelligence. To create an effective and efficient engagement strategy, ask your Best Customers how they buy and what appeals to them and who gets involved in their purchase decisions. In other words, focus on their knowledge of Target, Value, and Offer, and embed those insights right into your strategy.

BUILDING YOUR ENGAGEMENT STRATEGY

In the first of the 7 Steps, you identified your Fans. These are your Best Customers, the ones who happily circled 9 or 10 on your one-question survey. Now they're going to be instrumental in helping you develop the Target, Value, and Offer elements of your engagement strategy. Throughout this book, we're going to echo and reinforce the single most important rule for growth:

> *The fastest way to grow your business is to*
> *find more customers like your Best Customers.*

To find more customers like your Best Customers, you'll take the behaviors, characteristics, demographics, and buying habits of your current Best Customers and use them as a marketing template or filter: only the Beast Prospects get through. Which means we want you to ask your Best Customers some questions. To help smooth your job, we've designed an Engagement Questionnaire for you that lays out the fewest questions you need to ask to get a tight, meaningful profile that you can then use to go track down some fresh, new Beast Prospects for your business.

As you can see in Figure 4.1, your Engagement Questionnaire is structured into three parts according to the Laws of Engagement: Target, Value, and Offer. All the questions are brief and have the following objectives:

1. **Target: Who you'll be saying it to.** You need to confirm decision-making roles and profiles. Which deciders, influencers, and users are typically involved in the decision process? Whom do you need to target your marketing efforts to?

Figure 4.1 Engagement Questionnaire

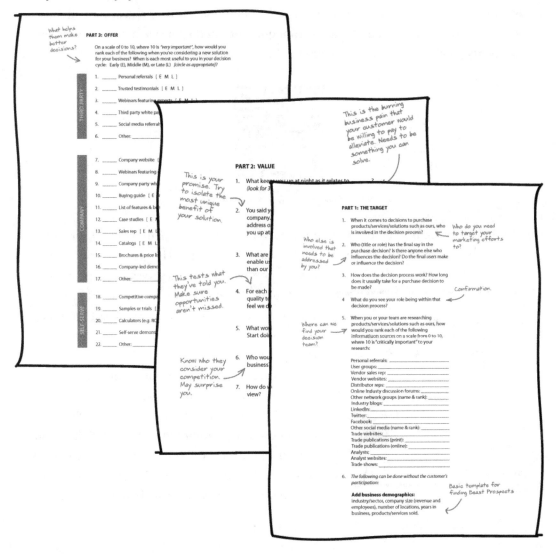

2. **Value: What you'll be saying.** You need to identify the burning business pain your Best Customer has that she is willing to pay to alleviate. This needs to be something you can solve in a unique way.

3. **Offer: How you'll be saying it.** You need to confirm what decision-making support your Best Customers value. What helps your Best Customers make better decisions? What content, tools, or approaches will allow you to best engage others like them?

It should take about one hour to complete the Engagement Questionnaire with your Best Customer, and it's truly worth the effort. If you'd like to preview it now, you can download it at http://tools.FeedTheBeast.biz (or use the QR Code below on your mobile device). Of course, you may need to modify the questions to better reflect your situation or your industry, but you'll find that the root questions in the Engagement Questionnaire do a pretty good job of covering the essentials.

QR Code
Engagement Questionnaire

Why go to the trouble of creating the survey? Because the path to Big, Hairy, Outrageous Sales Growth means zigging while others are zagging. The vast majority of your competitors will never do a survey like this, let alone develop an in-depth prospect profile. That means they'll be less certain who *their* Beast Prospects are, where they can be found, or how they buy. In fact, studies indicate that less than 20 percent of large organizations understand their customers' behaviors and buying processes.[1]

And don't worry. You won't be annoying your customers with another survey. They'll be more than happy to answer your questions because, as you'll recall, they're your Best Customers—they love you already. And besides, just about every customer

alive wants to be listened to, and who's more likely to welcome your attention than your Best Customers?

CONDUCTING THE INTERVIEW

Important breaking news: we don't want you to interview your Best Customers. We want you to interview your Very Best Customers. Who are they? They're the most profitable among your Best Customers. As you can imagine, if you have a low-margin, high-cost customer who just happens to love you, you won't necessarily be wanting to find more like him. So before conducting your interviews in Chapter 5, we'll help you identify the best of your best.

Once you've identified your Very Best Customers, you'll call (or email) up to 10 of them and ask for an in-person interview. Ten interviews is a good rule of thumb, because patterns and insights tend to emerge quickly—in many cases after as few as two interviews. However you contact them, your interview request should be brief and phrased along these lines:

> *Thanks again for completing my one-question survey. It was very helpful.*
> *I'd like to ask you for one more favor—I'd really appreciate an hour of your time.*
> *I consider you one of my best customers, and I'd like to better understand*
> *your experience with us and how we can use that input to do a better job for you.*

Given how much your Very Best Customers like you and want you to succeed, you should be able to set up these interview sessions fairly quickly. By far, the best way to conduct the actual one-hour interviews is in person.

Remember that no customer can ever be too far away. You need to meet them face-to-face at some point if you truly want your relationship to flourish (a tradeshow will do, if nothing else). That said, if travel just isn't in the cards for all of your Very Best Customer interviews, conduct them over the phone. Oh. And *you* should do the interviews. Don't drop them on the lap of a junior member of your team. Building a prospect profile is far too

important to your success; you need to *listen*, firsthand, to what your Very Best Customers have to say.

BUILDING YOUR ENGAGEMENT TEMPLATE

Because your interview questions will be brief, relevant, and highly focused, your Very Best Customers will generally be forthcoming with their answers. You'll gather very useful insights into the research habits, buying behaviors, and decision-making processes of your Very Best Customers. And once you've organized, analyzed, and interpreted those insights, a comprehensive profile of your Beast Prospects will emerge. This is called your Engagement Template, and it will instantly become one of your most valuable marketing tools.

Your Engagement Template (see Figure 4.2) is simply a profile of your Very Best Customers—who is involved in their buying decisions (Target); what they value in your product or service (Value); and what kind of outreach is likely to engage them (Offer). So it just makes sense that your Engagement Template, like the Engagement Questionnaire, is divided into exactly those three sections: Target, Value, and Offer.

Your Engagement Template will help you identify your Beast Prospects. And it's all based on this one, simple, powerful idea:

The fastest way to grow your business is to find more customers like your Best Customers.

Figure 4.2 Engagement Template

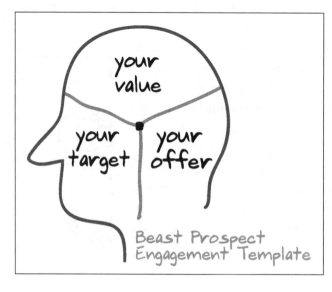

CAVE SCRATCHES

4

~ Identify your Very Best
   Customers and you'll identify
   your Very Best Prospects
~ Laws of Target, Value, Offer
~ Survey customers with
   Engagement Questionnaire

NEXT UP

Over the next three chapters, your Very Best Customers are going to help you build a profile of your Beast Prospects—which will become your Engagement Template. We call it that because it will guide you as you engage your Beast Prospects and transform them into Customers and Fans. We're going to help you build your template piece by piece, starting with part one, the Target. Along the way, you'll also get help from our three entrepreneurs—Sophie, Paul, and Karim. But to make your Engagement Template as accurate as possible, you need to do this: *listen* to your customers very, very closely. Listening is an important part of Big, Hairy, Outrageous Sales Growth, so make sure your Beast has a great set of ears.

Step 2 — LISTEN

CHAPTER 5

Target: The First Law of Engagement

What you'll find in this chapter:
• Most profitable = Very Best
• Sophie, Karim, and Paul discover their Very Best Customers
• Asking the right questions: your Engagement Questionnaire
• Building the first piece of your Engagement Template
• Sophie, Karim, and Paul target their Beast Prospects

Do you know who your Beast Prospects are or where they hang out? Most companies don't, which means they're wasting an awful lot of time and money. There's little point creating dazzling content and honing brilliant marketing pitches if you aren't reaching the right people. You already know that the keys to marketing success are patience, persistence, and a plan. The key to reaching your Beast Prospects is a fourth *P*—precision.

There are two things you will do in this chapter to achieve that precision. First, you'll identify the very best of your Best Customers, and then, once that's accomplished, you'll go out and talk to those best of the best in order to complete part one of your Engagement Template: the Target.

THE TARGET

Targeting is all about focus. Most companies focus on the forest. While keeping the picture of the forest in mind, the Big, Hairy, Outrageously Smart entrepreneur really zeros in on the trees. To build a precise targeting strategy, you need to:

1. Identify your Very Best Customers
2. Identify your best prospects (or "Beast Prospects") who most closely resemble your Very Best Customers
3. Identify the decision teams within those prospect companies
4. Determine where the key members of the team "hang out"

To reach and engage the right target group requires more than simple intuition or quick-and-dirty web research. You need to ask the people who most resemble your Beast Prospects—these of course would be your Very Best Customers. They're actually an even more select group than your Best Customers. Let's remember that your Best Customers—your Fans—are the ones who enthusiastically marked 9 or 10 on your one-question survey. That's great. But the truth is, not all of your Best Customers are your most profitable customers. In fact, some may not be profitable at all. A 2006 Booz Allen study found that as many as 50 percent of a company's customers are "likely unprofitable or marginally profitable" over the course of their relationship with that company.[1]

How can that be? It may be that some of your Best Customers require an excessive amount of service and support, or they buy less frequently than other customers. Your Very Best Customers don't behave like that because they're also your *most profitable* customers. They're the best of the best. They sing your praises like your *regular* Best Customers do, but they boost your bottom line far better than anyone else. Your Very Best Customers are the ones you want more of. They're the ones you want to build your Engagement Strategy around. They'll teach you what to say, to whom, and how to say it. In fact, you'll find that your Very Best Customers will make all the difference between your Beast being very happy or being very hungry.

IDENTIFYING YOUR VERY BEST CUSTOMERS

Determining who your Very Best Customers are is actually a fairly simple process. Using the criteria that follows, you can start to develop a short-list.

1. Total dollar volume
2. Purchase frequency (if customers place discrete orders)
3. Monthly Recurring Revenue (MRR) growth (if customers subscribe to an ongoing service)
4. Gross margin
5. Your gut

Dollar volume, purchase frequency, and/or MRR are usually pretty easy to uncover, but gross margin by customer may be harder to determine. It depends on how you approach your accounting. Once you've tagged your customers by these criteria, plot your customers in a grid like the one you see in Figure 5.1, first by total dollar volume/gross margin on the y-axis, then by purchase frequency or MRR (as applicable) on the x-axis. It's entirely possible that cash flow might be king in your company. In that case, it could be that you go after lots of high volume, high revenue, lower margin business. In that case, just worry

Figure 5.1 Your Very Best Customer Segmentation Grid

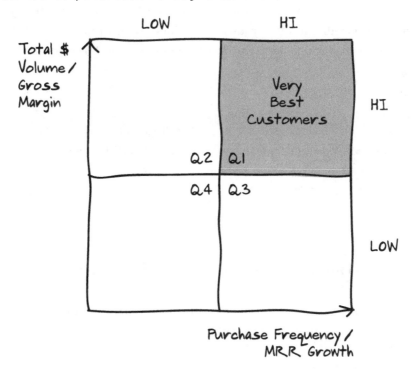

about total volume and not gross margin so much. If there's any doubt about where customers fall within the grid, use your gut. In general, your Very Best Customers will fall into quadrant one (Q1) because, of all your customers, they spend the most with you, spend the most often, and you generally make the most money on them.

In quadrant two (Q2), you'll find customers who spend a lot of money with you but who purchase sporadically, or else the growth of your subscription revenue from them (MRR) is low. This might suggest they're using you for a few specialized purchases, or, on the subscription side, they've run out of services they can or want to buy from you. This is very useful to know because you can think about strategies to encourage their move into Q1.

Quadrant three (Q3) customers purchase frequently or have good MRR growth, but their average order sizes are small. This might suggest they're "cherry-picking," possibly focusing on lower-cost sale items. Or, on the subscription side, they might be smaller accounts (or smaller divisions within larger companies) that have a limited budget. For the most part, these are customers with uncertain potential. But they might also be larger companies that are early in the adoption of your service and are testing their way in, which means they have good upside potential.

What about quadrant four (Q4)? This is where your worst customers lurk. They don't spend much with you, or they purchase infrequently, or they have low MRR growth. To make matters worse, they're often your worst Critics. In fact, only Q1 is likely to be a Critic-free zone, which is one more reason why you want your Engagement Template to be defined as much as possible by Q1 customers.[2]

big, hairy tip

We recommend segmenting all of your customers into quadrants, not just your most profitable ones, so you can quickly identify and filter out your unprofitable and marginal customers. Yes, this means we're suggesting that you might want to consider firing some of your less profitable customers and focusing on your more profitable customers.

SOPHIE IDENTIFIES HER VERY BEST CUSTOMERS

When Sophie, Paul, and Karim segmented their customers by quadrants, they were amazed to discover that some of their earlier assumptions were a little off-target. This is not surprising. We tend to think that our lowest maintenance customers, or the ones we're most comfortable with, are naturally our best customers. But that's not always the case.

When Sophie segmented her real estate agent customers into four quadrants, she realized, for the first time, that her highest purchase frequency, highest dollar volume customers were consistently among the top five agents in every agency (see Figure 5.2). And they skewed male more than female. *In fact, over 70 percent of her revenue came from her Q1 agents.* When she examined their gross margins, she found that her Q1 agents were also her most profitable. Her gut supplied a likely reason: the top agents (who tended to be male) were far more hands-off on staging, trusting *Staged2Go* to do its job. They were genuinely less interested in design because they were busy selling houses.

What's more, Sophie identified a number of top agents in Q2 who used her services less frequently but who were very profitable when they did. Once again, Sophie's gut told her that these were agents who used other staging companies but reached out to Sophie when they were in a pinch. From these findings, Sophie's marketing strategy evolved to:

Figure 5.2 Staged2Go's Very Best Customer Segmentation Grid

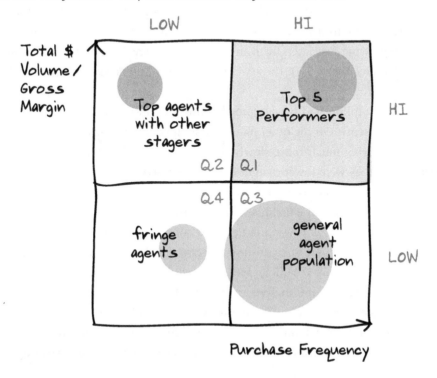

1. Focus on Q1 agents in her current market.
2. Raise the service levels on Q2 agents to win more of their business.
3. Stop actively marketing/selling to Q3 and Q4 agents.
4. When expanding into new markets, focus only on Q1 agents.

Sophie's Beast Prospects were clearly the top 5 to 10 agents in every agency (as measured by the revenue they generated for their agencies) in her current market and in any new markets she chose to enter. She assembled her list of Very Best Customers from her Q1 customers and included her Q2 customers so she could explore any differences between the two groups. Sophie was now ready to interview her Very Best Customers and start building the targeting section of her Engagement Template.

KARIM'S VERY BEST CUSTOMERS ARE CONSUMER ELECTRONICS RETAILERS

Because Karim has been in business for only a year and has just five clients, he was able to quickly plot his Very Best Customers by name onto his segmentation grid. He, too, found some interesting patterns that further supported his earlier Beast Potential score findings. Karim's fastest growing customers from an MRR point of view were his CE (consumer electronics) retailers (see Figure 5.3). These were his highest revenue customers *and* his highest margin customers.

His software solution had been expressly built for consumer electronics retailers, so this made perfect sense. On the other hand, it was clear that his mass merchandise (MM) retailers were growing much more slowly. They represented less than one-quarter of all his revenue, and they were lower margin because they required more customization and service to meet the broader needs of mass merchants.

This confirmed his hunch—that his solution wasn't addressing the needs of mass merchandise retailers as well as it was the needs of consumer electronics retailers. His segmentation also revealed that one consumer electronics retailer was showing low overall revenue contribution and low MRR growth. This would require further investigation.

Karim's segmentation and analysis opened up his mind to some new possibilities. Given his limited access to capital, his gut feeling was that he'd be far more profitable if he focused solely on the consumer electronics retail space, since his product for those customers was essentially built, and he could apply what resources he had to creating an even

Figure 5.3 BigFatData's Very Best Customer Segmentation Grid

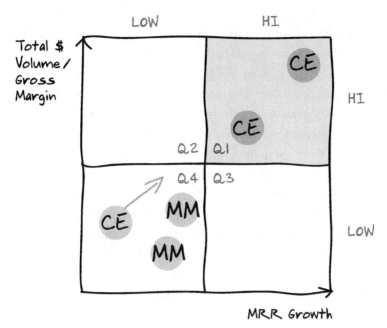

deeper solution for those retailers. Once he'd firmly established his consumer electronics base, he would be in a stronger position to reach out to the next most logical retail space and repeat the same strategy. Karim asked himself some "big fat" questions:

1. Is the consumer electronics retail space big enough for me to build my company out on?
2. How will my (seemingly) broader-solution competition be viewed, given my new focus?
3. Might I be able to sell mass merchandise retailers on a deeper, more focused solution that addresses only the consumer electronics portion of their business?

As a result, Karim decided first to size the consumer electronics retail market and second to personally interview all five of his customers, with an eye to answering questions 2 and 3 above. From there, based on what he found, he would build out a tentative Engagement Template that focused exclusively on the consumer electronics retail space.

PAUL IDENTIFIED THREE GROUPS OF "BEST" CUSTOMERS

Treadwater Chocolates had three distinctly different customer groups: small retailers, private label customers, and corporate gift basket suppliers.

The first group, small retailers, were his bread and butter: the tiny gift and confectionery retailers who represented over 85 percent of his customer base and accounted for 50 percent of his revenue. Private label customers, the second group, were large, national department stores and specialty food retailers who privately labeled Paul's products under their own brands. While these companies represented only 5 percent of Paul's customer base, they represented 40 percent of his revenue, but they were generally lower margin because they demanded such heavy discounts. Those discounts were balanced by up-front orders with only one or two shipping dates later in the year that allowed him to plan better. The last group was his unheralded corporate gift basket companies, who represented just 10 percent of his customer base and accounted for only 10 percent of his revenue. Nevertheless, the gift basket business is higher margin because it involves less service and support—in part because these resellers are very self-reliant, placing their orders through Paul's partner ecommerce site.

When Paul segmented his customers, he discovered a bit of a conundrum.

Figure 5.4 Treadwater's Very Best Customer Segmentation Grid

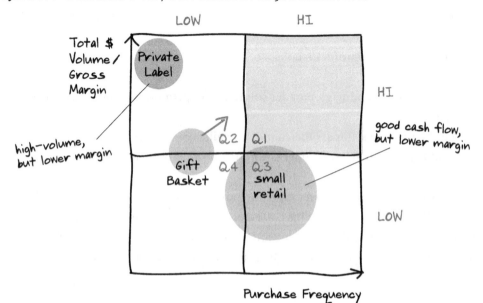

In a sense, Paul didn't really have any Very Best Customers. They were all valuable, but for different reasons, making up a kind of product "portfolio" for him. His private label retailers represented large, infrequent orders, which was actually good except the orders were lower margin. His small retail customers tended to be slightly lower margin because of higher servicing costs relative to their average order size, but they paid by credit card, so cash flow was good with this group. And while his gift basket customers offered reasonably good margins, they were very sporadic buyers, with 80 percent of sales coming in the December corporate gift-giving season.

What to Do?

Paul knew he didn't have the capital to turn Treadwater Chocolates into a national consumer brand that could result in much broader retail distribution, so standing back and putting on his 30,000-foot aviator goggles, he interpreted his segmentation opportunities this way:

1. He needed to lower his cost per sale to small retailers. That might mean reducing his number of SKUs and forcing more of them to place their orders online.
2. By better understanding the needs of private label retailers; by creating a full, turnkey program for them; and by actively marketing to them, he could probably increase his share of this market quite substantially while laying in a very dependable revenue base for his business.
3. By better understanding the needs of corporate gift basket companies, he could probably develop a better program for this market, which he could then more aggressively promote. While the business would remain mostly seasonal, it is profitable and is significantly underdeveloped in his business.

Paul decided to choose a sampling of customers from each of his three customer groups to help him further explore the opportunities his segmentation revealed. While his Beast Prospects appear to be private labelers, and the market growth among private labelers appears to be substantial, focusing only on private label business seemed to Paul a case of putting "too many eggs in one basket." Paul's gut was saying that his current customer diversification was good, but that each segment needed fine-tuning and balancing in order to optimize revenue and margin potential. He thought that, in the coming year, he would try tightening up his costs on his small retailers while expanding his business into more private label work. From that foundation, next year he would try a more aggressive push on corporate basket companies.

Paul's Very Best Customer list turned out to be broader than the other two entrepreneurs'. He decided to interview 20 customers in all—around six customers per segment. Paul needed to validate his possible market opportunities with his customers and then build the appropriate Engagement Template for *each* opportunity, because he knew that his Beast Prospects would be defined differently for each market. But for now, from a marketing point of view, he was going to start with the private label retailers.

THE ENGAGEMENT QUESTIONNAIRE

Now that our three entrepreneurs (and you, if you're following the bouncing ball) have identified their Very Best Customers, it's time for them/you to make appointments to actually talk to those Very Best Customers to start building the first part of the Engagement Template: the Target.

The key elements of the Target that you want to uncover with your Very Best Customers are:

1. Identifying your Very Best Customers' decision-making process.
2. Identifying your Very Best Customers' research habits when they're making a considered purchase for their business.
3. Confirming the identity and title of the primary decision maker for your category of product or service. This may be more than one individual.
4. Determining the identities and titles of the decision team (Deciders, Influencers, Users), as applicable.

To help you gather this information from your Very Best Customers as efficiently and effectively as possible, we suggest you use the questions from the Engagement Questionnaire, "Part 1: The Target" (see Figure 5.5). In part one, you're going to ask them to identify the key decision makers and the research sources they go to during their typical Decision Cycle.

Identifying the decision team. Before you interview your Very Best Customers, please note: If you're selling to a larger company, chances are you'll be selling to a "decision team," not an individual buyer. That team often includes a number of Deciders, Influencers, and possibly even Users. It's possible that the number of people on the decision team could be as high as 20, which is a lot of people to engage. Truth be told, you don't need

(continued on page 54)

Figure 5.5 Very Best Customer Interview Guide: Target

PART 1: THE TARGET

1. When it comes to decisions to purchase products/services/solutions such as ours, who is involved in the decision process?

    Who do you need to target your marketing efforts to?

2. Who (title or role) has the final say in the purchase decision? Is there anyone else who influences the decision? Do the final *users* make or influence the decision?

    Who else is involved that needs to be addressed by you?

3. How does the decision process work? How long does it usually take for a purchase decision to be made?

4. What do you see your role being within that decision process?

    Confirmation.

5. When you or your team are researching products/services/solutions such as ours, how would you rank each of the following information sources on a scale from 0 to 10, where 10 is "critically important" to your research:

    Where can we find your decision team?

    Probe for examples of each and rank as appropriate

    Personal referrals: _____
    User groups: _____
    Vendor sales rep: _____
    Vendor websites: _____
    Distributor reps: _____
    Online industy discussion forums: _____
    Other network groups: _____
    Industry blogs: _____
    LinkedIn: _____
    Twitter: _____
    Facebook: _____
    Other social media: _____
    Trade websites: _____
    Trade publications (print): _____
    Trade publications (online): _____
    Analysts: _____
    Analyst websites: _____
    Trade shows: _____

6. *The following can be done without the customer's participation:*

    Add business demographics: industry/sector, company size (revenue and employees), number of locations, years in business, products/services sold.

    Basic template for finding Beast Prospects

to reach them all. Through your Engagement Interview, you need to zero in on who the key decision maker and influencers are. The smaller the number, the easier and more efficient it will be for you to identify and reach them.

SOPHIE BUILDS HER ENGAGEMENT TEMPLATE

Thanks to the insights she gathered from her Very Best Customers, Sophie's targeting strategy has come into focus, and the first part of her Engagement Template has been completed (see Figure 5.6).

When those insights are analyzed and interpreted, a target profile begins to emerge. Sophie confirmed *who* her Beast Prospects are and what *role* they play in the purchase decision. Importantly for her, while the top agent wasn't the *de facto* decision maker (the homeowner was), the top agent introduced the sale and *strongly* influenced the outcome.

Figure 5.6 Staged2Go's Engagement Template So Far

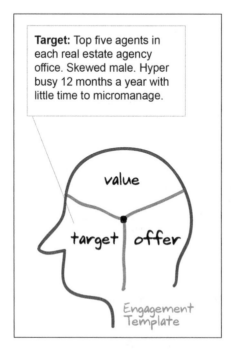

- Prospect companies: real estate agencies in prescribed geographic region dealing with higher-end homes
- Primary target: top five agents in each agency
- Decision maker: homeowner
- Decision Influencers: the agent, the homeowner, possibly the broker principal
- Users: homeowners

KARIM BUILDS HIS ENGAGEMENT TEMPLATE

Karim, too, has completed the first part of his Engagement Template (see Figure 5.7).

Karim has not only discovered *who* his Beast Prospects are—the decision team and the primary target—but what *role* they play in the purchase decision.

Figure 5.7 BigFatData's Engagement Template So Far

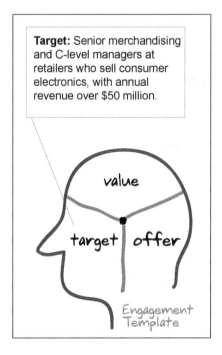

- Prospect companies: $50+ million national retailers who sell consumer electronics
- Primary target: senior merchandising managers and C-level managers
- Decision makers: senior merchandising manager and possibly CFO and/or CTO
- Decision Influencers: other IT managers, marketing managers, sourcing/procurement managers
- Users: merchandising managers/buyers, pricing specialists/analysts

PAUL BUILDS HIS ENGAGEMENT TEMPLATE

Finally, the first part of Paul's Engagement Template for his private label retail prospects was completed (see Figure 5.8).

Like the two entrepreneurs before him, Paul now has a stronger picture of who he needs to include in his Beast Prospect List:

- Prospect companies: $100+ million national mass merchandise and specialty food retailers
- Primary target: confectionery and/or food category buyer

Figure 5.8 Paul's Private Label Engagement Template So Far

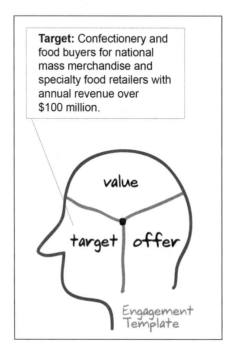

- Decision makers: confectionery and/or food category buyer
- Decision Influencers: assistant buyer, category manager, inventory manager, market analysts, region managers, store managers
- Users: category buyers and/or assistant category buyers

CAVE SCRATCHES

5

- ~ Segment your customers into quadrants based on profitability
- ~ Use Engagement Questionnaire to identify decision makers
- ~ Target: First part of Engagement Template

NEXT UP

To complete your targeting strategy, you will need to build a Beast Prospect List. You'll find the secrets to building a high-quality list in Chapter 14, "The Beast Prospect List." Although you can skip to that chapter if you're in a hurry, to get the most out of the book, it's best to follow the roadmap step-by-step. In the next chapter, you're going to discover how to unearth your company's true value *as your Beast Prospects see it*. Once you begin speaking their language, you'll be amazed at how much easier it is to get your Beast Prospects' attention.

Value: The Second Law of Engagement

Chances are you think you know your value story inside-out for each of the market segments that you serve. After all, like any passionate entrepreneur, you're repeating your value mantra to anyone who'll listen, every day of the week (including evenings). In fact, you may be saying to yourself: "Value. Yup, got it. Think I'll skip this chapter and see what's going on in Chapter 7." Stay with us for at least one more paragraph.

It's quite possible that your current value proposition is doing your business more harm than good. How so? If your value story doesn't resonate with your Beast Prospects at a visceral level, then it's probably coming across as white noise, and you've just dropped your chance to create your first engagement. If you want to successfully feed your Beast, you can't afford to do that too often. Big, red flags in your value proposition include words like "best," "more," "world-class," "high-quality," and the mention of "price" in any form. Another big, red flag is if your Very Best Customers didn't write your value proposition.

TELLING THE RIGHT STORY

So how do you know if you're telling the right value story? You may have your sales pitch down pat, but a sales pitch and a value proposition are often miles apart. A sales pitch generally frames the story around *you*, the seller. This often means that you're presenting a list of features and benefits to your Beast Prospects, and you're expecting them to figure out how those features and benefits can be applied to their situation. Here's an example from the data storage business:

THE WRONG STORY

Prospect Pain	Sales Pitch	Required Prospect Translation
"We need a simpler way to make sure all the right data is available to all the right people throughout the company."	• More storage • More secure storage • Lower cost • User-friendly admin portal	"I guess if we had more storage, our data could all be in one place, and presumably, it would be more available. I wonder how we'd manage permissions."

The reality is, your Beast Prospects have a pain that needs to be solved, not a brochure that needs to be read. A sales pitch makes the prospect work too hard—it introduces unnecessary friction where you don't want any. A value proposition, on the other hand, is message grease. It frames your value story around the business problems your Beast Prospects are trying to solve, and it does so in the prospects' own words (or in the words of your Beast Prospects' able proxy, your Very Best Customers).

THE RIGHT STORY

Prospect Pain	Value Proposition	Required Prospect Translation
"We need a simpler way to make sure all the right data is available to all the right people throughout the company."	We securely and easily centralize all your data and give you a simple way to control who can access it.	None.

To ensure your value proposition is well grounded, you need to complete the second part of your Engagement Template for each market segment you're going after, with the help of your Very Best Customers. Once that's completed, you'll add the third and final law, the Offer, and you'll have a complete template with which to go out and find more customers like your Best Customers. So right now, let's formally define "value proposition" and then give you the three questions that will help you create a truly compelling value proposition.

YOUR VALUE PROPOSITION

Your value proposition is the pressing business pain you solve for your Beast Prospects, in their own words. This is a pain that you consistently solve *better than anyone else* and that your prospects are *willing to pay you money* to alleviate.

Over the years, we've found that the best and simplest way to develop (or sharpen) your value proposition is to have your Very Best Customers answer three questions under the headings Pain, Promise, and Proof:

1. **Pain.** What significant business pain do your Very Best Customers have that they are willing to pay to have resolved?
2. **Promise.** How does your product or service uniquely address that pain in a way that is superior to your competition?
3. **Proof.** What three facts about your product or service prove your promise to be true?

Of course, to get true, unvarnished answers, it often helps to be a little more circumspect in an interview. Sometimes, because of their tendency to want to please the interviewer, people have trouble answering direct questions. To help you formulate your own value story, let's follow Sophie as she uses her Engagement Questionnaire to explore her value story with her Very Best Customers. You can download the interview guide at http://tools .FeedTheBeast.biz (or use your mobile device to scan the QR Code).

QR Code
Engagement Questionnaire

HOW SOPHIE GOT HER GROOVE BACK

When we last saw her, Sophie had decided to delay expanding her business into new markets, had added a bookkeeper to smooth out some "wrinkles" in her business that were possibly holding back her growth, and had decided to focus her marketing efforts on the top 5 to 10 real estate agents per agency. These are the very people Sophie will now interview to help tighten her value proposition for use within her Engagement Template.

Before she started her Engagement Interviews, we talked to Sophie about her value story and asked her to articulate it. Sophie admitted she hadn't thought through her value proposition, let alone documented it, but when pressed to come up with something she could hang her hat on, she offered us this: "Staged2Go provides the best staging services to real estate agents and homeowners at a very competitive price."

Not a very compelling value story, is it? There are three main reasons it fails to do the job. There's no empathy with the customer's business *pain*, no *promise* to resolve that pain, and no *proof* that she's even able to keep her promise. In fact, it could easily be the value proposition for any staging firm in town.

Sophie's thinking on her value story had been influenced by her perception of all her real estate agents' needs, not the needs expressed by those who were in fact her Very Best Customers, the top-performing agents. As a result, Sophie believed:

1. Real estate agents think that all staging firms offer essentially the same service, with the difference being who has the best staging inventory and design skills.
2. Real estate agents just want the home to look good, so they can sell it quicker.
3. Real estate agents want to be involved in the staging process (because they always seem to be).

Fast forward to Sophie's Engagement Interviews. At least two of the three assumptions Sophie had made were proven less applicable *to the top agents in the market*—her Very Best Customers. Below you'll find the Value section of the Engagement Questionnaire (see Figure 6.1). These are the questions Sophie asked to get at the root of her Very Best Customers' pain and find out how they perceived the *value* of her services.

Figure 6.1 Engagement Questionnaire: Value Section

This is the burning business pain that your customer would be willing to pay to alleviate. Needs to be something you can solve.

PART 2: VALUE

This is your promise. Try to isolate the most unique benefit of your solution.

1. What keeps you up at night as it relates to _____?
   (look for 3-5 relevant monsters in the closet)

2. You said you would be very likely to recommend our company. What is the best thing we do to help you address *one or more* of the things that are keeping you up at night?

This provides the proof that makes your promise believable.

3. What are 3 qualities of our business that you think enable us to address your closet monsters better than our competitors?

This tests what they've told you. Make sure opportunities aren't missed.

4. For each of the qualities in (3), how important is each quality to you (scale of 0-10), and how well do you feel we deliver on each quality (scale of 0-10)?

A great trick to find out more!

5. What would you tell us to stop doing? Keep doing? Start doing?

Know who they consider your competition. May surprise you.

6. Who would you say are our competitors for your business?

Another cross-check on what they've told you.

7. How do we differ from those competitors, in your view?

From these seven questions, this is what Sophie found out about her Very Best Customers' pain: Her top agents' most valued commodities are time and money. The more time they spend selling any one house, the less money they make in a year. As one agent put it, "I wish I had two of me."

And here's what they value most highly about Sophie's business:

1. **Her services are complete, and they are turnkey.** The best agents want to be involved as little as possible in the staging so they can manage the many other matters that arise in the emotion-laden sale of a home.
2. **Her business is professionally run.** Most staging firms aren't. They err on the side of design over business, with limited or no service and support staff.

Figure 6.2 Sophie's Value Proposition

Staged2Go

Value Proposition: Top-Performing Real Estate Agents

Pain

"I want to sell more homes, faster. Fix 'em up, and move 'em out. Wish I had two of me."

Promise

Staged2Go is a trusted business partner who will save you time on every home you sell by handling the complete home transformation in an efficient, professional, and turnkey manner.

Proof
- *Track record.* Staged2Go pioneered home staging 10 years ago and has transformed thousands of homes for hundreds of the city's top agents.
- *One-stop shop.* Staged2Go will manage every aspect of the staging so you don't have to—from cleaning to staging to painting to renovations—with full-time, on-staff stagers and contractors, ensuring availability and the quality of work.
- *Professionally run business.* Staged2Go has a dedicated customer service team, and all stagers receive twice-yearly sales and customer service training.

3. **They trust Staged2Go.** They trust that Sophie's team will make them look good in the eyes of their clients, the homeowners.

4. **Staged2Go saves them significant time.** Sophie's team does so by accomplishing all of the above, to say nothing of helping to sell the home faster.

From these findings, Sophie was able to build a strong value proposition that was more likely to resonate with other top-performing real estate agents in her market (see Figure 6.2).

Now that Sophie has nailed down her value proposition (the second Law of Engagement), she can fill in the value component of her Engagement Template (see Figure 6.3).

If your product or service doesn't consistently solve a monetizable customer problem better than your competitors', no amount of marketing will keep your ship from sinking. In fact, it will just accelerate it. If you have any doubts as to whether you can deliver on the value proposition you've just developed, go back and read Step 1 (Ask). Knowing your Beast Potential is the critical factor in determining whether your marketing dollars are being put to good use or are being wasted.

Figure 6.3 Sophie's Engagement Template So Far

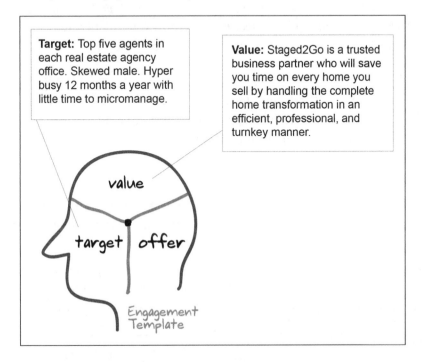

Target: Top five agents in each real estate agency office. Skewed male. Hyper busy 12 months a year with little time to micromanage.

Value: Staged2Go is a trusted business partner who will save you time on every home you sell by handling the complete home transformation in an efficient, professional, and turnkey manner.

value

target | offer

Engagement
Template

KARIM SHARPENS HIS FOCUS

Using the same Engagement Questionnaire as Sophie, Karim was able to confirm his Very Best Customers' pain and build a tighter value proposition for the merchandising executives he wanted to focus his resources on (see Figure 6.4).

Figure 6.4 Karim's Value Proposition

Value Proposition: Mid-to-Large Consumer Electronics Retailers

Pain
"I can't measure the impact of my pricing decisions. I'm pricing my products in a near vacuum because the data I'm using—competitive, store level, even inventory levels—can't be trusted."

Promise
BigFatData provides reliable, competitive pricing intelligence that will improve your product pricing decisions and give you insight into the effect those pricing decisions have on your unit and dollar sales.

Proof
Accurate. BigFatData examines millions of products across the Internet using proprietary artificial intelligence technology to match product and price data at a 98 percent accuracy level—the highest in the consumer electronics business.

Usable. BigFatData maps its data delivery to your workflow—as integrated data feeds, customized portals, or customized spreadsheets—ensuring that your team will be able to incorporate the competitive pricing intelligence into their decision making.

Measurable. BigFatData provides an A/B testing environment that allows you to assign sales results to each pricing action, either manually or via integration to your revenue reporting systems or data warehouses.

PAUL TRIPLES DOWN

Finally, our chocolate entrepreneur, Paul, developed three value propositions from his Very Best Customer interviews—one for each of the segments he wanted to optimize: small retailers, corporate gift basket companies, and private label retailers. Here's how his value story for private label retailers emerged against a very specific market pain (see Figure 6.5).

Figure 6.5 Paul's Value Proposition

CHOCOLATES

Private Label Value Proposition: Retail Buyers for Large, National, Mass Merchandise and Specialty Retailers

Pain

"Making gross margin (and my bonus) using the limited resources I have to reliably analyze, forecast, source, select, and then manage and promote my product mix in what's become a very unpredictable market."

Promise

Treadwater will become your "buying assistant" for private label confectionery products, applying our expertise to plan out a complete, high-margin, high-demand program to help anchor your gross margin achievement.

Proof

Market analysis and forecasting support. Treadwater deepens your planning resources with category expertise that helps to reduce costly out-of-stock and overstock situations and to maximize sales opportunities and margins.

The right product line. Treadwater's core product is Belgian-style, small-batch chocolate, and the company embellishes that core product annually with a focused selection of interesting-to-exotic line extensions based on significant R&D investment. Treadwater will custom develop your product,

continued on next page

brand, and packaging to meet your assortment and market requirements.

Proven sell-through. Treadwater's innovative, award-winning packaging and its innovative merchandising support have a demonstrable track record of producing high shelf-turns for its private label customers.

———

Now that you've had a chance to see how value propositions are constructed, it's time to develop and refine your own. Make it easy on yourself by building it around Pain, Promise, and Proof. Once you've nailed your value story, you'll have completed two-thirds of your Engagement Template. Your Engagement Template is more than a prospect profile. Think of it as your little black book, your quick reference guide. Keep it close and keep it safe, because all the big, hairy, outrageous marketing successes to come will flow out of it.

CAVE SCRATCHES
- "Why should I buy from you?"
- Pain, Promise, Proof
- Value is solving your prospects' pain
- Value: Second part of Engagement Template

NEXT UP

You know who your Beast Prospects are. You know what story they want to hear. What about the third piece of the engagement puzzle? *How* do you tell your story in such a compelling and timely way that your Beast Prospects raise their hands and engage in a relationship with you? That's what the third Law of Engagement, the Offer, will help you do.

Offer: The Third Law of Engagement

What you'll find in this chapter:

- The Decision Cycle
- Why offers work
- Content and the Engagement Ladder
- Be a dolphin in a sea of sharks
- Paul's Engagement Ladder
- Completing your Engagement Template
- Paul's offer hooks a customer

More than 3 billion searches are conducted online every day, and that number is increasing exponentially. Among those 3 billion searches are business buyers looking for solutions to their problems. In fact, today those buyers will be nearly 60 percent through their purchase Decision Cycle before they even have a conversation with a sales rep.[1] That's why the key to Big, Hairy, Outrageous Sales Growth is to become part of their exploration. Your goal is to become their trusted resource as they research, evaluate, and consider the solutions they need to ease their business pain.

Do you want to be that resource? Then offer them something different. Something they can't find anywhere else. Something that will help make their job easier.

Content.

Not just any content. Content that's valuable, timely, relevant, matches your prospects' Decision Cycle, and focuses on *their* needs, not yours. But in order to be able to match your content to their needs, you have to better understand their needs.

YOUR PROSPECT'S PURCHASE DECISION CYCLE

The Decision Cycle is a series of fairly well-defined steps in the considered purchase decision process, beginning with awareness of a need (stage one in Figure 7.1), moving through a process of education, and concluding with vendor selection and purchase (stage five). It can take weeks or months or even years to complete, depending on the complexity of the product being considered. In Sophie's business (home staging), the decision would likely be measured in weeks. In Karim's business (enterprise software solutions), months are more likely. Early in the process, when a new purchase is being investigated and possible solutions are being evaluated, business buyers will frequently tap their peers and personal networks for information. But beyond that, studies now show that vendor websites and web searches are topping word-of-mouth as the most common source of early stage purchase information.[2]

Stage 1: Problem Awareness

"Hmmm . . . I've got a problem."

At some point, buyers decide they need to seek a solution for a business problem they have. At that point, their need becomes an *active need*, and depending on the urgency, the buyer is motivated to start exploring whether a reasonable solution can be found. Reasonable, in this case, can mean many things, including affordable, effective, timely, and manageable from a risk tolerance point-of-view.

Stage 2: Solution Education

"What's available to help me solve my problem?"

At the solution education stage, buyers are trying to frame their problem to see if a reasonable solution exists. They need to understand the lay of the land and will talk with colleagues, possibly read analyst and industry reports, and generally try to educate themselves on what is possible, often developing a list of requirements along the way. Clearly,

Figure 7.1 Your Prospect's Decision Cycle Journey

the most opportune time to insert yourself into the Decision Cycle is stage two, if you're able to do so in an unbiased, helpful fashion.

Stage 3: Vendor Education

"Which solutions are credible and relevant?"

At the vendor education stage, buyers are actively exploring which vendors offer a solution that seems to address their list of requirements. Still heavily web-based, their research is intended to cast a wide net to make sure that they're not missing what might be the best solution for their business. This stage might be considered creating the vendor "long list."

Stage 4: Vendor Consideration

"Which are the best solutions for my needs?"

At the vendor consideration stage, buyers are interested in creating a vendor "short list"— vendors who seem most capable of addressing the buyer's requirements in the most reasonable manner. At this stage, buyers will often review peer reports, seek easily found references and testimonials, download analyst reports, and visit company websites in order to compare vendors and product specifications. Some buyers will reach out to the companies at this stage to begin a conversation. When this happens, it's your sales team who should be having that conversation.

Stage 5: Vendor Selection

"I choose . . ."

At stage five, most buyers are ready to speak with their candidate vendors. At this point, your sales team needs to be fully engaged because the buyer is moving toward a purchase decision. That said, in larger companies the purchase decision may still take months to complete as vendors are put through a selection process often involving a "decision team" of several individuals within the buyer company.

That helps. So how do we connect content to need?

HELLO
Karim

How do we connect content to need? Very good question. You use offers.

THE THIRD LAW

If you were to create some of the most helpful and *findable* content out there, you would likely attract a number of buyers (who we'll call prospects, at this point) who happen to be looking for what it is that you sell. At the same time, if you were to target likely prospects and put your helpful content under their noses, some of them too would scoop up your helpful content. But if you gave these prospects all of this valuable content for free, what happens next? How do you turn that free content into a sales lead for your company? Well, the trick is, you don't give it to them for free. Or at least, not quite. The Third Law of Engagement states:

Never give anything of value away for free.

You create valuable content, yes, but you require an exchange before your prospect can access it—a value exchange. What do you want from your prospects? You want a serious expression of their interest that you can *measure*, because measurement, as you'll see, drives your entire Beast Marketing System. The simplest way to measure their interest is to have them give you their contact information in exchange for your content. You make them an offer: *in exchange for this, you get that.* They decide whether that exchange is worthwhile to them or not.

Will asking for contact information cause a bunch of your prospects to leave without accepting your offer? Quite possibly, but here's the thing: If prospects are seriously researching a topic, and if you provide a piece of content that promises to make their lives far easier at this point in their Decision Cycle, don't you think they'd give up their name for it? If they're serious, and if your content is good, most will. If they're not serious or, alternatively, if your content isn't that compelling, they may walk away. The former situation—prospects who aren't serious, walking away—quite likely saves you a bunch of cycles that you can't afford to waste anyway. The latter situation—content that's not compelling—is one you can't afford to let happen.

There are two qualities of a successful offer: it must be valuable in the eyes of your prospects, and it must be relevant to them. The first you'll solve with your Engagement Questionnaire; the second you'll solve with a ladder. Let's start with the ladder.

YOUR ENGAGEMENT LADDER

Information loses its power to inform and persuade unless it's relevant and timely. The trick is to develop and organize your content and then time its delivery to make it as relevant as possible to your prospects based on where they are in their Decision Cycle. You do this by creating an Engagement Ladder, which is simply a series of escalating offers that are developed to address the different needs your prospects have during their Decision Cycle, making an effort to "engage" them each step along the way. See the sample Engagement Ladder that follows.

A SAMPLE ENGAGEMENT LADDER

Touch	Offer	Lead Grade Goal	Decision Cycle Support
8th	Custom analysis, plan, or assessment	A	Decision support
7th	Aids: ROI calculator, forecast tool		
6th	Samples, demos, or trials	B	Vendor consideration
5th	Video testimonials		
4th	Webinar	C	Vendor education
3rd	Case studies or white papers		
2nd	Generic buying guide or competitive comparisons	D	Solution education
1st	Analyst reports or industry studies		

Each "rung" of the Ladder, working from the bottom up, contains high-value content that best matches the prospect's needs at a given Decision Cycle stage. Whether your prospects *find you* (via inbound marketing like search engine optimization and pay-per-click ads on search engines) or you *find them* (via outbound marketing like email), you want to have a full Engagement Ladder of content ready *before* the two of you interact. That way, if one of the shiny objects on your Ladder captures their attention, you're immediately ready to tempt them up your Ladder with the shiny object on the next rung. When you're trying to build a new relationship, responsiveness is everything, and your prebuilt Engagement Ladder gives you the ability to be *very* responsive.

The higher your prospects go up the ladder, the closer they get to becoming customers. To get on the Ladder, prospects either find you (when they're researching on the web), in which case you make sure there is an unmistakable and very attractive path directly to your offer. Or you find them (when you're prospecting for leads), in which case you again make sure that you lead them to your offer. Either way, they end up on the same Ladder with the same offers and same content because they're on the same Decision Cycle, regardless of how they come to you. And if the offers are well conceived, high-potential prospects will be drawn up your Ladder and then down into your sales funnel.

The typical Engagement Ladder is made up of eight rungs. Why eight? It's said that it takes eight touches before a relationship is created between two people. At touch one, I don't really know who you are. By touch eight, I pretty much feel like I know you. You have become familiar to me. Hanging off each rung is an offer. Exposing your prospects to a series of high-value offers over time not only deepens their engagement but keeps them engaged *throughout their Decision*

Cycle until they're ready to be contacted by you. And because they'll be exchanging information (i.e., their name and email address) for each offer they accept, you'll have a measurable record of where they are on your Ladder, giving you insight into how to reach out to them next. What's also important to note is that this measurable record allows you to deal with hundreds of prospects simultaneously by grouping like-needs together and responding to them in a personalized yet very efficient batch-like way. For that reason, you'll notice that each rung of the Ladder in the previous sample shown also contains a lead grade that you'll use to track and group your prospects over time.

You might also have noticed that the sample Engagement Ladder doesn't include the usual stock-in-trade-like product brochures and spec sheets. That kind of content *should* be on your website, and it *should* be free (i.e., no value exchange required). The content on your Engagement Ladder needs to be a cut above and entirely focused on adding value to your prospect's Decision Cycle journey—content they'd be willing to *exchange* for. If it is, you'll be able to engage your prospects and begin a relationship with them.

big, hairy tip

If you're a good writer, your offers probably won't cost you anything but time and effort (neither of which we take for granted). But most entrepreneurs don't have the time or ability to produce consistently good content. Spending money on content creation can pay big dividends, as you'll discover later in the chapter. In addition, you can and should complement your original content with high-value, third-party content. This can take the form of webinars, podcasts, videocasts, newspaper articles, newsletters, infographics, white papers, case studies, and so on. Quality third-party content is readily available if you know where to look. Just make sure you personalize it and give it context by adding an introduction.

HOW TO BE A DOLPHIN IN A SEA OF SHARKS

It may seem counterintuitive, but the content of your offers should never be about you or your products or services. At least, not initially. Not if you want to start building trust.

Paul, our chocolatier, knows that if he wants to stand out from his competitors, his offers and messaging must be all about his prospects: *their* industry, *their* opportunities, and above all, *their* pain. In other words, Paul's goal is to be a dolphin in a sea of sharks.

Dolphins are known for their acute eyesight, advanced hearing, remarkable intelligence, and protective attitude toward humans in trouble. Just as the dolphin becomes the swimmer's best friend when the swimmer is attacked by sharks, Paul can become the business buyer's most trusted ally during the complex buying decision process. This is not by chance—Paul has carefully targeted his Beast Prospects, understands their pain, and is planning to keep them informed throughout their Decision Cycle.

Because your goal is to be always building a value-based relationship with prospects, as well as to be *tracking* the stages of that relationship so you can better respond to your prospects, all of your marketing efforts should contain a "rung" offer that directs your prospects back to a web-based Engagement Page that allows them to transact for the offer. Engagement Pages, more often called landing pages, are web pages that are completely dedicated to your offer, promoting it in the best light possible and containing a web form with a "submit" button that allows the value exchange to take place (see Figure 7.2). In Chapter 8, you'll learn how to create an Engagement Page for each offer on your Engagement Ladder. It's easier than you might think.

Why are Engagement Pages so important? Because a stunning 70 percent of B2B buyers rate how vendors *engaged* with them as being more important to their decision process than *what those vendors were selling*, according to Forrester Research.[3] In other words, buyers are saying, "Make my life easier." And yet studies show that three-quarters of B2B companies direct their prospects to the home page of their websites to essentially fend for themselves. The likely thinking is that the home page has all the information prospects are looking for, but the trouble is that most home pages are closer to being information dumps than they are to being guided tours. Your website, as you'll see in Chapter 8, needs to be a guided tour to your Engagement Pages so your prospects' lives can be made easier. That said, when you find a prospect or a prospect finds you, you want the line to your Engagement Pages to be as short as possible.

Figure 7.2 One of Paul's Engagement Pages

PAUL'S ENGAGEMENT LADDER

Let's take a look at an actual Engagement Ladder—one that Paul created to engage his private label prospects, whose business he's chosen to focus on in the next year. As you can see in Paul's Engagement Ladder that follows, there are eight rungs on his ladder, and they're grouped according to the stages of his prospects' Decision Cycle.

PAUL'S COMPLETED ENGAGEMENT LADDER

Touch	Offer	Prospect Grade Goal	Decision Cycle Support
8th	Custom analysis and sample plan	A	Vendor selection
7th	Confectionery forecasting tool for private label		
6th	Treadwater private label sample kits	B	Vendor consideration
5th	Treadwater private label success stories		
4th	Treadwater private label program kit	C	Vendor education
3rd	"Private Label: The Treadwater Difference" (video)		
2nd	"Holding Margin with Private Label" (analyst study)	D	Solution education
1st	"Exotic Flavors Drive Sales" (trends report)		

Paul's D-rung offers include a trends report and an analyst study. This is partly to appeal to the largest number of prospects, because at this point he doesn't know where they are in their Decision Cycles, and partly because he hasn't yet established a relationship. But keep in mind what he *does* know. He knows that the audience he's targeting has an interest in private label products and that private label confectionery products are high on their list. How does he know? Because his Very Best Customers told him so during his Engagement Interview, and Paul's out to find more customers who look just like his Very Best Customers. (See Figure 7.3 for Paul's completed Engagement Template.) It's also worth noting

Figure 7.3 Paul's Completed Engagement Template

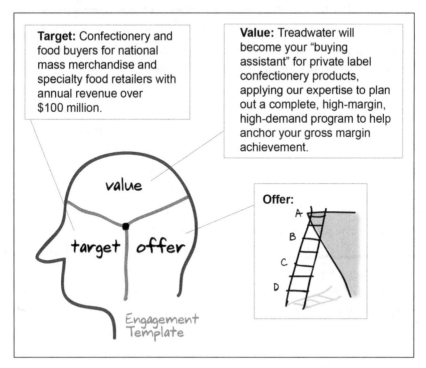

that his first two offers have little or nothing to do with his company or his products. This low-key, non-hard-sell approach is important because he's still a stranger—he hasn't yet earned his prospects' trust or confidence.

What if some of his prospects are further along the Decision Cycle, say in the vendor education stage? If Paul has put a solution education offer in front of them, doesn't he risk missing the mark and losing the prospect? Possibly, yes. There's no practical way for Paul to know exactly what stage prospects are at in their Decision Cycle when he first encounters them. So he starts by casting as wide a net as possible (using his D-rung offers), hoping to engage them at some level and then qualify them based on what they show interest in next (we'll explain more fully in Part Two of the book).

But there is something he can do to help. He can always include an Escape Hatch Offer. An Escape Hatch Offer says to the prospect, "Close, but not quite what you're looking for?" and then provides a link to something you'll come to know as your Learning Hub. In your Learning Hub, your prospects will be able to see the entire range of your Engagement Ladder content and self-select whatever is most relevant to them. More on Escape Hatches and Learning Hubs later.

Paul sequences his offers so that his prospects are encouraged to climb his Ladder from bottom to top. If a prospect "reaches" for the offer on the next rung, Paul will "see" it in his reporting (Chapter 9) and will graduate that prospect up to the next Prospect Grade. For tracking purposes, every prospect is assigned a grade from D to A, with D being the least engaged. The moment a prospect reaches for an A-rung offer, Paul knows he needs to get that prospect into the hands of his sales team (who, in the case of his private label programs, is him). The prospect has become "sales ready."

So, for example, if Paul's D-prospects respond to his *Exotic Flavors Drive Sales* trends report offer, it suggests that Paul has struck a relevant chord with them. So on his next outreach, he would feature his *Private Label: The Treadwater Difference* video to see if his prospects are ready to be enticed up the Ladder to become C-prospects. Paul always leaves an Escape Hatch open by featuring his Learning Hub.

If they reach for his C-rung offer, Paul moves them up a rung, including them in his next monthly mailing to aspiring B-prospects, featuring a new offer (Treadwater sample kits). And so on up the Ladder until they become A-prospects, ready to be passed to his sales team for conversion into a sale. Typically, the marketing person/team owns and nurtures the prospect relationship all the way up to the B-rung; then, if a prospect reaches for the next A-rung offer, the sales team is called in. Or Paul puts on his sales hat.

There's no particular magic to eight rungs other than, as we discussed, relationships generally become bound after eight "touches." We've seen for ourselves that financial services prospects usually require eight to ten touches before they make a decision to move forward, while in software and high tech, the number of touches can vary widely, from two or three in some software categories to over ten in some hardware categories. But again, in our experience eight is a good working number for most industries.

That said, the "graduate by action" process we've been describing isn't perfect by any means. For example, prospects may decide to select and download all the information available to them in order to save time later on. What stage are they at? Hard to say. Even so, a repeatable, structured approach like the Engagement Ladder will, over time, produce a more consistent flow of opportunities through your Beast Cave than most other approaches because of its *consistency*. As always, slow and steady wins the race.

PAUL'S OFFER HOOKS A CUSTOMER

As you'll recall, during his survey of his Very Best Customers, Paul confirmed that his best private label prospects were larger mass merchandise and specialty retailers. The prospects responsible for what he had to sell were food and confectionery buyers whose primary concern was managing the gross margin of their product mix. They earned their bonuses, a significant part of their compensation, based on how well they hit their gross margin goals.

Sandra is the assistant confectionery buyer for a trendy, national chain of upscale food supermarkets. She's one of Paul's Beast Prospects, but Paul has not reached out to her yet. Sandra's job is to research, source, purchase, and manage all confectionery products carried by the chain—both in-store and online—a total of about 300 SKUs. The contract for her current private label chocolate line was up for renewal, and she wanted to explore all her options. Her margin on chocolate products overall had been soft, and the markdowns she was taking weren't good for her bonus. Sandra had recently read that her core customers' tastes were shifting toward the slightly more adventurous—involving unusual and exotic combinations of flavors. Sandra had contacted her current private label chocolate supplier about broadening the flavor selection, and they'd promised to get back to her with some ideas. That was over two weeks ago. Sandra didn't want to wait any longer, and thanks to the glowing, ubiquitous monitor in front of her, she didn't have to.

Knowing she could talk to her private label rep after she learned more about what she wanted, Sandra turned to the web for ideas. She began her search process with one question in mind: "What's available to help me solve my problem?"

On a hunch, Sandra Googled "savory chocolate." She noticed several vendors she'd heard of before, but she also noticed an ad at the top of the page for Treadwater Chocolates. They were offering a trends report demonstrating the significant growth of savory chocolate snacks over the last several years. Because Sandra wanted to learn more about the trends she'd recently discovered for herself, she clicked on the ad and landed on a web page that described the report in greater detail and contained a web form that she would need to complete in order to get the report. The bullet point summary of the report piqued her curiosity, and she decided it was worth handing over her name for the report itself.

D-rung offer. In exchange for her name, company name, and email address, Sandra was able to download the report, which strongly supported her idea of adding savory chocolate items as impulse purchase items. Interested in the company that brought this report to her attention, Sandra clicked on the link to Treadwater's website that she saw on the "thank you" page that appeared after she had downloaded the report. Sandra was impressed with Treadwater's well-organized website and wondered why she'd never heard of them before. On the right side of the home page, she noticed a small banner ad for a private label program kit, which she clicked on.

C-rung offer. Clicking on the banner ad brought Sandra to a web page that featured Treadwater's private label kit, which would be shipped within three days and would include a cold pack to ensure the chocolate samples arrived as intended (see Figure 7.4). The sample pack cost $15 to cover the cost of shipping. Sandra thought that was more than fair and proceeded to place her order online. While she didn't use Paul's Escape Hatch, there it was, sitting patiently at the bottom of his Engagement Page.

Sales-Ready Lead. By the end of the week, Sandra had received and tasted the samples. Overall, the presentation and intelligence of the private label kit impressed Sandra tremendously. She decided she would invite Treadwater Chocolates to bid on her private label business and began a relationship with a firm she hadn't known existed a few weeks earlier.

Timing is everything. Making prospects an offer they're not ready for (e.g., a discount) will fall on deaf ears (meaning lower response rates) if they're still educating themselves about the category you're in. For example, if Paul's Google ad had offered Sandra a shipping discount on savory chocolate, it would have gone wide of the mark on many levels, and Sandra probably would never have clicked on the ad. Remember, at the time, she didn't even know who Treadwater Chocolates was or whether they were suitable for her needs, so a shipping discount would have been meaningless.

Figure 7.4 Another of Paul's Engagement Pages

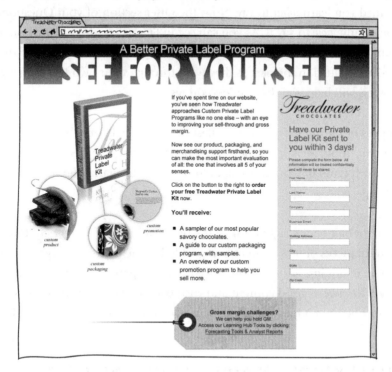

When you make your offer on your Engagement Page, try to keep the number of links and buttons to an absolute minimum. You want to make it as easy as possible for your busy prospects to quickly access and download the information they want. If they have trouble understanding or accessing what you're offering, a large percentage of your prospects will just swim away.

HOW TO CHOOSE THE RIGHT OFFER
(USING YOUR ENGAGEMENT TEMPLATE)

If you're wondering what to offer your prospects, not to worry. Your Very Best Customers will tell you during the Engagement Interview. As you'll recall, part one of your

Engagement Interview (the Target section) clarified *who* to say it to. Part two (the Value section) helped you learn *what* to say. Now, the Offer section of your Questionnaire will help you determine *how* to say it. As you can see in Figure 7.5, there is only one question. You're simply asking your Very Best Customers to rate which sources of information they've used and valued in the past as they went through their own Decision Cycles.

The answers will help you discover two things:

1. The sources of information your Very Best Customers rely on when purchasing
2. The content, tools, or approaches you'll need to engage others like them (in other words, which types of worms you should put on your marketing hook to attract your Beast Prospects)

Having the right bait on the right hook in the right fishing hole at the right time is critical. With billions of pieces of new content being added to the Internet every year, you want to make sure you're not just adding more content to the sprawling online landfill. There's a huge difference between good content and *great* content. Great content doesn't waste the prospect's time because it has value and focus. Great content engages the reader.

THE CHALLENGE OF CREATING GREAT CONTENT

The key to a successful Engagement Ladder is ensuring that it's filled with lots of great content. Unfortunately, most entrepreneurs fall short in this area. They find it difficult to continually develop relevant new content that will engage prospects, so when the prospect is ready to make a move, the entrepreneur too often isn't. Forty-one percent of respondents surveyed by the Content Marketing Institute said they faced challenges "producing the kind of content that engages prospects"[4] (see Figure 7.6). You won't face this problem because you're going to stock your Engagement Ladder in advance with a combination of engaging content you've created mixed with relevant third-party content and possibly even informative, "curated" content.

Content curation (not the same as content aggregation) involves finding content and making editorial choices, so your content is always high quality and consistently relevant to your Beast Prospects. In addition, adding your own comments and insights to the content creates value by personalizing it, stamping it with your signature, and thus enhancing your reputation as a thought leader.

Figure 7.5 Engagement Questionnaire

What helps them make better decisions?

PART 3: OFFER

On a scale of 0 to 10, where 10 is *"very important,"* how would you rank each of the following when you're considering a new solution for your business? When is each most useful to you in your decision cycle: Early (E), Middle (M), or Late (L) *[circle as appropriate]*?

THIRD PARTY

1. _____ Personal referrals [E M L]

2. _____ Trusted testimonials [E M L]

3. _____ Webinars featuring experts [E M L]

4. _____ Third party white papers [E M L]

5. _____ Social media referrals [E M L]

6. _____ Other: _____ [E M L]

COMPANY

7. _____ Company website [E M L]

8. _____ Webinars featuring company execs [E M L]

9. _____ Company party white papers [E M L]

10. _____ Buying guide [E M L]

11. _____ List of features & benefits [E M L]

12. _____ Case studies [E M L]

13. _____ Sales rep [E M L]

14. _____ Catalogs [E M L]

15. _____ Brochures & price lists [E M L]

16. _____ Company-led demonstrations [E M L]

17. _____ Other: _____ [E M L]

(continued)

Figure 7.5 Engagement Questionnaire *(continued)*

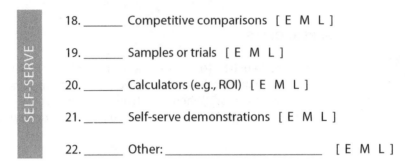

18. _____ Competitive comparisons [E M L]

19. _____ Samples or trials [E M L]

20. _____ Calculators (e.g., ROI) [E M L]

21. _____ Self-serve demonstrations [E M L]

22. _____ Other: _____ [E M L]

SELF-SERVE

Content curation can be useful, but ultimately, the biggest challenge isn't how to create *enough* content but rather how to make sure your content has high value and matches up as closely as possible with the prospect's Decision Cycle.

There are four secrets to creating high-value content—which, incidentally, search engines love—so that your Beast Prospects are better able to find you:

1. Allocate sufficient resources
2. Develop your content up front
3. Make sure that your content is "findable" by search engines
4. Make sure your content helps solve a business problem for your prospect

Figure 7.6 Biggest Content Marketing Challenges

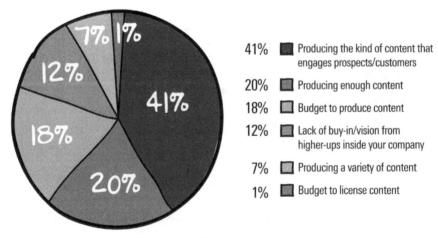

41% ■ Producing the kind of content that engages prospects/customers

20% ■ Producing enough content

18% ■ Budget to produce content

12% ■ Lack of buy-in/vision from higher-ups inside your company

7% ■ Producing a variety of content

1% ■ Budget to license content

The first secret is pretty self-explanatory, yet content creation is very frequently under-resourced. The second secret, developing all your content up front, ensures that you don't lose prime prospects. For instance, let's say you've developed a C-prospect who wants to pursue a relationship with you. If you delay responding because the material necessary to nurture the relationship isn't ready, you risk disappointing (and possibly losing) your prospect. The third secret, making your content "findable," is about creating content that's visible and valuable to your prospects when they're researching on the web. We'll show you how to do this in Chapter 11.

The fourth secret—ensuring your content solves a problem—may be the most misunderstood part of content creation. High-value content is a lot easier to create if you remember two key words: *pain* and *proof*. You identified your prospects' pain in the Value part of your Engagement Interview, and you identified the solution when you clarified your value proposition. Use these to hone your message, but make sure that you resist the temptation to sell too hard—especially early on in your relationship with prospects. Like any entrepreneurial thought leader, you want to hint at the solution without giving it away (or being too self-serving) so they come back, hungry for more.

What about the quality of the writing? Good writing is a skill acquired over time. Even the most casual reader will be gripped by a good story well told. Conversely, even the most committed reader will disengage if the writing is mediocre. Interestingly, the larger the company the more likely it is to outsource its content development, as you can see in Figure 7.7.

Figure 7.7 Percentage of Companies That Outsource Content Marketing

	2011	2010
Micro (fewer than 10 employees)	53%	48%
Small (10-99 employees)	60%	42%
Mid-sized (100-999 employees)	62%	54%
Large (1000+ employees)	74%	77%
Average	58%	55%

Unless you're a very good writer, the best way to develop compelling content that consistently engages the reader is to assign it to a professional content developer with writing experience in, or a passion for, your industry or vertical market. That makes sure it gets done well and, even more important, makes sure it gets done.

KARIM'S AND SOPHIE'S ENGAGEMENT LADDERS

We've seen how Paul built his Engagement Ladder and used it to engage, nurture, and convert prospects. Because we'll be referring to the Engagement Ladders of all of our entrepreneurs throughout the book, here's what Karim's and Sophie's Engagement Ladders look like. Like Paul, their ladders were focused by the insights they obtained from their Very Best Customers as recorded in their Engagement Templates (see Figures 7.8 and 7.9).

Figure 7.8 Karim's Completed Engagement Template

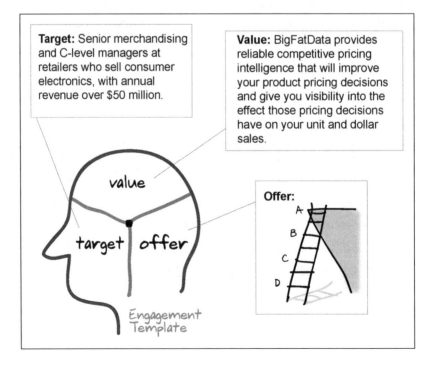

KARIM'S COMPLETED ENGAGEMENT LADDER

Touch	Offer	Lead Grade Goal	Decision Cycle Support
8th	Live data test drive (using the prospect's data)	A	Decision support
7th	ROI calculator		
6th	"Selecting Your PI Vendor: 12 Questions Retailers Should Ask"	B	Vendor consideration
5th	Interactive case studies		
4th	Self-guided online demo	C	Vendor education
3rd	"5 Secrets" (webinar featuring actual customers)		
2nd	"5 Retail Price Intelligence Secrets" (analyst paper)	D	Solution education
1st	"Competitive Price Intelligence: UNMASKED"		

Figure 7.9 Sophie's Completed Engagement Template

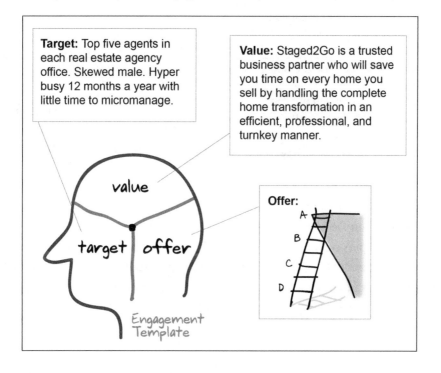

Remember, the goal of your Engagement Ladder is to make your prospects' lives easier—to help resolve, bit by bit, a little of what is keeping them up at night—from first encounter through to final sale. Start with non-company-specific offers until you've built trust. Only then should you make the shift to company- or product-specific information.

SOPHIE'S COMPLETED ENGAGEMENT LADDER

Touch	Offer	Lead Grade Goal	Decision Cycle Support
8th	"What to Expect: S2G Pledge of Service" (includes terms of satisfaction guarantee)	A	Decision support
7th	S2G warehouse tour		
6th	Annual S2G homeowner satisfaction survey results	B	Vendor consideration
5th	Testimonial papers (rave reviews from agents and homeowners)		
4th	"S2G Home Staging Guide" (branded, 16-page booklet agents can offer to homeowners)	C	Vendor education
3rd	S2G before-and-after catalog (mostly visual, but includes high-level sales results)		
2nd	"Staging Works" (before-and-after pictures, testimonials, and case studies an agent can offer to a homeowner; unbranded)	D	Solution education
1st	"6 Ways to Clone Yourself (and Make More Money in a Day)"		

The Third Law of Engagement is about exchanging value with your prospects by creating offers that make their Decision Cycle journey easier and, hopefully, more directed toward you. Patience and persistence are the order of the day. Too many entrepreneurs just send out a pitch or two, and if they don't get the response they want, they give up and move on. You can do it that way, but we guarantee that creating a consistent, high-value Engagement Ladder will move you a whole lot closer to Big, Hairy, Outrageous Sales Growth—which, we're assuming, is why you're reading this book.

CAVE SCRATCHES

7

~ Offers motivate prospects to put up hands

~ Valuable, timely, and relevant

~ Engagement Ladder

~ Create "findable" high-value content

~ Offer: Final part of
    Engagement Template

NEXT UP

Now that you know how to hook your prospects, you're ready to begin reeling them in and to start building a relationship with them. To do that, you not only need to capture the tracks of those who raised their hands and responded to your offer, you need to convert them into Engaged Prospects so they can be nurtured into paying customers. It's all about preparing your Beast Cave and turning passive websites and landing pages into active Engagement Tools.

Step 3

1: ASK
the right
question

2: LISTEN
to your best
customers

3: FOCUS
your resources

4: ATTRACT
your best prospects

5: PURSUE
your best prospects

6: NURTURE
your engaged
prospects

7: GROW!
measure your
success

7 Step Beast
Marketing
System

Organizing your resources for the engagement

The Paths to Engagement

> **What you'll find in this chapter:**
> - Your website's prime directive
> - Creating value exchange
> - Turning visitors into Engaged Prospects
> - Portals of higher learning

Until now, your customers have pretty much been driving the bus, but now it's your turn to take the wheel. In this chapter, we want you to clear the dust off your long-in-the-tooth website and get it selling for you like, well, a Beast. You can't afford to let your website be that lonely general store in the middle of nowhere where visitors (the few that do visit) flit in and out in seconds. To pull its weight, your website pages (including your Engagement Pages) have to *engage* and *convert*. They must engage visitors with content written in your prospects' language, and they must convert those visitors into higher-level relationships until you have a sale.

If you remember *Star Trek* of old, Captain Kirk and his team were obligated to follow the prime directive—there can be no interference with the internal development of alien civilizations. We're going to mess with that a bit. We want you to interfere (in a good way) with the development of your (non-alien) prospects' Decision Cycle. To do that, you're going to make sure that all roads your prospects might be on lead back to your website. You not only want every marketing campaign you put out there to get attention, but you also want them to lead your Beast Prospects back to your website.

Figure 8.1 Your Beast Cave

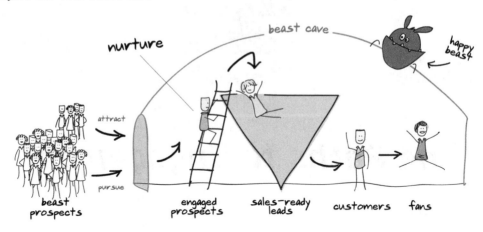

Keep one thing in mind throughout this chapter: your website's prime directive is to *engage and convert* those prospects. Anything else is wasted energy because your website, along with your Engagement Pages, is the beating heart of your marketing universe. It's the cave where your Beast resides, engages, enlightens, and persuades (see Figure 8.1). Let's see how you can make it so.

THINK OF YOUR HOME PAGE AS A GIANT BILLBOARD

Your prospects are rushing by at 60 miles per hour. What will stop them and get their attention? A well-thought-out billboard that tells a quick but compelling story by making use of big images and emotional headlines that prospects immediately identify with. So too should your home page. Design it so that it immediately expresses *empathy* (an understanding of their pain, which you are promising to relieve) and *humanity* (the people who will keep that promise) to anyone who visits. Above all, make sure your value proposition is front and center, embedded in the headline.

As you'll recall, Sophie's Value Proposition spoke of her Beast Prospect's pain ("time is my enemy") and her unique solution for that pain ("a turnkey staging service that lets you get back to the business of making money faster"). However, Sophie would have made a mistake if she'd just taken her Value Proposition and cut-and-pasted it onto her home page as a block of text. Figure 8.2 shows how Sophie laid out her home page billboard.

Figure 8.2 Sophie's Home Page

The Home Pages of Paul and Karim

The key to Paul Treadwater's home page (see Figure 8.3) is that it isn't all about his company. Paul has wisely taken the three Value Propositions he carefully built into his Engagement Template for each of his target audiences (we showed you one of his target groups in Chapter 6) and has made sure that his home page immediately reveals an understanding of the business pains that each of his prospects are experiencing (empathy is the first step toward relationship). Only then does Paul reveal his promises to each of those audiences.

Karim has also made his home page (see Figure 8.4) a billboard that focuses first on his Beast Prospect's pain ("I can't measure the impact of my pricing decisions") and then offers his promise ("price intelligence that will let you see and measure the market effects of your pricing decisions").

The biggest mistake most businesses make with their home pages is to use them to shout out what they do, entirely from their point of view. Go surf the web, and have a look. While saying what you do is important, more important is creating an immediate connection with your prospects that gives them a reason to stroll further into your Beast Cave.

Figure 8.3 Paul's Home Page

Figure 8.4 Karim's Home Page

YOUR WEBSITE IS A PROMISE

What should your prospects find when they're drawn into your website? Remember why they're there. Your Beast Prospects are there for only one reason: to understand whether their business pain can be reasonably solved—possibly by you. And if they're in the later stages of their Decision Cycle, they're looking for a promise that it *can* be solved by you.

Your promise needs to be embedded in the story your website tells. It should be educational and very soft-sell because you're trying to build a relationship based on trust, not club a baby seal who happened to wander into your igloo. As you might expect, your Value Proposition will play a big role in defining your story, creating a pathway through your website for your prospects (see Figure 8.5).

1. **Establish your credibility.** The quickest way to establish your credibility is by showing your prospects that you're trusted by other companies just like them. The more your prospects can identify with these companies, the better. This is most often achieved on the home page via some display of your existing customers' logos, thereby quickly removing this price-of-entry requirement. Of course, if you're a startup and don't have any customers yet, you have a bit of a challenge. One approach many startups use is to feature the logos of third parties who have reviewed them in some way (e.g., the press, relevant websites or blogs, analysts, or other industry influencers). Or, if you've created any kind of loose relationships with other recognizable companies (e.g., resellers, strategic partners), their logos can serve in a pinch. If you don't have any credible references, this will be a handicap throughout your entire marketing and sales process. The best answer, as it was back in Step 2 when you needed Best Customers to profile, is to go out and get a customer. Every startup has to start somewhere.

   The "About Us" page is an important part of your credibility story and will likely be one of the most frequently visited pages on your website. (See Figure 8.6 for Karim's "About Us" page.) Make sure that your passion for what you do shows here. Most people are moved by passion because, surprisingly, so few seem to possess it or at least express it. Images of your team on this page (the "whites of their eyes") will also enhance the potential connection you make with your prospects.

Figure 8.5 The Engagement Path

Figure 8.6 Karim's "About Us" Page

2. **Frame your promise.** This comes directly from your Value Proposition and should be detailed on your products, services, or solutions page. (See Figure 8.7 for Karim's product page.) Create empathy with your prospects by restating the pain that they're experiencing, and then proceed to explain how your product or service supports your promise to alleviate that pain. Diagrams and anything else that improve the readability of your promise are helpful. So too are relevant third-party quotes relating to each of your promises (you may have more than one promise for each of the markets you serve, as Paul Treadwater would for his three target markets).

3. **Deliver your proof.** The proof that you can actually deliver on your promise should also be a prominent part of your products, services, or solutions page. Highlight each proof point (of which there should be three or four) and, as on your Value Proposition, lay them out in list or bullet form so that they are easy to scan and absorb.

Figure 8.7 Karim's Product Page

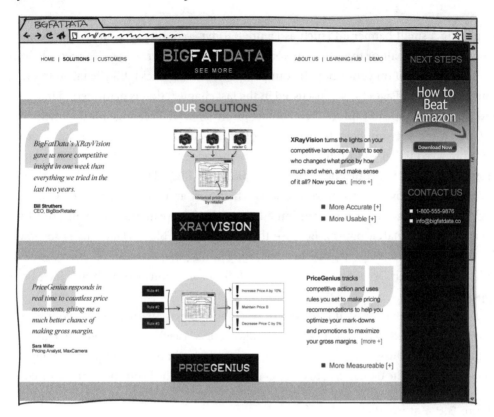

4. **Lead to next steps.** The path to your next steps will involve your "Contact Us" page—another highly visited page on your site—but mostly the path we want you to set up will be the persuasion sequence that's described next. Once your prospects get the sense that you may be able to solve their business pain in a reasonable way, they're frequently open to suggested next steps, if those next steps are a good match with their Decision Cycle needs. Enter your Engagement Ladder. As you'll recall from the last chapter, you developed a series of offers that, conveniently enough, match content to the Decision Cycle needs of your Beast Prospects. What you want to do is expose the prospects on your website to the offers that sit on your Engagement Ladder, making it easy for them to take that meaningful next step with you. How do you do that? With *banner ads, Engagement Pages,* and *Learning Hubs.*

BANNER ADS

By placing a small banner ad (such as Figure 8.8) *on every page* of your website, you can promote any and all of the offers in your Engagement Ladder. As you've seen, the offer serves as the worm on your hook. If your prospects bite (or click), they're taken to one of your Engagement Pages (as we discussed in the last chapter) that is dedicated to that offer, and where you hope to capture their contact information in exchange for the offer.

The banner ad simply states what the offer is—and nothing more. If the offer was well-conceived when you built your Engagement Ladder, it should hold interest for the prospects who match your Engagement Template. On BigFatData's website, for instance, Karim might choose to appeal to prospects who are at an earlier stage in their Decision Cycle by featuring one of his "solution education" offers (e.g., the "5 Retail Price Intelligence Secrets" analyst paper). Because the solution that BigFatData sells is so new to the retail category, it's a pretty safe bet that many of his prospects are still at an early-education stage of their Decision Cycle. So the "solution education" worm should have broad appeal.

Depending on how easy it is for you to insert and manage banner ads on your website (a Wordpress-based website, for example, makes it dead easy), you can judge whether you feature one offer throughout your site or a variety of offers on different pages. At any rate, you should limit the banner ads to one per page, including the home page of your website.

Figure 8.8 Karim's Banner Ad

While your general web content is designed primarily to be educational in nature, your banner ads are more sales-y, representing an opportunity for your prospects to get more involved with you.

YOUR ENGAGEMENT PAGES

The purpose of the banner ads on your website is to deliver your prospects to a place where they can take advantage of your offer. That place is your Engagement Page. Engagement Pages do two things: they *present* each of your offers in as appealing a light as possible, and they *create* a call to action that will encourage as many prospects as possible to exchange their contact information for the offer.

When your prospects put up their hands in this way, it becomes a measurable action that you can use to track the progress of prospects up your Engagement Ladder and through their Decision Cycle. If you're thinking Engagement Pages sound an awful lot like landing pages, you're right. They are. We believe the term "engagement" much more closely reflects what these pages do, because they help turn visitors into Engaged Prospects and Engaged Prospects into Sales-Ready Leads. Your Engagement Pages sit at the heart of your entire 7-Step Beast Marketing System.

BUILDING YOUR ENGAGEMENT PAGES

There are two ways you can build your Engagement Pages: the more expensive way, and the cheaper way. The more expensive way is to use a web coder, which you may already be doing for your website. In that case, this person can help you build your banner ads and construct your Engagement Pages for you. One of Karim's Engagement Pages is shown in Figure 8.9.

The easier way is to use web-based landing page services like Unbounce (see Figure 8.10), Optimizely, InstaPage, or KickoffLabs, which let mere mortals develop really useful Engagement Page systems. These services host your Engagement Pages, so you don't need to worry about the technology. They offer you an easy way to build Engagement Pages by dragging and dropping elements onto your page, as well as a number of best-practice templates that follow many of the above design principles. These services also let you set up URLs that match your own website URL, so to your prospects, it looks like they're still on your website when they hit your Engagement Page (even though they're not really).

Figure 8.9 One of Karim's Engagement Pages

Figure 8.10 Unbounce's Page Setup Area

To really make your marketing system work, you'll need to capture and track the data footprints that your prospects leave as they interact with you through your Engagement Pages. To simplify things, we'll take a closer look at Unbounce, one of the landing page services we like best. The costs for Unbounce are very reasonable, and by signing up, you'll be able to create as many Engagement Pages as you want (one page for each Engagement Ladder offer). You can use the prebuilt templates that Unbounce provides, but in order to take advantage of the automated tools we're going to give you in Chapters 9 and 19, you'll need to set up the web forms so they match the data structure we'll be using. To do that, go to http://tools.FeedTheBeast.biz to download our simple how-to guide. Next, you need to figure out the content for your Engagement Page. Figure 8.11 offers some content guidelines.

In the Engagement Page templates you'll find on Unbounce, you'll notice that some do not include a web form. There may be times when you want to violate the Third Law of Engagement and give your prospects an "obligation-free" offer they can download without having to fill in a web form (laws were made to be broken, after all). This is typically done early in your relationship with prospects, and as your relationship evolves and your prospects' needs move up your Engagement Ladder, you can start asking for their contact information in exchange for your offer.

Figure 8.11 Engagement Page Basics

URL - Unbounce.com will provide you with URLs you can use initially, but you'll want to use your own. Ask your webmaster/web designer for help.

Engagement Page Basics

Banner Image - You'll need to create your own banner artwork. You may want to call on your designer for some help to create one banner for each of your Engagement Ladder offers.

Banner Headline - Your banner headline (and your banner image) should speak to solving your prospect's pain. Think like a prospect.

Left Image - You should try to include an image of your offer. It helps your prospect to visualize the value they'll be receiving. You may need the help of your designer, again.

Webform - Unbounce.com will automatically capture prospect information for you. You'll find out how to access it in the next chapter.

Submit Button - Tell them what to do next (e.g., "Download now"). Big, compelling buttons get more clicks.

Body Text - The text describing your offer should be no more than 100 words. Focus only on one question: Why should my prospect care?

Bullet Points - Bullet points are almost always the most read element on any page (print or web). Summarize your offer's benefits in 3-4 bullet points.

Contact Info & Links - Avoid putting website links in the top three-quarters of your Engagement Page to limit distractions. The sole focus of your page is your offer.

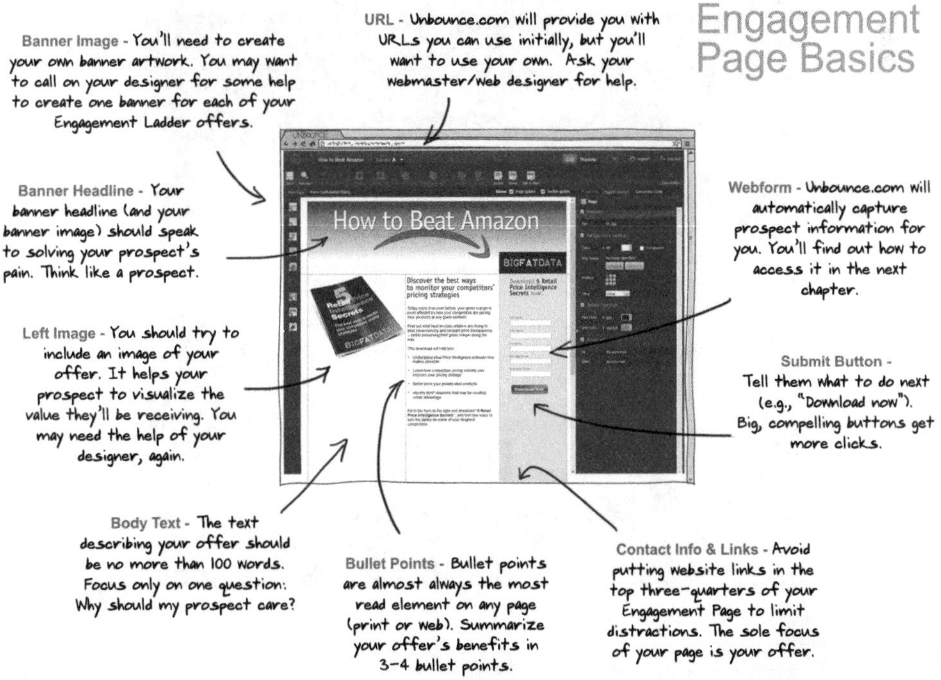

DELIVERING ON YOUR PROMISE: YOUR FULFILLMENT PAGE

Once your prospects complete the web form in order to receive your offer, you want to deliver on your offer's promise (of course), as well as give them some "next steps" to entice them into a deeper relationship with you. Oh, and you want to say "thanks." That's what your Fulfillment Pages are for. You build your Fulfillment Pages within your Engagement Page tool, and once again, we've created a quick "how-to" at http://tools.FeedTheBeast.biz that you can use to simplify your life. You'll find that we've included the best approaches to Fulfillment Page design in this "how-to."

If your offer is a download (e.g., a white paper) or a link to some other site, provide your prospects with the required link on your Fulfillment Page (see Figure 8.12). If you need to send the prospects something (e.g., a book or a gift card), use the Fulfillment Page to thank them and let them know when they can expect to receive the item. In general, it's always better to fulfill the prospects' request immediately (e.g., via download). This falls into the "strike while the iron is hot" department.

Since you have your prospects' attention on the Fulfillment Page, you might as well suggest some "next steps" via links to additional offers that sit at the same rung and

Figure 8.12 Karim's Fulfillment Page

possibly up a rung or two from the feature offer your prospects requested. These "next step" links point your prospects to the Engagement Pages that correspond to each offer (see Figure 8.13). This gives you a second chance to engage your prospects and have them tell you more about their needs. For example, if Paul's main feature is a trends report, his "next step" offers might be the analyst study, a private label kit, or a video case study, all leading to the corresponding Engagement Pages. You might also offer your prospects a link to your Learning Hub, which features the full range of content from your Engagement Ladder and allows them to self-select.

You may have noticed that each time your prospects take you up on one of your offers, they're providing the same web form information (first name, last name, etc.) over and over again. This is not optimal, but if you want to keep your Beast Marketing System simple and achievable, it's an acceptable trade-off. Reentering the same information is

Figure 8.13 Paul's Fulfillment Page

not really that big an imposition on your prospects. In the worst case, they may scratch their heads. Still, if you feel this is a problem, you can get a web coder to build you a custom system that follows the principles outlined here. Or you can explore more advanced solutions like the BeastMachine or marketing automation systems. (See the Beast Briefing at the end of Chapter 9 for more information.)

MAKING YOUR LEARNING HUB WORK

If website visitors want to learn more about market or industry trends or the latest product developments, they should be able to find that kind of information by clicking on your Learning Hub. If you don't have one, you should, because you're missing out on a great opportunity to engage your prospects more deeply. It also hooks them onto your Engagement Ladder as they work their way through their Decision Cycle.

Your Learning Hub sits on your website and conveniently organizes all of the offers you've developed into categories so your prospects can browse (see Figure 8.14). Some

Figure 8.14 Karim's Learning Hub

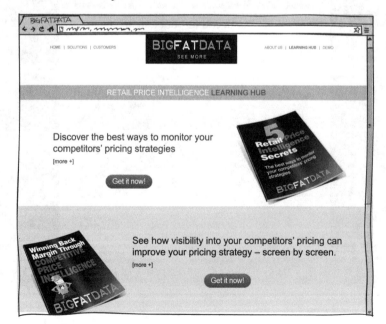

of the offers on the lower rungs of your Engagement Ladder may be "free" (that is, your prospects can download the offer without having to give you their contact information). Offers higher up on your ladder generally require a "value exchange"; in other words, prospects must provide their contact information. It's often useful to have some or all of your banner ads point to your Learning Hub. One benefit of this approach is that you don't have to guess what content/offers your prospects will find relevant to their needs. They can self-select from the Learning Hub and self-identify to you.

You can hire someone to build your Learning Hub (time to call your web coder again), or you can use the Beast Learning Hub template you'll find on Unbounce. This template is set up to accommodate from two to eight offers, and you can easily customize it to match your content. Each offer then links to the corresponding Engagement Pages you built earlier. To ensure the appeal of your Learning Hub and Engagement Pages, you may want to hit your other speed-dial button and call your designer.

Undoubtedly, you'll come across those who say that prospects do not like to fill in forms and that you shouldn't use them. We disagree. If prospects really value the thing you are offering, they'll be willing to pay a price for it—like their contact information. That is the concept of *value exchange*. If they feel the offer isn't worth that price, then either your offer is weak, mistimed, or the prospect isn't really a very good prospect. The first two you will need to address. The last actually works in your favor, filtering out less qualified prospects and saving your valuable resources.

CAVE SCRATCHES
- All ads and links lead to your website
- Credibility, promise, proof, next steps
- Build your Engagement Pages
- Fulfillment Page
- The BeastMachine

NEXT UP

Now that you have these key building blocks in place, you can probably delete the speed dial numbers for your designer and web coder for a while. What you've built through this chapter should see you into the next year. Now you need to set yourself up to track all the invaluable prospect data you'll be producing from your website, Learning Hub, and Engagement Pages so you can monitor your prospects' progress up your Engagement Ladder. Don't worry. No coders required.

Step 3 FOCUS

CHAPTER 9

Your Engagement Engine

> **What you'll find in this chapter:**
> - Keeping things simple
> - Getting insight into your Beast Prospects' needs
> - Setting up your Engagement Spreadsheet
> - Putting your Engagement Spreadsheet to work

If you're like many B2B entrepreneurs, your immediate goal might be to land, say, 10 or 20 profitable, new customers. With those kinds of numbers, why in the world would you need to think about scaling your marketing? Here's why. If you want to land 10 new customers, you might need to tempt as many as a thousand new prospects into your Beast Cave. Prospects have a way of wandering off, or losing interest, or buying from someone else, so you need to have many, many more in the top to get a few out the bottom. And marketing to and engaging with that number of people, so that each feels personally attended to, could take countless hours—*if* you did it the old way.

But the old way is not the Beast way. And the Beast way is grounded in this inescapable truth: you can't measure what you can't see, and you can't make smart decisions about what you can't measure. If you want to *see*, *know*, and *engage* hundreds of Beast Prospects at the same time, you need a tool to help keep track.

That tool is your Engagement Spreadsheet.

Why is seeing so important? Because if you're able to see which of your offers your prospects are responding to, you'll have a pretty good idea where they are in their Decision Cycle, and that means you'll be in a better position to anticipate what they'll need *next*—which is crucial to building a good relationship. Your Engagement Spreadsheet will help you organize, track, and manage thousands of relationships all at the same time, letting you scale your marketing efforts—and still get you home in time for dinner. So how does it work? How do you get to "see" and interpret everything your prospects do with you, and how do you effectively manage your prospect relationships using a spreadsheet? The answers are surprisingly straightforward.

MAKING EVERYTHING WORK

The secret to keeping your Engagement Spreadsheet simple, usable, and effective can be found a few chapters back. Remember when you constructed your Engagement Ladder so that each offer on the eight rungs would appeal to a different stage of your prospect's Decision Cycle? In other words:

offer selected = Decision Cycle stage

Let's use a simple example to illustrate. John the Prospect has a particular business problem he needs to solve. John has just started researching potential solutions, and while he has a number of options, web search engines are the first research choice of more and more business buyers. Since John is in the very early, solution-education stage of his Decision Cycle, if he finds a white paper on the web that introduces him to an overview of "what's possible," that document would likely hold more appeal for him than a fancy ROI calculator that shows him how much money he can save.

At his current decision state, John doesn't know whether a solution is appropriate for his business or even how that solution works, much less what numbers to plug into an ROI calculator. So if John were to find you (or you, him), he would be more likely to respond to one of your D-rung offers (those providing "solution education") than any of the other offers on your Ladder. And since John is responding to your D-rung offer, you would be quite safe in assuming that John is early on in his Decision Cycle.

On the other hand, if Carol the Prospect has been thinking about the same problem for several weeks or months, she will likely have already educated herself on what's possible and may have moved through her Decision Cycle to "vendor education" ("Which solutions are credible and relevant?") or "vendor consideration" ("Which are the best solutions for my needs?"). If you and Carol find each other at this point in Carol's Decision Cycle, she might well respond to your ROI calculator offer *because she is ready for it*. So from Carol's response, you could reasonably conclude that she is much *later* in her Decision Cycle.

It's important to point out that this approach is not perfect, and that there are far more sophisticated lead scoring systems out there. But maybe that's the point. "Sophisticated" doesn't always mean better, and "good enough" often wins the day. In our experience, the simpler your scoring system, the more you'll use it, and the better it will serve you. Assessing your prospects' Decision Cycle state based on the type of content they respond to is a very good shortcut to being more relevant to your target audience. And that, as mentioned earlier, is the key to building effective, two-way relationships.

All of this ultimately leads back to your Engagement Page. Your Engagement Page is the physical place where you and your prospects transact for your offer. That transaction is measurable and, based on the offer selected, highly revealing. So here's the trigger that makes the Engagement Spreadsheet work: it will track *every transaction* your Beast Prospects make for the content you're offering from your Engagement Ladder. That's to say, if they want your offer, they have to fill in the web form, and filling in the web form leaves a record you can see. Seeing how many prospects are becoming *engaged* tells you whether your marketing campaigns are producing enough Engaged Prospects to meet your goals. And knowing which offer they last took tells you a lot about what offer you should make to them next.

Before we look at how responses to your Engagement Pages feed your Engagement Spreadsheet (so you can keep track of what's working and what's not), let's talk about how you'll set up your initial Engagement Spreadsheet.

WHERE TO START?

Well, to start, you need some basic spreadsheet software. While you're free to use any spreadsheet software that works for you (e.g., Open Office, Google Docs), we're going to recommend that you use Excel. Why? Because you can download a free starter Engagement

Spreadsheet template at http://tools.FeedTheBeast.biz that has all the very cool reporting tools that you'll be using in Chapter 19 already built in. In addition, we've built a free Beast Plug-In for Excel that you can download from the same site that will make managing your Engagement Spreadsheet a breeze and will allow you to easily create and export the lists you'll need to run your marketing campaigns. If you choose not to use Excel, then you'll have to do everything we describe manually, which is certainly possible but would really be a big pain in the Beast. Your call.

QR Code
Engagement Spreadsheet

Okay, assuming you're with us on the Excel thing, go to the Beast site above and download both the template and the Plug-In. Open the template in Excel, and then save it with a meaningful name somewhere on your hard drive that you'll be able to easily locate later. Next, double-click on the Beast Plug-In for Excel, follow the instructions, and install it on your computer. It should work equally well on either PC or Mac.

big, hairy tip

Strongly consider saving your Engagement Spreadsheet to the cloud in a Dropbox or a SkyDrive folder. These are folders on your computer that are automatically mirrored "up in the cloud," meaning that a copy of everything you put into the folder is kept on a remote server managed by, in the cases above, Dropbox and Microsoft. Here are the big benefits: One, you will have an automatic backup of your Engagement Spreadsheet. We cannot stress how important this is. Once you start depending on this spreadsheet, it will hurt severely if you lose it. Two, another person (say, a marketing assistant) will be able to access the same file from her computer, no matter where she is. This might be insanely convenient for you, as you'll see.

OK. Now open your Engagement Spreadsheet and have a look around. You should see exactly what's in Figure 9.1. The first row has a bunch of titles at the top of each column, many of which will mean nothing to you yet—but they will later. What's important is

Figure 9.1 Your Engagement Spreadsheet

	A	B	C	D	E	F	G	H
1	date_submitted	time_submitted	ip_address	variant	page_uuid	current_grade	channel	campaign
2								
3								
4								
5								
6								
7								
8								
9								
10								
11								
12								
13								
14								
15								
16								
17								

that you *never* remove or rearrange any of these column headers—*not if you want your Engagement Spreadsheet to continue making your life easier*—because the calculations in the sheet depend on these headers being in place.

Running along the bottom of the spreadsheet (see Figure 9.2) you'll notice a series of tabs. The first tab on the left is "Beast Prospects." This is where you place your prospect list. (If you don't have a list yet, we'll show you in Chapter 14 how to buy one, build one, or improve the one you already have.) The "To Sales" tab is where you'll be placing all prospects who achieve an A grade through the course of your marketing campaigns and need to be handed off to your sales team for prompt closing. The last two tabs, "Beast Dashboard 1" and "Beast Dashboard 2," contain the aforementioned cool reports that you'll use to stay on track toward Big, Hairy, Outrageous Sales Growth.

Okay, let's look at the three main activities you'll need to manage as you swing your Engagement Spreadsheet into action: getting data in, getting data out, and adding data. You'll likely want to refer back to these when you reach Chapters 15 through 17.

1. Loading Your Spreadsheet

As you've seen, when you open your Engagement Spreadsheet onto the "Beast Prospects" tab for the first time, the spreadsheet is blank except for the column headers (see Figure 9.1). If you buy a list, it will almost certainly be delivered to you as a spreadsheet. In that case,

Figure 9.2 Engagement Spreadsheet Tabs

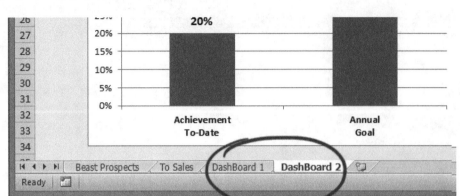

you would need to rearrange the columns in your purchased list to match those in your Engagement Spreadsheet. Where your purchased list doesn't have a particular column that appears in your Engagement Spreadsheet, just create a blank column in your purchased list. Once the columns are in matching order, cut and paste all rows (except the first header row) from the purchased list and paste them into the first empty row of your Engagement Spreadsheet (presumably row two). On the other hand, if you're building your own list, simply build it within your Engagement Spreadsheet (see Figure 9.3).

In either case, what you'll have when you're finished is your starting Engagement Spreadsheet containing your initial Beast Prospects List. Important to note is that the "current_grade" column will be empty for all prospects in your spreadsheet at this time. The "null" value in this column indicates that you have not yet marketed to any of these prospects. When you do run campaigns to some or all of the members in your Engagement Spreadsheet, your Beast Plug-In for Excel will help you automatically grade your prospects.

2. Creating Your Lists

Each of your marketing campaigns needs its own list. And one of the most important jobs your Engagement Spreadsheet performs is to produce different lists of prospects (for each group of P—your unEngaged Prospects—D, C, B, and A prospects) so you can send the appropriate campaign with the appropriate offer to the appropriate prospect. For example, you would send your D prospects a C offer to try and move them up your Engagement

Ladder. If they took you up on your C offer, the next time you would send them a B offer, and so on. To save you the hassle of always keeping track of who's on first, your Beast Plug-In will do the heavy lifting for you. Let's use your very first campaign to illustrate how it works.

For your first campaign, you've decided to do a test run to 50 random prospects from your Engagement Spreadsheet. On your Engagement Spreadsheet, you open up your Beast Plug-In (see Figure 9.4), and you click on "Export Lists" and then on "New Prospects." A

Figure 9.3 Loading Your Prospects List

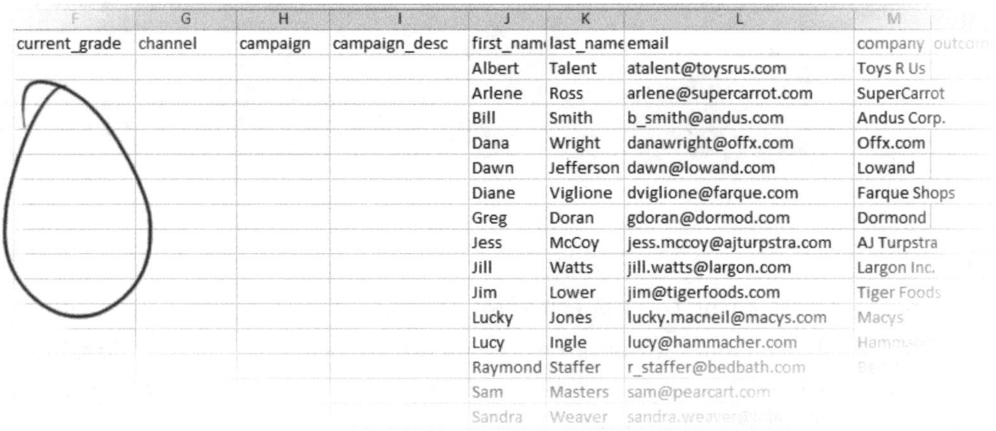

Figure 9.4 Beast Plug-In for Excel

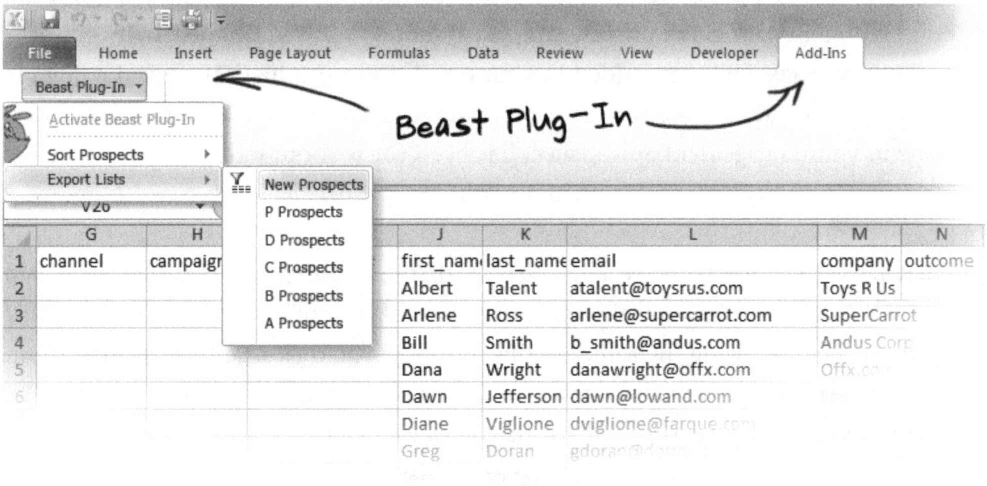

Figure 9.5 Exporting Our New Prospects List

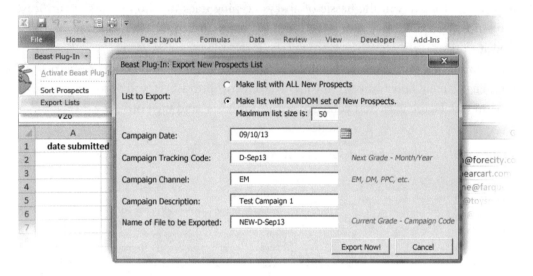

dialog box will then pop up (see Figure 9.5) into which you'll place the details of your test campaign. We'll talk about the bottom five fields you see here in the next section, but at the top of the dialog box, you choose whether you want to create *one* list from *all* your new prospects, or a smaller, randomized list.

By clicking the "Export Now!" button, two things happen.

1. Your list of 50 new prospects is saved as a new text file (.TXT) on your hard drive. It can now be used in your email pursuit campaign (more on this in Chapter 16).
2. The 50 prospects who were added to your new list are automatically given a P grade in the "current_grade" column of your Engagement Spreadsheet. Anyone who has a P grade in your Engagement Spreadsheet has been (or is about to be) sent a marketing campaign but is still, to this point, an unEngaged Prospect.

What if you wanted to send a D offer to all the P prospects who had remained unengaged (that is, they haven't taken you up on any of your offers yet)? You'd make a list of P prospects by following the same routine, but now you'd choose "P Prospects" from the "Export Lists" menu. You'd be presented with a slightly different dialog box and the option to export a P-prospect-specific list, as you can see in Figure 9.6.

Figure 9.6 Exporting a P Prospects List

3. Updating with New Data

Over time, you'll be running many marketing campaigns, engaging with each Beast Prospect several times over the course of your relationship (up the ladder), before each hopefully converts to a Sales-Ready Lead (down the funnel), and then to a sale. Each engagement will take place over a different Engagement Page—one page for every campaign that you run. As you'll recall from Chapter 8, web-based Engagement Page tools (like Unbounce) sit behind your Engagement Pages.

One of the great things about these tools is that when your prospects fill out a web form, the tools automatically capture that information, as seen in Figure 9.7.

Looking at Unbounce's Campaign Report in Figure 9.7, you can see two leads have come in for your "ARM Analyst Study" offer so far. Every time a prospect requests an offer from you, your Engagement Page tool will record it by date and time in the Campaign Report. One of the new leads is Sandra Weaver, who came in as a P prospect. The report would automatically turn her into a D prospect because she requested a D-level offer (the "Arm Analyst Study"). Make sense? Sandra takes the offer, Sandra's prospect grade gets moved up. Now all you have to do is get that new information back into your Engagement

Figure 9.7 Campaign Report

	Date/Time Submitted	IP Address	Variant	Current grade	Channel	Campaign	Campaign desc	First name	Last name	Email
	You have 2 leads from your "D-Rung: ARM Analyst Study" page Create CSV of Leads									
2	10/10/2013 08:22 AM UTC	00.000.000.00	a	D	EM	D-Oct13	ARM Analyst Study	Sandra	Weaver	sandra.weaver@tobys.com
1	10/10/2013 08:07 AM UTC	00.000.000.00	a	D	EM	D-Oct13	ARM Analyst Study	Jill	Watts	jill.watts@bla...

© Copyright Unbounce.com. Used with permission.

Spreadsheet so Sandra can be promoted to a D prospect, ready to receive your next C campaign, so you can continue trying to tempt her up your Engagement Ladder.

So how do you update your Engagement Spreadsheet?

Simply go to the "Download CSV Here" button you'll find within the Engagement Page tool (see Figure 9.8). By clicking the button for each campaign you run, you download all of the new offer transaction data from your Campaign Report (or equivalent) as a spreadsheet you can add to your Engagement Spreadsheet. You do this every time you run a marketing campaign, for all the prospects who accepted the offer that campaign was promoting. *And prospects within the Campaign Report automatically bring their new prospect grade with them.*

Now, what would happen if you combined all the data from those Campaign Report spreadsheets into your Engagement Spreadsheet (see Figure 9.9)? You'd be able to sort all of your prospects using the Beast Plug-In (see Figure 9.10), allowing you to *see* the complete history of offer transactions for every prospect who has ever engaged with you. And at the top of each prospect history, you would see the latest prospect grade assigned to that prospect. Combining spreadsheets is easy. In each Campaign Report you download, copy every line except the first line (the header line), and paste it into the next empty row of your Engagement Spreadsheet, making sure that the column headers line up. That's it!

Your Engagement Spreadsheet is key to your overall engagement strategy because it helps you propel hundreds and even thousands of prospects up your Engagement Ladder by making the campaigns (and offers) you put in front of them more *personally* relevant, better matching the stage they are in within their Decision Cycles.

Figure 9.8 Updating with New Information

Figure 9.9 Combining the Data into Your Engagement Spreadsheet

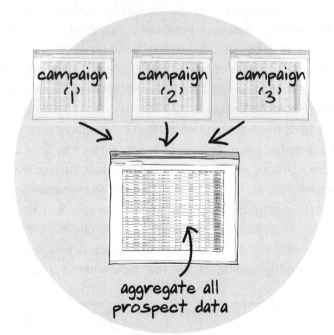

Figure 9.10 Sorting Your Engagement Spreadsheet

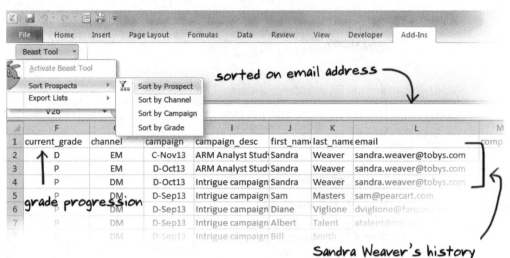

You probably have a bookkeeper for your accounting and consider that to be a critical function in your organization. In the same way, you need to have someone to take care of your Engagement Spreadsheet. This could be a part-time marketing assistant, or it could even be a student who's good with spreadsheets. Here's why it's important: the job we've described above will get done; it will get done properly; and you will have the information you need to power your Big, Hairy, Outrageous Sales Growth. Your marketing assistant is the oil that keeps your Engagement Spreadsheet running smoothly.

If your budget is tight (and whose isn't?), you might justify hiring someone to manage your Engagement Spreadsheet by broadening that person's responsibility to include related functions such as managing email marketing; tracking and managing website performance; producing sales lead reports for the sales team; managing your Beast reports (see Chapter 19); managing offer content; managing marketing digital assets, competitive analysis, and review; and acting as a point person for marketing with the sales team.[1] But the Engagement Spreadsheet has to be job one.

CAMPAIGN TRACKING CODES

Okay. How does the Engagement Page tool know what grade belongs to which campaign, so it can assign it to a newly Engaged Prospect? There's not a lot of magic here. You have to tell it. But that's easy too. We suggest that you adopt a consistent naming convention for all of your marketing campaigns using the format in Figure 9.11.

To get these campaign tracking codes into the Engagement Spreadsheet, you first have to enter the campaign tracking codes into your Engagement Page tool. When you set up each Engagement Page for every campaign you run in Unbounce (or other Engagement Page tools), you can double-click on the web form in the page-building section of the tool. If you followed the web form instructions at http://tools.FeedTheBeast.biz, on the resulting screen pop-up (see Figure 9.12), you'll see four grayed-out, "hidden" fields (that is, the prospect will never see these fields) into which you can place your campaign tracking code for that campaign.

When your prospect requests an offer from this Engagement Page by filling in the web form, the campaign tracking code is attached to the prospect in the Campaign Report. That's all there is to it.

Figure 9.11 Campaign Tracking Code

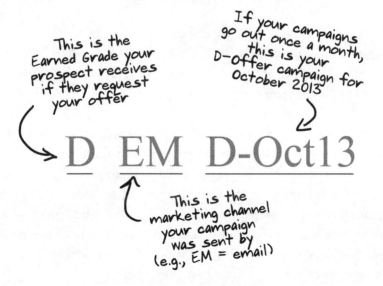

Figure 9.12 Entering Tracking Code in Unbounce

BEAST BRIEFING: GETTING AUTOMATED

Because marketing is a game of numbers, you need to *engage and convert* over and over again. Lots. So you need two things to help you be successful:

1. A way to efficiently manage a large volume of prospects to make the numbers game work in your favor.
2. A way to ensure that your prospects don't feel like cattle. As much as possible, they have to feel like you are reaching out to them personally.

In Chapter 9, we introduced you to a bit of simple technology (your Engagement Spreadsheet) that allows you to scale your marketing efforts dramatically, all the while preserving that one-to-one feeling between you and your prospect.

The Engagement Spreadsheet is free, and it makes it possible for you to do all of the above quite efficiently. However, there may come a time when you want to explore solutions that provide even more scalability and ease. When you reach that point of pain, you'll become a prospect for the BeastMachine and possibly even for full-blown marketing automation systems. We'll describe both briefly here.

THE BEASTMACHINE

We didn't set out to build a software solution. We just found that when we were looking for a way to easily manage a high volume of prospects in the most practical, cost-efficient, and effective way possible, we came up wanting. So we built a solution ourselves. While the Engagement Spreadsheet you learned about in this chapter, in combination with your Engagement Page tool, will do everything you need, here are a few things the Beast-Machine will do in the "above-and-beyond" department:

- Personalized Engagement Pages.
- Prospect's contact data can be prefilled on the Engagement Page web form.
- You can track prospects by name and present personalized Engagement Pages if they come in via nondigital channels (e.g., direct mail).
- Have your Engagement Pages and reporting all in one place—no more manual downloads, cuts, and pastes.
- Quicker list building and one-button exporting to your email tool.
- Tracks your prospects by name as they explore any page on your website or Engagement Pages.
- Automatic, offsite backup of all your prospect data.
- Broader reporting that is entirely automatic, including:
  o Email results
  o Results by marketing channel (i.e., PPC, banner ads, email, etc.)
  o Prospect history, including campaign history and web page activity history
- Integrates to several of the more popular web-based email services as well as sales management applications like Salesforce (http://www.salesforce.com/).

The BeastMachine is priced under $200 per month at the time of this writing. You can find out more about the BeastMachine at http://www.TheBeastMachine.com/.

MARKETING AUTOMATION PLATFORMS (MAP)

These are the toys for the big boys, although lots of not-so-big boys use them. MAPs can set you back a thousand dollars a month, but they are all-inclusive. MAPs offer a full email and landing page system as well as complete prospect tracking through your website, with reporting to track everything by prospect.

The main advantage of MAPs is that they allow you to set up your own scoring system for your prospects, based on many more factors. So, for instance, you might assign the following characteristics to a C prospect:

- Visited website at least five times and reviewed products pricing page at least once.
- Requested and downloaded white paper "X."
- Opened and clicked through on at least four emails.
- Watched the product video.

As you can see, this is quite a bit more sophisticated than the Beast Marketing System we're taking you through in this book. However, therein lies the catch. The very complexity of MAPs makes them quite hard to use effectively. Some users struggle to get value from their systems months and even years after those systems have been deployed. And the actual deployment can require a significant investment over and above the monthly fees.

The biggest challenge MAPs create for marketers is that it's very hard to automate a process that may not exist. Many companies, especially small companies, have not developed an executional process for their marketing programs and, as a result, are ill-equipped to adopt a sophisticated third-party process that may or may not suit their industry and business style.

Which is why the Beast Marketing System you're reading about here is a great starting point. It will give you a grassroots system that you can use to drive real business in the short term. In the longer term, if your marketing and company reach the point of needing more scale, you'll have a strong foundation on which to overlay solutions like MAPs.

Four of the leading marketing automation solutions today that you may want to investigate are:

Marketo (http://www.marketo.com/)
Eloqua (http://www.eloqua.com/)
HubSpot (http://www.hubspot.com/)
Infusionsoft (http://www.infusionsoft.com/)

CAVE SCRATCHES

- Engagement Engine is a simple spreadsheet
- Organizes, tracks, and scales your marketing efforts
- Campaign reports categorize prospects, help nurture by engagement level

NEXT UP

So now you have a place (your Engagement Pages) to send your Beast Prospects and an Engagement Spreadsheet that lets you better coax them up your Engagement Ladder (by letting you *see* what's going on). Next, let's focus on what happens when you successfully graduate your Beast Prospects to A-status, making them Sales-Ready Leads for your sales team to start working on. The truth is if your sales team (or channel partners) receive better quality sales leads, and if they're more focused and motivated to pursue those leads, you'll close more short-term business. Sound good? Let's go.

Fine-Tuning Your Sales Conversion

> **What you'll find in this chapter:**
> - The planets of sales and marketing
> - A partnership agreement to align the planets
> - How sales fingerprints create buy-in
> - Marketing follow-through means more conversions

The best marketing campaigns in the world will struggle to achieve real success if your sales team doesn't support them. Why? Because once your Engaged Prospects become Sales-Ready Leads and you drop them into the sales funnel, it's up to the sales team to close the opportunities you worked so hard to produce. This chapter is for you if you have sales reps in your employ, resellers who are not, and/or third parties who are contracted to sell for you. If you make use of any or all of these, Chapter 10 will help you align your marketing and sales objectives to significantly improve your chances of success. If you don't have a sales team yet (as in, *you* are currently the sales team), you can skip over this chapter if you like, and come back to it when you're in need.

THEY LOVE ME, THEY LOVE ME NOT

They share the same goal; they work for the same company; and you can't have one without the other. Even so, your sales and marketing teams can develop a love-hate relationship if you're not careful. Salespeople and marketing people are often very different types of beings with very different world views. And when a traditionally independent group (sales) has to rely on another group (marketing) *for much of their livelihood*, it can get a little sticky at times. Especially if sales feels they're not getting an adequate number of what (they believe) to be high-quality leads, and marketing feels that sales is letting too many leads slip through the cracks.

By necessity, marketers need to have a farming mentality. They need to patiently plant seeds and nurture those seeds until they have the potential to feed someone. A salesperson is the opposite. The most successful salespeople are hunters: they can't afford to wait around for green things to pop above the soil. They go out and shoot things that they can eat right away. This doesn't mean that salespeople won't sit outside a rabbit hole and wait for food with legs to appear, if they know it to be there for certain. Good reps are impatient to get results but patient enough to hunt for those results if they're confident that they'll be rewarded.

Farmers and hunters most often see the world from slightly different vantage points. The farmer is more inclined to watch the ground. The hunter is more inclined to watch the sky.

It can be said that the sales team provides the *immediate* lifeblood to the company and the marketing team provides the *future* lifeblood to the company. When the objectives of these two groups are aligned, beautiful things start happening. A recent study of

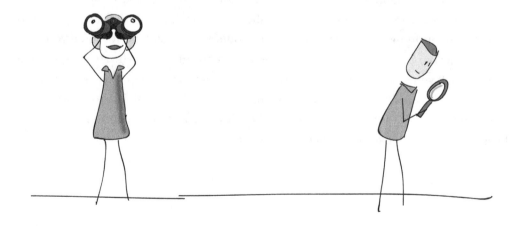

1,400 companies by MathMarketing in conjunction with MarketingProfs (http://www .marketingprofs.com/) showed that companies that aligned the objectives of the sales and marketing teams grew 5.4 percent faster, closed 38 percent more proposals, and kept 36 percent more of their customers.[1]

If the two groups are out of sync, however, marketing can lose its way, and sales can lose trust in the quality of the leads they're getting. There are three things you can do to ensure alignment:

1. Create a sales/marketing partnership agreement based on mutual performance
2. Get sales and marketing speaking the same language
3. Get sales' fingerprints on your marketing strategy

CREATING A PARTNERSHIP AGREEMENT

The best way to ensure that two parties see things the same way when the fur starts flying is to set up a formal agreement that details the responsibilities of each group. This is true in marriages, in matters of estate, and in making sure that marketing and sales are singing from the same song sheet. Enter the partnership agreement.

A partnership agreement between marketing and sales accomplishes a couple of things:

1. It gives both groups a context in which to evaluate each other's actions.
2. It establishes numeric targets that hold each group accountable and, when added up, should support the overall sales objectives of your business.

For the agreement to even be understandable, sales and marketing need to agree on language. Think of them as members of a relay team passing the baton. To win the race, they need to clearly understand the rules—how and when the handoff will take place. In other words, they need to agree on how a prospect is graded, how the prospect's Decision Cycle is defined, and which team "owns" the prospect each step of the way. They need to agree on the definition of terms like "Engaged Prospect," "Sales-Ready Lead," and "Fan."

Figure 10.1 From Prospect to Fan

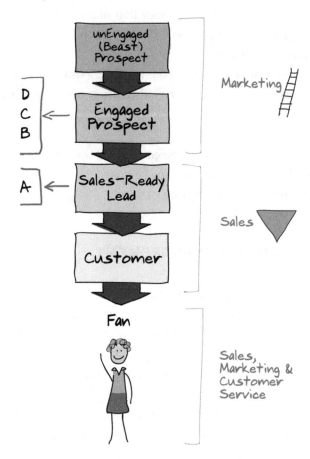

These are the terms and this is the language that will underlie the partnership agreement and define your marketing and sales processes, so you need to get it right. This chapter will provide you with a good starting point. See Figure 10.1 for an overview of the process and the terminology we use.

MARKETING OWNS THE FIRST TWO GROUPS

The unEngaged Prospects and Engaged B, C, and D Prospects (Beast Prospects all) are "owned" by marketing.

The *unEngaged Prospects* represent all the prospects who match your Engagement Template who you may or may not have found, or who may or may not have found you, but who haven't yet engaged with you—that is, they haven't reached for one of your rung offers and made an overt, measurable declaration of their interest. We'll be calling them "Beast Prospects."

Engaged Prospects are those who've taken the next step and accepted one or more of your offers. As prospects become engaged, you use your Engagement Spreadsheet to coax them up your Engagement Ladder to become more deeply engaged. They start as D prospects and move up the ladder from there:

> **D Prospects:** *These (generally) newly Engaged Prospects have shown themselves to be exploring the category in which you sell and are asking themselves, "What's available to help me solve my problem?"*

> **C Prospects:** *These Engaged Prospects have shown themselves to be exploring the different solutions available to them within this category that seem to meet their needs and are asking themselves, "Which solutions are credible and relevant?"*

> **B Prospects:** *These more deeply Engaged Prospects have chosen to include your company in their evaluation of a solution to their pain and are asking themselves, "Which are the best solutions for my needs?"*

> **A Prospects:** *These fully Engaged Prospects want to explore a possible sales engagement with your company. They're handed over to the sales team as "Sales-Ready Leads."*

SALES OWNS THE NEXT TWO GROUPS

Sales clearly owns the customer, but they also own the A prospects above—the "Sales-Ready Leads."

Sales-Ready Leads, in our book, are B prospects who have reached for an A-rung offer, triggering an immediate transfer to the sales team. In larger companies, these leads may be qualified against some additional criteria, often via a phone call by an inside sales rep or a lead development rep, and are passed to the sales team for *acceptance by an assigned sales rep.* If accepted, the prospect becomes an "opportunity" for that rep. If the prospect is not accepted by the rep for reasons of ineligibility, the prospect is either recycled back into marketing (the prospect is not quite ready for a sales engagement) or rejected and discarded (the prospect will never have need for your solution).

Customers, of course, are Sales-Ready Leads that the sales team has successfully converted to a sale.

Fans belong to everyone in the company. Fans are your best customers, the ones who are extremely likely to recommend your product or service to their colleagues and associates. So turning Customers into Fans should be the responsibility of virtually everyone inside your company, from sales (who would continue their relationship with the customer for the purposes of selling more to them in the future) to customer service to marketing (who will be involved in ongoing customer referral and satisfaction programs—see Chapter 18).

Remember that the average B2B prospect today is two-thirds of the way through his purchase Decision Cycle before he elects to engage a sales rep, so there's a lot of nurturing for marketing to do before that prospect is introduced to sales. Some sales reps struggle with this thinking. It wasn't so long ago that every prospect went directly to the sales rep. Because the leads weren't well qualified, typically *70 percent of those prospects were thrown away or ignored.* The reps who struggle with the new approach to B2B marketing may feel disenfranchised, and so the partnership agreement is critical to a common understanding of the responsibilities of both groups and the benefits of the process.

ADDING SOME MEASURES OF SUCCESS

In order for your company to achieve its big, hairy sales goals, you have to have a predictable flow of prospects, leads, and sales. By working backwards from your sales goals, you can determine how many of each group you need, based on your *conversion rates*.

Conversion Rates

There are seemingly hundreds of metrics you can pick from to try and figure out if your marketing programs are working or not. It's very confusing, and yet knowing what works and what doesn't is critical to the success of you and your sales team. To cut through the confusion, here are four marketing and sales measures you can track to make sure you're on the path to Big, Hairy, Outrageous Sales Growth:

1. **Prospect Engagement Rate (PER):** PER measures the percentage of your Beast Prospects who've engaged with you by filling out a webform for one of your offers. They're identified, and they're on your Engagement Ladder. (Beast Prospects are those you defined and selected in the "Target" portion of your Engagement Template.)
2. **Marketing Conversion Rate (MCR):** MCR measures the percentage of Engaged Prospects on your Ladder who've become Sales-Ready Leads because they've expressed a level of interest that's best handled by a sales rep.
3. **Sales Conversion Rate (SCR):** SCR measures the percentage of Sales-Ready Prospects who've been converted into Customers by your sales team.
4. **Fan Conversion Rate (FCR):** FCR measures the percentage of customers who've been converted into Fans through your efforts to service and build relationships with them.

A full description of these metrics can be found in Chapter 19, "Unleashing Your Beast." MCR is an excellent measure of marketing performance, while SCR is a solid measure of sales performance. What better numbers to include in your partnership agreement between marketing and sales? If everyone hits their conversion rates, everyone gets to go to Hawaii, right?

The annual benchmarks for Paul's marketing efforts: an overall 38 percent Prospect Engagement Rate and an overall 20 percent Marketing Conversion Rate. The annual benchmark for Paul's sales team: a 35 percent Sales Conversion Rate. If everyone hits their numbers, Treadwater will increase its private label business by 143 percent this year (much more on this in Chapter 19). Your expected engagement and conversion rates will vary according to your specific market situation. With time, your numbers should become more robust and will serve as the benchmark that your marketing and sales teams will measure themselves against.

Let's look a little deeper at Paul's situation. At the beginning of the year, Paul developed his Engagement Template and sized his market. He believed that if he ran some consistent marketing programs (which he had never done before) that also took advantage of the Beast Marketing System, he could find 10 new private label customers this year at an average selling price of $60,000 per account. This would achieve the kind of growth that he considered big and hairy for his private label business.

To reach this goal, he assigned the following annual metrics (see table below) to the partnership agreement between his marketing team and his sales team. We're using the term "team" loosely, because Paul was the sales team and a big part of the marketing

Figure 10.2 Treadwater Chocolates Conversion Rates over 12 Months

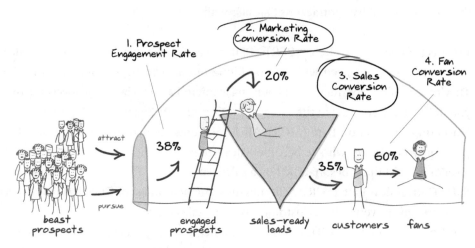

team (although, to be fair, Paul envisioned adding another salesperson to help him this year).

TREADWATER ANNUAL SALES AND MARKETING GOALS

Team	Conversion Action	Conversion Rate	Conversion Goals
Sales	Sales-Ready Leads to Customers	Sales Conversion Rate 35%	10 customers
Marketing	Engaged Prospects to Sales-Ready Leads total	Marketing Conversion Rate 20%	30 Sales-Ready Leads
	unEngaged Prospects to Engaged Prospects	Prospect Engagement Rate 38%	152 Engaged Prospects
	unEngaged Prospects		400

You'll notice this table starts with Paul's sales goal. He then works the numbers backwards to figure out just how many unEngaged (Beast) Prospects he'd need to engage (both by *finding* prospects and by *being found* by them). This language and these numbers would form the partnership agreement between Paul's sales and marketing teams.

In a larger company, you can see how the marketing and sales teams would become mutually dependent on each other to achieve the company's new customer goal. Both teams would be compensated against these numbers. It would matter less where prospects came from or how they were converted than it would that each team lives up to its conversion promise. For Paul's part, he'll monitor these numbers monthly to make sure he's on track to meet his annual sales objective, giving him more insight into his annual revenue outcome than he had ever had before. We'll delve into all the metrics of success in Step 7.

SALES FINGERPRINTS

Once your sales and marketing teams are aligned on objectives, you need to invite sales in to muck around and leave their fingerprints on your marketing work. *No, we're not kidding.* There are two good reasons to do this. The first is that the sales team is closer to the customer than anyone else in the organization. The sales team's input on the elements that make up your marketing thinking will make your programs stronger and more widely supported, and it may increase your program response rates several percentage points (potentially representing thousands of dollars in incremental revenue).

The second reason to let sales fingerprint your marketing process is that they're more likely to support the programs when those programs reach the market, because the sales team will feel some ownership of them. This will contribute to improved follow-up rates and improved conversion rates, and it will also serve to better integrate the sales and marketing teams. By being involved, the sales team will view the marketing executions and the marketing team as more grounded and more relevant. This will go a long way toward aligning the two teams. Here are three marketing areas where sales' fingerprints could prove useful:

1. **Get Sales' Input on Your Engagement Template.** When you're developing your Engagement Template by surveying those whom you identified as Best Customers, include your sales team in the exact same survey. The sales team will provide a template of who, in their experience, represents the company's Best Customers, and this template can be held against the template that your Best Customers themselves complete. Your job is to look for gaps and insights between the two. The Engagement Template provides a composite view of your Very Best Customer, heavily weighted by your Best Customers' input but tweaked by the input of the sales team. You should get the head of sales (you?) to sign off on the document because your Engagement Template defines the Beast Prospects whom you're targeting to get onto your Engagement Ladder and on whom everyone's success will depend.

2. **Get Sales' Input on Your Value Proposition.** Because your newly refined Value Proposition is an easy-to-read, one-page document, it shouldn't be a problem getting your sales team to read and comment on it, right? Actually, you can expect the exercise to be like coaching penguins. Once your Value Proposition reaches its first draft form, based on input from your Engagement Interviews, you need to let the sales team fingerprint the document. Feedback can be provided via email, or you can present the document to your sales team during a regular sales meeting and get feedback from the sales reps during the meeting or afterward via email.

   Select a handful of sales reps who you know will take the time to give you a thoughtful response, and meet with them one on one. The goal is to acid test the communications strategy with the people in the company who are closest to the customer. Overall, for this portion of the exercise, you can expect your response rate from the sales team to be quite low unless you have a very small sales team. Just make sure the head of sales signs off on the final draft of the Value Proposition.

3. **Get Sales' Input on Your Creative.** You might also consider running your creative executions by your sales team before committing to sending them out. Again, the lens through which you'll ask the sales team to evaluate the creative is the Value Proposition. The rules are simple. You must *not* ask your sales team to critique the creative. This is asking for trouble because it's too subjective. Instead of twisting everyone into knots, ask them which execution best satisfies the requirements identified by the Value Proposition. There's an important distinction here. Voting that something is "on strategy" or not is very different from voting on which creative execution a person prefers. The former is far less contentious. Once the sales team has gone through one cycle of this preparation phase, they'll likely be more attentive when asked to participate again because they'll have lived with the results.

You might not escape criticism by the sales team for work that you've done, but you'll definitely see more acceptance of your work, and your work will probably be better for having involved the sales team. The simple act of involving the sales team to this degree, which is unusual in most marketing circles, should earn you the sales team's respect and trust.

MARKETING FOLLOW-THROUGH

In golf, a good follow-through helps keep your golf ball on the fairway and out of the woods. In marketing, good follow-through keeps your marketing balls on the fairway by extending your marketing team's responsibility *beyond* the point where they normally throw Sales-Ready Leads into the sales funnel. Do that and only good things can happen. Here are four Beast Practices to help you follow through, improve your conversion rates, and land more of your marketing balls on the green.

Beast Practice 1: Create a Sales Portal

No matter how small (or big) your company is, if you have staff, a sales portal is a good idea. Your sales portal is a web-based tool that gives all your staff (not just your sales reps) a single place to go for everything marketing-related. If you believe that everyone at your company should be on full-time marketing and sales duty (and you should), this portal will give everyone the tools they need to be more successful at building profitable relationships with prospects and customers (see Figure 10.3).

A great, affordable, web-based sales portal you can use with all your staff and third-party contractors (and even customers, if you like) is Microsoft's SharePoint Online (http:// sharepoint.microsoft.com/). It costs under $5 per month per user, is password protected, and lets you post a marketing calendar displaying all the documents used to support each marketing campaign (see Figures 10.4 and 10.5).

You can also use your sales portal to post the documents you want your sales team to fingerprint, with room for them to make comments and provide feedback.

Beast Practice 2: Give Your Reps Some Silver Bullets

There's an old direct response rule called the 30-20-10 rule[2] that says if 100 prospects respond to your marketing campaign, 30 percent of them will likely buy a solution in your space *from some vendor* within 6 months; 20 percent will likely buy a solution between 7 and 12 months; and 10 percent will buy in over 12 months. The other 40 percent are just tire kickers.

While this rule isn't perfect, it provides some good directional indicators. You can expect that up to 30 percent of the prospects who request one of your offers are going to buy within 6 months, so they ought to be in the hands of your sales team pretty quickly. To make sure your sales team is ready to speak to those 30 percent in the language of the marketing campaign that got them in the door in the first place, you need to arm your sales team with some silver bullets. And the more remote your sales team, the more true this becomes.

Figure 10.3 Treadwater's Sales Portal for Its Contract Sales Team

Figure 10.4 Treadwater's Sales Portal: Marketing Events Calendar

Figure 10.5 Treadwater's Sales Portal: Campaign Details

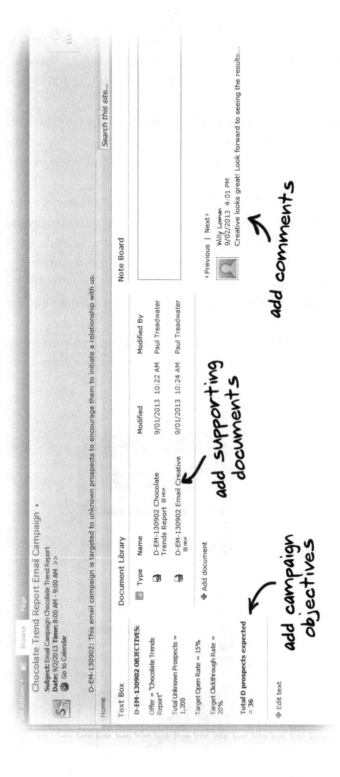

Silver bullets are marketing campaign crib sheets for your sales team. For example, when Paul ran a B-rung marketing campaign promoting his "Private Label Sample Kits" offer, he made sure his sales reps knew what the key selling points were for his campaign (see Figure 10.6).

Even though his sales reps weren't actively involved in the sample kits program, knowing the details of the campaign would prove invaluable for targeting those prospects who converted up to sales-ready status as a result of this campaign. The reps had to know what their prospects were responding to.

Silver bullets can be delivered via small "crib cards" the size of a playing card that a rep can refer to during a sales encounter; they can be interactive videos that run on a mobile device and are played for the prospect; or they can be well-produced PowerPoint presentations. Whatever form they take, your silver bullets can be made available to the sales team on the sales portal, under the corresponding campaign folder. The important point is that you're influencing the message that reaches the prospect and making sure that the message is integrated into your overall campaign.

Silver bullets should be employed with every campaign you create. And because they can be affected by environmental factors (e.g., competitive activity), they should change

Figure 10.6 Paul's Campaign Silver Bullets

from program to program. That said, repetition is one of the best ways to learn, so if some of the bullets are reused from campaign to campaign, there's no harm done.

Beast Practice 3: Survey Your A Prospects (Sales-Ready Leads)

Here's a radical thought. Email your A prospects who were recently converted into Sales-Ready Leads. Positioned as a courtesy follow-up, the email asks if the sales prospect wouldn't mind completing a one-question satisfaction survey, using a 0–10 scale, to rate the level of follow-up they've received so far (sound familiar?). Why go to the trouble? There are a bunch of good reasons. It will take only a few moments; it shows responsible follow-up to the prospect; it gives the prospect an opportunity to say thank you (for good follow-up) or to complain (about lack of follow-up); and it puts the sales team on notice that follow-up is required and expected.

Because Sales-Ready Leads are generally assigned to specific sales reps, they can be held accountable for their level of follow-up in a specific campaign. With senior management's buy-in (which should be a snap), this can be a very powerful tool to dramatically increase follow-up rates to any new business program you're considering.

Beast Practice 4: Sales Contests (Of Course)

What would a chapter on sales be without some mention of a contest? Some might disagree, but a well-designed sales contest can be used to motivate and focus your sales team, not just your top performers. We've found that most sales contests suffer because the top-performing reps usually win. If you follow the Pareto Principle, that means 80 percent of your reps are never even in the running and, as a result, aren't very motivated to try. When you structure your contest criteria, try to select behaviors that will lead to the hoped-for outcome (presumably, increased sales) but which are more achievable by your entire rep population.

For example, running the contest based on *number of calls made* rather than *number of deals closed* can really level the playing field for all reps. And yet, you can argue, if more opportunities are being followed up on, that should still translate into desired sales objective. Think of it this way: *what if you could get your lower-performing reps (maybe 80 percent of all your reps) to improve their performance by, say, 5 percent? What kind of impact would that have on your business?*

Surprisingly, online sales contest solutions are a relatively new and growing area. If you use Salesforce.com, there's a great solution called "Contest Builder" from Level Eleven (http://www.leveleleven.com/). "Contest Builder" is a highly regarded tool that uses "gamification" to drive participation. A newer solution (at time of writing) that's also worth investigating is Incenteev (http://www.incenteev.com).

Sales and marketing are often at odds, not because their goals are different but because of misunderstandings and poor execution between the two as they work together (but more often alone) to identify, nurture, and manage leads. It's actually quite easy to moderate this natural divide, creating a team that's more focused, more consistent, and that closes more business for you.

CAVE SCRATCHES

10

- Sales/marketing partnership agreement
- Mutual metrics establish accountability
- Conversion rates for each group
- Agree on language (leads)
- Get sales involved
- Marketing follow-through

NEXT UP

You've now completed Part One of your quest for Big, Hairy, Outrageous Sales Growth. Congratulations! Now that all the foundational work has been done, it's time to get out of that easy chair and hit the street. Part Two is focused on *execution*—taking all the good work you've done and getting it out in front of your Beast Prospects so you can start producing reliable revenue streams for your business.

PART TWO

Grow Your Beast

BEAST BRIEFING: READY TO START GROWING YOUR BEAST?

Ready to start growing your Beast? It's time. All the planning you did in Part One is about to pay off.

In Part One, you began your journey by talking and listening to your Very Best Customers. You used their insights to establish and confirm a laser-targeted engagement strategy based on the Laws of Engagement—Target, Value, and Offer. You created an Engagement Template to help you get *inside the minds* of your Beast Prospects so they could come to know and trust you and begin building relationships. And you installed the machinery that would help you effortlessly and effectively *scale* these Beast-building relationships.

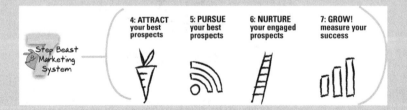

Now the road has brought you to Part Two. It's here that you'll learn how to *find* new customers and *be found* by them, so that Engaged Prospects turn into Sales-Ready Leads, and Customers turn into Fans. As your Beast Prospects go in search of solutions to their business pain, you'll *attract* them with high-value, "findable" content that draws them into your content-rich Beast Cave. You'll also reach out and *pursue* your Beast Prospects, proactively starting relationships by inviting them to take advantage of the targeted offers you've strung across your Engagement Pages.

As a result of your efforts, you have the opportunity to become an online authority in your space. Your Beast Prospects will regard you as one of their most trusted sources, so when *they're* ready to make a decision, *you're* ready to convert them into high-quality, Sales-Ready Leads and new Customers. But prospects can't connect with you if they can't find you. And they won't find you unless you're findable. That's what the next step is all about. Many moons ago, a movie star named Gloria Swanson famously said: "All right, Mr. DeMille, I'm ready for my close-up." Are you ready for your close-up? Get ready to get findable.

1: ASK
the right
question

2: LISTEN
to your best
customers

7: GROW!
measure your
success

7 Step Beast Marketing System

3: FOCUS
your resources

6: NURTURE
your engaged
prospects

5: PURSUE
your best prospects

4: ATTRACT
your best prospects

The secret to being found by prospects

Step 4

ATTRACT

CHAPTER 11

Getting Found by Search

What you'll find in this chapter:
- A needle in the organic search haystack
- Be relevant, be focused, be found
- Making your content search-friendly
- Making your website search-friendly
- Pay per click, but mind your keywords

Getting "discovered" by Hollywood is the goal of every aspiring actor. Getting "discovered" by search engines is the goal of every aspiring entrepreneur. Fortunately, entrepreneurs have a slightly easier road to travel in their quest to become "findable." What do we mean by "findable"? We mean *attracting* those Beast Prospects who are actively researching solutions on the web *into* your Beast Cave by being *visible* and *valuable*. In a nutshell, here's what you have to do:

1. Make your Beast *valuable* by producing high-value content.
2. Make your Beast *visible* by optimizing your content for search through search engine optimization (SEO).

But before we dive into these topics, you should know that the tools of being found—SEO, pay-per-click, social media, blogs, and banner ads—can be massive time sinks that don't necessarily provide a good return on your investment unless you're able to dedicate substantial resources to them. The volume of work required to maintain a great blog or a well-followed Twitter feed, for example, is almost as significant as the number of blogs and tweets on the web that nobody (except their author) ever reads. Remember, just because everyone is doing it doesn't mean that it's the right thing for your business to do. The most important consideration for you is: *What are your Beast Prospects paying attention to?* Everything we have to say aside, *that's* what should determine your Attraction strategy. Fortunately, much of the information about what your Beast Prospects value will have been unearthed by you when you developed your Engagement Template.

While becoming truly *findable* is really hard work, the payback for being found by your Beast Prospects *when they're shopping for a solution* can be immense. And so, in keeping with our dedication to the 80/20 rule—to maximize your payoff while minimizing your work—we're going to flag the key Tools of Attraction and prioritize them for you according to your Beast's hierarchy of needs:

Of course, these recommendations will ebb and flow depending on what business you're in, but out of all the tools you'll find in the next three chapters, here are the top five:

 1. **SEO.** These are the table stakes. You're tying your Beast's arm behind its back if you're not taking advantage of SEO.

 2. **Join the conversation.** Involve yourself in professional social communities like LinkedIn, Viadeo (popular in South America and Europe), or Ushi (LinkedIn's Chinese version) where your Beast Prospects are (*if* that's where they are).

 3. **Pay-per-click ads.** These get you on page one of search faster than anything else and are highly measurable.

 4. **Retargeting.** Retargeting (or remarketing, as Google calls it) is almost too good to be true. Ads that follow your prospects around the web providing free branding at the very least, and valuable click-throughs in the best-case scenario. We're giving this one two thumbs up.

 5. **Blog.** Blogs can be brilliant, but they're just *so* much work. If you want to do this, you may want to get help.

 6. **Everything else.** We'll discuss more as we go.

Here we go. Let's start with the number one "gotta do," SEO.

GETTING FOUND WITH SEO

 SEO stands for search engine optimization, and it matters a great deal to your Beast because SEO keywords help search engines like Google to find your content and potentially place you near the top of their search results. There are two things to keep in mind when it comes to SEO: (1) you have to create content on all of your web properties that your Beast Prospects value, and (2) you have to make your valuable content visible to the web world through the judicious use of keywords. Believe it or not, that's 90 percent of what there is to know about SEO.

By the way, if you've got any ideas about trying to game the search engines and maybe even puzzle out the shortcuts to getting on page one of the search results, you might as well go and get that degree in rocket science you've always wanted, because you'll be going toe-to-toe with a bunch of *actual* rocket scientists. Google's current head of research, for example, was NASA's leading computer scientist.

> *SEO is simply about promoting your high-value content with the right keywords. Keywords are two or more words used in combination that help search engines identify what your content is about.*

What about hiring an SEO expert? If that's the route you want to go, a good place to begin might be a search on "SEO consultants [your town or city]." You can also try the user blog at http://www.seomoz.org/. But if you want a much more affordable way to become findable, or if you just want to dip your toes into the SEO waters, the good news is that you can do much of it yourself. To get your Beast up and running on a simplified, do-it-yourself SEO basis, your Beast needs these five basic ingredients:

1. Focus
2. Content
3. Keywords
4. Links
5. Tweaks

Let's walk through each ingredient.

focus   content   keywords   tweaks
(offers)

1. Focus

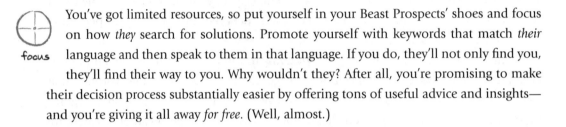

focus

You've got limited resources, so put yourself in your Beast Prospects' shoes and focus on how *they* search for solutions. Promote yourself with keywords that match *their* language and then speak to them in that language. If you do, they'll not only find you, they'll find their way to you. Why wouldn't they? After all, you're promising to make their decision process substantially easier by offering tons of useful advice and insights—and you're giving it all away *for free*. (Well, almost.)

2. High-Value Content

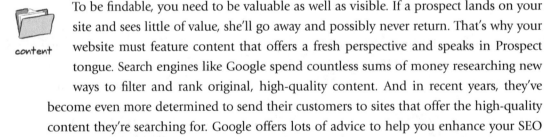

content

To be findable, you need to be valuable as well as visible. If a prospect lands on your site and sees little of value, she'll go away and possibly never return. That's why your website must feature content that offers a fresh perspective and speaks in Prospect tongue. Search engines like Google spend countless sums of money researching new ways to filter and rank original, high-quality content. And in recent years, they've become even more determined to send their customers to sites that offer the high-quality content they're searching for. Google offers lots of advice to help you enhance your SEO efforts, including: "Make pages primarily for users, not for search engines." Translation: create content-rich websites and thought-provoking blog posts that focus on your prospects' needs, not on what you think search engines are looking for. Then you'll rank well.

3. Keywords

keywords

Keywords are the words and phrases that prospective buyers type into search engines such as Google and Bing and Yahoo! to find the information they're looking for online. Keywords also help search engines identify what your content is about. Think of keywords as "signage" for your website and blog, so choose them carefully. When business buyers search online, they're focused, single-minded, and in a hurry. It's as if they're driving down Main Street at rush hour on their way to an important meeting looking for a hardware store because the screw on their license plate is falling off and they need a screwdriver, real quick. They're intensely scanning the store signs as they drive by, looking for one keyword, "hardware." If they don't see the word, they keep driving, missing the convenience store that carries small screwdrivers simply because that store's keyword, "convenience," didn't match the drivers' search criteria.

Without the right keywords, your web content is unlikely to be found online. To help you find and refine the best keywords for your purposes, the major search engines offer a number of tools including Google's Keyword Tool, Google Trends, and Yahoo Buzz Log.

There is a difference between organic and paid search. Search engine results pages (commonly known as SERPs) combine paid and unpaid search results. Paid results (advertising) are separated from unpaid results by shading or some other identifier. When prospective buyers search on Google, Yahoo!, or Bing, the unpaid results they receive are generally considered more valuable because there is presumably no commercial interest behind those results. They were produced by the search engine's algorithms, which are trying to best match content to the search term.

4. Links

links

When a prospect types a keyword phrase into, say, Google, Google searches for sites that are relevant and "important." Important, in Google's world, means your site has relatively high traffic volume and is being linked to by other "important" sites. "Important" sites would be those run by experts and key influencers in your industry. Why? Because these are the people your Beast Prospects follow. Beast Prospects read the blogs and the white papers of influencers and experts and subscribe to their industry reports. And if your content is referenced and linked to by those influencers, you're halfway home.

5. Tweaks

tweaks

There is some basic web housekeeping you need to do, which can pay off with higher traffic and more inbound influencer links to your site. For example, one of your first things to do is make your website as search-friendly as possible. Get rid of any broken links. They are an annoyance to visitors and do you no ranking favors. Make your website easy to navigate because your audience's patience is usually pretty limited, and their cost to go elsewhere is zero. Your conversion rates will rise if prospects can quickly find your Engagement Pages and easily download your offers.

KARIM ENTERS THE WORLD OF SEO

Let's see how Karim focused his SEO efforts by selecting keywords that would match the needs of his Beast Prospects as they searched the web for solutions. We'll also have a look at how he tweaked his website and keywords to further increase his attraction quota. Unlike many entrepreneurs, Karim had a head start on his SEO program because (as we saw in Chapter 7) he'd already stocked his Engagement Ladder with plenty of high-quality content. He knew that when his fast-moving prospects came calling, he'd better have something valuable and timely to offer them, or they would just disappear into the night.

To choose the right keywords and phrases to improve the chances of being found during organic search, Karim knew that the logical place to start was his Engagement Template. *Who needs my product and services?* His Engagement Template told him. *What content are they looking for?* His Engagement Template told him. He knew from the Value section of his Engagement Template that his Beast Prospects lacked competitive pricing information and, as a result, were pricing their products in the dark. The solution to their pain, as Karim's research supported, was to offer them some form of "competitive price monitoring" or "retail price intelligence."

The above phrases became Karim's starting keywords. But he wasn't done. He expanded his keyword research using Google's free Keyword Tool and then refined his keyword strategy with Wordtracker, one of the many affordable, pay-as-you-go keyword research tools available. (Keyword tools show you what people are searching for by collecting search query words and phrases from the search engines and ranking them by popularity and level of competition.) There are many other keyword tools Karim could have chosen, but he liked Wordtracker's user-friendly interface.

Combining his keyword research with his industry knowledge, Karim came up with this set of SEO keywords to start testing: "retail price optimization," "retail price intelligence," and "retail price monitoring." While he could have added misspellings of his keyword phrases to his test set (because many web searchers aren't big on spelling), he chose not to because most search engines now take misspellings into account in their search results. Karim then repeated the above keyword process for every page in his website and his blog to best match page content to likely Beast Prospect search terms. (Google and others frown on mismatches.) For example, on his pricing page, one keyword phrase he developed was "price intelligence pricing"—which makes sense if someone were searching on solution pricing as opposed to general solution information.

Google will probably drive most of your SEO efforts because it's the world's biggest search engine. In the United States, for example, Google accounts for over 66 percent of all searches, dwarfing its main competitors Microsoft (Bing) and Yahoo![1] In addition, a number of B2B-specific sites have sprung up over the past few years. Three of the more popular B2B search engines are Business.com, ThomasNet.com, and GlobalSpec.com. While their percentage of the overall search pie may be tiny, their traffic is extremely targeted and therefore very high quality.

KARIM PUTS THE RIGHT "SIGNAGE" ON HIS WEB PAGES

Where did Karim put the keywords he developed? He began with the title tags on each page of his website and blog. Title tags are little snippets of HTML code that use your keyword phrases to inform search engines what a given page is all about. Search engines

look at hundreds of signals to determine page relevance, but they love title tags most. In fact, 35 of the 37 SEO experts in industry leader SEOmoz's annual Search Ranking Factors survey said that the title tag was *the most important place* to use keywords to achieve high rankings.[2] Your title tag is not only your signage; it's a mini-ad with a maximum of 63 characters that's highlighted on the first line of the search result for each page of your website and blog (see Figure 11.1). Your web person can easily insert your title tags for you. It's a very easy job and shouldn't cost you much, unless your sites have thousands of pages. Then you'd be paying for the chore of going through a large number of web pages.

Karim knew from his keyword research that of the hundreds of merchandising managers at consumer electronic retail firms who were searching for ways to accurately monitor their competitors' prices in near real time, a large number would type in the phrases "price intelligence" and "competitive monitoring."

It's no coincidence that Karim's title tag read "Price Intelligence & Competitor Monitoring." That's part of the reason why BigFatData's solution showed up on page one of Google's search results. His title not only fit the search engine's criteria—accuracy and

Figure 11.1 BigFatData's "Title" Tag and Resulting Search Listing

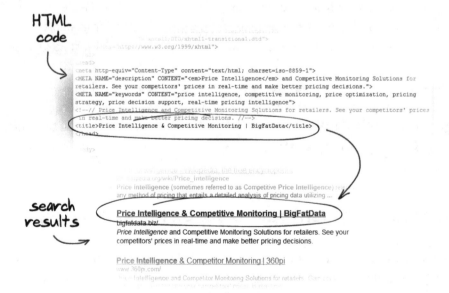

relevance—it gave an accurate and relevant glimpse of what his prospects could expect to find *if they were to click* on the link, so when they clicked, they'd be rewarded for their time and effort.

Where else did Karim put his keywords? In the headlines and subheadings on his website pages (H1 and H2 tags), in the paragraphs of his body copy (within P tags), and in some of his image captions and ALT tags. (Your web designer can help you with this, although if you've built your website in a content management system like WordPress, it's quite easy for you to do yourself.)

Make sure your headlines and body copy read well and make sense, or your visitors will turn away. And don't go overboard and start packing in keywords everywhere you can. In fact, having a keyword density level higher than 5 to 8 percent of your content is a big no-no. The search engines are clever (remember the rocket scientists), and they'll happily knock the stuffing out of your "keyword stuffing" trickery by dropping your content in their rankings.

KARIM WORKS HIS LINKS

Karim already knew who some of his influencers were and where they hung out online, thanks to his Engagement Template. His company is in the data mining space, a subset of what's often called "Big Data." So when Karim searched online using the keywords "top ten influential bloggers big data," a very useful Forbes.com article appeared at the very top of the first page entitled "Who Are the Top 20 Influencers in Big Data?" by Haydn Shaughnessy.[3]

Karim visited a number of the bloggers who were listed, observed how many links (backlinks) there were between blogs, noted how many comments were attached to the posts they made (this can suggest how popular their posts are), noted whose names were referenced again and again, and so on. He also narrowed down his influencers to those whose own business interests most closely matched his own. From that, he built a list of his top 10 influencers who he planned to become more involved with (see more on influencer strategy in Chapter 18).

From there (as we'll see in Chapter 13) the goal is to become a valuable part of the conversation by commenting on influencer posts (and the comments of others) with a view to advancing the discussion by adding your own insights. One of the most effective ways to contribute to a discussion is to ask the author of a given post a relevant question. This often leads to an engagement with several of the forum participants, and gives you a chance to gradually feed your insights into the discussion.

Importantly, you do not want to self-promote or sell in this forum. What you do want to do is make sure that you have a profile set up within every forum you participate in, with the appropriate links back to your website and/or blog. That way, if someone likes what you're saying, they can click on your forum name and link to your profile. From there, prospects, influencers, and experts may choose to link back to your website or blog postings, explicitly approving your insight, analysis, post, or article. But be realistic; it may take months before they notice you. And when they do, you need to be in a position to add value to their existence, you need to be trustworthy, and your website/blog must walk the walk.

It's not a good idea to trade or exchange links. You might think this would be an easy way to build traffic and page ranking, but Google frowns on artificial link-building, and if you're caught, your site could be penalized. If people contact you asking to trade with them, say no.

A TWEAK HERE AND A TWEAK THERE

Business buyers won't stay on your site very long (and they're unlikely to return) if they find the experience frustrating. Karim made sure his website loaded quickly and eliminated Flash from his site. Most mobile devices such as Apple's iPhone and iPad do not support Flash, and search engines have trouble recognizing the text within Flash, rendering much of your Flash-rich content invisible. Karim also ditched the "welcome" page because it slowed access and actually handicapped his search rankings. Vanity welcome pages are a bad idea for prospects and search engines.

Google can't read text that is part of an image, so Karim (actually the web guy who worked for him) used ALT tags alongside the images on his site so Google could index the text associated with the images, thereby helping to give his website, which was loaded with images, a higher ranking. That's as far as Karim wanted—and needed—to take his SEO strategy.

Here are a few more tweaks that can pay big SEO dividends:

- Think about installing analytics software such as Google Analytics, Clicky (excellent Twitter interaction tracking), KISSmetrics (which focuses on an individual's activity with you rather than the usual aggregated data), or CrazyEgg (which is excellent for optimizing your site's usability). They range from free to affordable, and in the very least will give you the baseline information on how many Beast Prospects are *finding* your site, for use in your Prospect Engagement Rate metric (introduced in the last chapter). In particular, look for where your traffic is coming from (by city), how long they're staying on your site, and what pages they're spending the most time on. You can also use pay-per-click tools to track which keywords are actually being used to seek what you sell (more on this in Chapter 12).
- Always try and position your keyword phrases near the top of your web pages.
- Use meta tags to describe your page. Meta tags are plain English text that describe your web page. While they don't count for much in the way of SEO value, they're often used by search engines as the text that describes your site in the search results (see Figure 11.2). Since usability can be as important as findability, you should make sure your meta tags are clear, descriptive, and well maintained.
- Search engines do assign some value to links, so make sure you embed relevant keywords in the anchor text that describes your links. Anchor text is simply the descriptive text you use (like "click here") whenever you create a link on your site. An optimized alternative to "click here," for instance, would be "click here for price intelligence pricing," where the entire phrase is used as a link.

Figure 11.2 BigFatData's Meta Tag and Resulting Search Listing

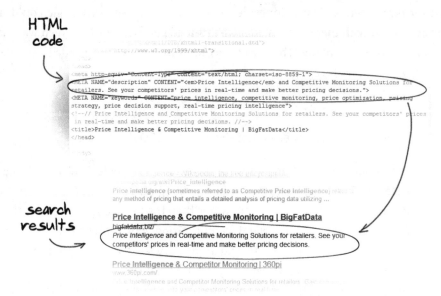

If you're wondering what impact Penguin—one of Google's latest major algorithm changes—will have, you needn't worry (unless you've been trying to game the system). If your site contains good content, relevant keywords, and valuable backlinks, nothing will change. If your site ignores what's been discussed in this chapter, however, it will be penalized with a much lower search ranking, resulting in lower visibility and lower traffic.

SEO NO-NOS

Don't bother slapping together pages and pages of me-too content in the hope you'll gain "visibility" on the web. It won't happen. Search engines are too smart for that. Search engines like Google need to give their customers the highest quality, most accurate search experience possible, and that means your website will lose visibility if it undermines that goal by being:

- Poorly written
- All about your products and services instead of your prospects' needs
- Lacking insights and best practices
- Thin on content or having excessive advertising-to-content ratios
- Too derivative—lifting too much content from other sites
- Stuffed with keywords
- Stuffed with bought or low-quality links

CAVE SCRATCHES

11

~ Focus SEO on your prospects' needs
~ Build findable, high-value content
~ Content and keywords match prospect search terms
~ Tweak website and keywords

NEXT UP

In this chapter we've covered the most important tools you need to maximize your website's visibility and value—from an organic search perspective. But what about pay-per-click and other forms of paid advertising? Paid search is another "gotta do" and can be an important part of your Attraction strategy. That's what's up next.

Step 4

ATTRACT

CHAPTER 12

Getting Found by Placement

What you'll find in this chapter:
- Bidding on keywords
- Making pay-per-click work for your business
- Maximizing your ad content
- Making the right impression
- Target, then retarget
- PR vs. online wire services

To pay or not to pay—that is the question when it comes to search. Organic search may deliver 20 to 30 times the number of visitors as paid search (according to Google), but organic visitors view only half as many pages and have twice the bounce rate.[1] Translation: unpaid search delivers higher volume but lower quality prospect leads. Bounce rate refers to the number of visitors who leave a site after viewing only a single page. High bounce rates usually mean that the page or the site wasn't relevant or helpful to the visitor.

As we've just seen, unpaid search (SEO) costs you little but time. The downside is, it requires time to take root. *Paid* search, on the other hand—those sponsored pay-per-click (PPC) ads that appear at the top and the sides of most search engines' results pages—will give you almost instant gratification in the form of your company appearing on page one of the search results, provided your competition for the keywords you've selected isn't too great. Your ad will start working in minutes, not weeks or months, and pay-per-click ads are more easily measured than SEO. So why isn't everyone using it? Well, quite a few are (see sidebar). And Google, so far, has been the biggest beneficiary.

Paid Search Fast Facts[2]

- Paid search revenues in 2011: $34 billion

- Paid search revenues four years from now: $61.1 billion

- Paid search is already bigger than radio and outdoor advertising

- Paid search represents half of all online advertising

- Google's AdWords owns the majority of the PPC market

- Microsoft and Yahoo! (Bing Ads) own most of the rest

Advertisers generally agree that pay-per-click ads complement their organic search strategy. While studies show that organic search generates a great deal more B2B traffic than PPC, PPC is a better lead generator.[3]

Karim, our software entrepreneur, decided to invest in a pay-per-click advertising campaign to complement and build on his SEO program. When executives and managers at major consumer electronics retailers (Karim's Beast Prospects) start looking for solutions to a problem—lost sales due to smartphone-based comparison shopping—they key in a variety of phrases to start their search. Karim's keyword research revealed that "retail price intelligence" was one of their most popular search phrases, so to begin his PPC campaign, he bid on this phrase. You can see the search results for "retail price intelligence" in Figure 12.1. It's easy to set up a PPC account with any of the search engines (just search on "PPC"), and once you do, you'll have access to a range of PPC tools that allow you to manage your keywords, your ads, and your budget.

Notice that on the search results page (Figure 12.1), Karim's company name, Big-FatData, appears less prominently than "retail price intelligence," which is boldfaced. That's because Google bolds keywords, and his prospects, like many B2B buyers who are surfing the web, are using *solutions*-oriented keywords because they're in the early stages of their Decision Cycles. Karim's ad won a spot on page one for a number of reasons, including limited competition. But his Quality Score was high as well. We'll explain what this is in a moment, but first let's look at the big picture.

Figure 12.1 Karim's PPC Results on Page One

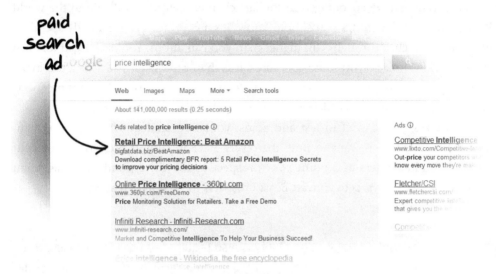

FOCUSING YOUR PPC GOAL

A targeted PPC advertising campaign can be a great way to "accelerate" your SEO efforts and grow your Beast *if it's done right.* Horror stories abound of PPC campaigns sliding off the rails and into a bottomless pit, but your campaign won't be one of them. It's going to be focused and monitored. To get your Beast up and running on PPC, you need to feed it four ingredients:

1. Focus
2. Content (Offers)
3. Keywords
4. Tweaks

Sound familiar? Of course. They're four of the five SEO ingredients we learned about in the last chapter. The one exception, links, isn't included because that's what PPC ads

focus   content   keywords   tweaks
(offers)

are—paid links. You're buying links to your own content, as opposed to the organic links from influencers that we encouraged in the last chapter. Before you dive into the world of PPC, there are a few things you should know. It's a good idea to set a daily spending limit in case your click-throughs run higher than you can afford. You're charged for each click on your PPC link, so you could get more clicks than expected if you attract too many poor-quality prospects (if your keywords aren't focused enough), or if the right prospects respond more than planned (which is a good thing, but needs to be managed).

In both cases, you'll want to test and adjust your PPC strategy while limiting your cost exposure. You'll also want to note that every PPC ad should present one of your Engagement Ladder offers and point your prospect to the corresponding Engagement Page. Your goal, as always, is to convert Beast Prospects to Engaged Prospects.

A certain amount of writing ability is also required to produce a successful PPC campaign—quite a bit of rewriting if you decide to do it yourself. Google AdWords allows you only 95 characters, so strong verbs and descriptive nouns are crucial in getting your message across succinctly. Strip out adjectives and adverbs wherever possible, because every word has to pull its weight.

Some of the top PPC blogs and PPC experts include Joanna Lord, Search-EngineJournal (SEJ), PPC Hero, and of course there's Google's AdWords blog. We mention these because PPC is complex, and reading blogs devoted to PPC can be a good way to speed your learning curve. You may decide to hire PPC expertise rather than do it yourself, because if you don't know exactly what you're doing (and what are the chances of *that*?), you can end up spending a lot of money with little to show for it. If you do want to try PPC yourself, be comforted by the fact that you can limit your spending and you can easily test what works and what doesn't work, allowing you to optimize your PPC strategy over time.

PRICING YOUR PPC CAMPAIGN

Speaking of price, if you're wondering how much Google AdWords costs, there's no simple answer. The price you pay depends on a host of factors, including the industry and market you're in, the kind of product you sell, and the popularity of the keywords you've chosen.

AdWords users have the option of choosing a pay-per-click model (most do) or CPM (cost per thousand impressions). Typically, you'll indicate the maximum amount that you're willing to pay per click based on the keywords selected. To protect yourself, you can also set a maximum spend per day. But keyword bidding is at the heart of the AdWords system.

How Much Should You Bid?

To answer this precisely, you have to determine your average conversion costs. And if you're like most B2B entrepreneurs, that isn't always so easy to do because B2B conversion is not a single monetizable step. If you're new to PPC, have a limited budget, and can't easily establish a conversion cost from PPC, we'd suggest using Google's automatic bidding process. You set a daily budget and the AdWords system automatically adjusts your maximum cost-per-click (CPC) bids based on your budget. You can also set a maximum bid limit so your bids don't go over a certain amount. But there's another factor to consider besides cost. Google wants to ensure the highest quality search results for its customers. To do that, a few years ago they instituted what they call a Quality Score.

Google defines Quality Score as a measure of "how relevant your ads, keywords, and landing page are to a person seeing your ad." Higher Quality Scores are in your best interest because they can lead to lower prices and better ad positions. This means companies can no longer win the rankings war by simply being the highest bidder. Ranking is based on keyword relevance, ad relevance, content relevance, and content quality. That all seems clear enough, doesn't it? You're good to go. Well, not exactly. Not if you read Google's guidelines. For example, here's their suggestion for getting on the first page:

> If it's important for you to have your ad show on the first page of Google search results, first page bid estimates will show you an approximate CPC [cost per click] bid needed for your ad to regularly reach the first page of Google search results when a search query exactly matches your keyword. The estimate is based on the keyword's Quality Score and current advertiser competition for that keyword, so there's no guarantee you'll consistently be on the first page.[4]

Note those last few words: "There's no guarantee you'll consistently be on the first page." There's no guarantee because Google not only wants to get the best results possible for their users, they don't want to be pinned down to a formula, at least not a *simple* formula. A simple formula can be "gamed," and Google wants its users, not you, to determine if your ad deserves a top ranking and top placement. That said, your ad ranking is determined by the following formula:

$$\text{bid price} \times \text{Quality Score}$$

Clearly, if the quality of the offer on your Engagement Page isn't deemed high enough, it doesn't matter how much you spend to promote it; you'll probably be wasting your money. Here's a very simplified example of how the process works: Let's say entrepreneur #1 has bid $4 per click for his ad and has a Quality Score of 3 (out of 10). Entrepreneur #2 has bid half that price ($2 per click) but has a much higher Quality Score (7 out of 10). Who wins the placement game? The winner is the lower bidder, #2, because 14 total ranking points beat 12 ranking points. But that may not *always* be true, because the weighting of the elements in the Quality Score formula is a closely guarded secret, and it's always changing.

HOW TO MAXIMIZE YOUR QUALITY SCORE

Your own experience surfing the web should tell you that a PPC ad has only a few seconds to do its job. If you can't convince enough prospects to read your PPC offer and then click your link, you've failed. What's the key to success, then? *A relevant ad combined with a relevant offer.* Relevance is critical from a PPC perspective no matter which search engine you're using, because relevant information is essential if the user is to have a quality experience online, and that's what all the search engine companies want for their customers.

The higher your Quality Score, the more money you'll save *and* the better your placement on the search page. So how *exactly* does one meet Google's standard of quality? Google's chief economist, Hal Varian, does a good job of explaining. (You can catch his nine-minute video presentation on YouTube using the keywords "Introduction to the Google Ad Auction" or watch it on Google's blog.)

According to Google's Varian, there are three components to a Quality Score:

1. **Click-through rate.** More than half of your Quality Score is determined by your CTR (click-through rate). CTR does not refer to your ad's popularity (the *number* of clicks your ad receives) but rather to your ad's effectiveness (the *percentage* of viewers who decide to click). The higher your CTR, the higher your quality rating.
2. **Relevance.** Another big chunk of your score is determined by your ad's relevance, which is defined as how closely its "content and context" relate to your keywords.

3. **Engagement Page.** The final, if smaller, piece of the quality puzzle is determined by the quality of your Engagement Page at the other end of your PPC ad. It must have original content, be easily navigable, quick to load, and have a minimum number of pop-ups. And it should be "transparent," meaning it should tell the prospect exactly what the page is about—all things your Engagement Pages are designed to do (see Chapter 8).

Of course, for entrepreneurs like you, there's a big silver lining to this decision by Google and by all the search engines to increasingly emphasize quality over quantity. If you focus your efforts on creating and delivering relevant ads that buyers want to click on, and then you back up your ads with relevant, high-value content, you'll win—*even if your keyword bids are relatively modest.* This really helps level the playing field. Instead of competing on price, you're now competing on "relevance," which is just Google's word for usefulness.

On its keyword tools site, Google uses the term "competition." Competition refers to popularity—how many people are bidding on and using the keyword you've selected. Companies compete for keywords, so every keyword or phrase has either a "low," "medium," or "high" level of popularity—and cost—associated with it. Low competition keywords cost less but attract less traffic.

OPTIMIZING YOUR PPC AD

Like any marketing tactic, PPC won't work for you unless you're absolutely clear about your objectives and the value of the information you want to offer. Again, you have only a few seconds to get a potential prospect's attention, so to maximize your results, you need to make the content of your PPC ad campaign as persuasive and compelling as it can possibly be.

Ad Content

- Make sure your title keywords match what your prospects are looking for. For example, Karim's title, "Retail Price Intelligence," has three words in total (see Figure 12.2).
- Build on your value proposition in the body copy. Karim's value proposition is about using software intelligence to gain a competitive advantage.

Figure 12.2 Karim's Pay-Per-Click Ad

Ads related to **price intelligence** ⓘ

Retail Price Intelligence: Beat Amazon
bigfatdata.biz/BeatAmazon
Download complimentary BFR report: 5 **Retail Price Intelligence** Secrets
to improve your pricing decisions.

Pricing Success Kit - 360pi.com
www.360pi.com/SuccessKit

- Make sure to include a strong action verb. Karim's descriptor copy began with "download."
- Offer something of value. Karim offered his D-rung "5 Retail Price Intelligence Secrets" analyst paper, addressing his prospects' need for "solution education."
- Add pain-oriented keywords that will be familiar to your B2B buyers. Karim included researched pain point keywords like "beat Amazon" (his prospects' number one competitor), "retail price intelligence," and "improve pricing decisions."
- On the corresponding Engagement Page, use the same title keywords you used in your PPC ad title.
- Get to the point.
- Make an offer. One offer and one Engagement Page per PPC ad (see Figure 12.3).
- Provide a clear path and a call to action.
- Direct with next steps.

8 STEPS TO A SUCCESSFUL GOOGLE ADWORDS CAMPAIGN (OTHER PPC SERVICES WILL DIFFER)

If you follow these eight steps, you'll greatly increase your chances of success with Google's AdWords service. But keep in mind, the following is only a summary, and it's AdWords-specific. (Before undertaking your own campaign, we recommend an extended visit to the AdWords website.)

1. Set a daily or weekly budget. Google suggests starting off with a budget of $5 to $10 per day. If you decide to test one campaign with one set of keywords for a week, your cost would be anywhere between $0 and $70. If no one clicked on your ad, the good news is it would cost you nothing. The bad news? You need to rework your ads.

Figure 12.3 Karim's PPC Offer Engagement Page

2. Select the automatic bidding option, which automatically adjusts your bids to maximize the number of clicks possible within your budget.

3. Many people set a CPC (cost-per-click) bid limit. Karim, for example, did not expect many clicks per day because of the technical nature of his product category and the specificity of his keywords. How much are you willing to pay for a click? Hard to say until you measure it. Karim started out with a $5-per-click limit knowing he could change his CPC bid at any time.

4. Select your keywords using your Engagement Template and Engagement Ladder offers for reference. Start off with about 10 phrases. Use Google's keyword tool to find keywords with reasonable levels of competition and view the volume of monthly searches.

5. Write your ad, framing it around the keywords and offers you've chosen.

6. Karim created three ad groups around the three keywords he created—retail price intelligence, retail price optimization, and retail price monitoring—and rotated them equally to see which performed best for him.

7. If you have multiple products, create ad groups for each product.

8. Test and refine your keywords, offers, and bids by running multiple PPC ad campaigns. Your PPC management panel will show you how many views your ad received and

what percentage of those views clicked through to your Engagement Page. Your Engagement Page reporting (discussed more fully in Chapter 19) will show you how many of those click-throughs completed your web form to become Engaged Prospects. All of this data can be plugged into your Prospect Engagement Rate (PER) metric. Testing different PPC ads is quite easy to do inside your PPC account (on the PPC management panel) and allows you to find the combination of keywords, offers, and bids that produces the best ROI on your PPC spend. If it hasn't already occurred to you, this is a great job to have a marketing assistant do for you.

IS PAID SEARCH RIGHT FOR YOUR BUSINESS?

It depends on your goals and budget and the accuracy and completeness of your Engagement Template, in particular the Target portion (revisit Chapter 5 for a refresher on the Law of the Target). Your success also depends on the quality of your Engagement Pages and your Offers. Hubspot offers a free ebook on the subject, while Brad Geddes' *Advanced Google AdWords* offers a more comprehensive study of PPC.[5] (Yes, AdWords equals PPC for most users.)

Success in a PPC campaign can easily be measured by your Prospect Engagement Rate. PER tells you how efficiently you're converting those who are outside your Beast Cave into cave-dwelling Engaged Prospects. For PPC, you would compare the number of PPC click-throughs you received on a given offer against the number who converted to Engaged Prospects by accepting that offer by completing the web form.

You can also calculate your cost per conversion and compare its efficiency to the other marketing channels you use. For example, if you spent $300 in a given month on a PPC ad for white paper "A," and you converted five new Engaged Prospects, you would have a cost of $60 per Engaged Prospect to compare to your other marketing channels. By tracking these numbers, you can decide to increase or decrease your PPC spending based on the channel's effectiveness for you. You'll learn more about this in Chapter 19.

Your basic PPC keyword themes should be reflective of your SEO keywords, but modified to reflect the Engagement Ladder offers you'll be making. For example, the three keyword themes for Karim's PPC campaign were "retail price monitoring," "retail price intelligence," and "retail price optimization," the same as for his SEO campaign. While it's true that Karim's product category is a very defined one, he was careful not to choose generic keywords in the hope of attracting a larger audience. Karim wanted quality, not quantity, and keywords like "retail price intelligence" are much more specific and more effective than "data mining," for example. Not only did these choices help raise the quality of click-through traffic to his Engagement Page, they significantly lowered his cost per click.

BANNER ADS

 Banner ads, also known as display ads, are ubiquitous throughout the web, probably because they're the closest in style to traditional placement advertising. Many advertisers find them attractive because they're familiar. This, of course, is not always the best reason to do something (see the Fast Facts sidebar that follows). One of the biggest issues with banner ads is so-called banner blindness—web surfers have simply trained themselves to ignore display ads. As a result, banner ads have very low click-throughs, with some studies estimating average click-through rates at just 0.25 percent. B2B display ads were increasingly less effective in 2011, according to Forrester Research, because most weren't optimized for mobile. That will need to change because studies show a growing percentage of business buyers are using their smartphones to do online research.

As if banner blindness wasn't a big enough obstacle, 31 percent of display ads never even get the chance to be seen according to a recent study by ComScore,[6] because the ads were served "below the fold" (below the first screen that is presented), and most users don't scroll down the page. Banner ads are usually priced by CPM, or cost per 1,000 impressions, which means you pay whether they generate click-throughs for you or not. An impression is simply a page view. It doesn't matter whether the page your banner is on is viewed for a minute or a second, or whether your ad is the only one on the page or one of several. For most industries, banner ad rates run between $0.50 and $5 CPM. This is an older-style advertising model that's likely to get a refresh before too long.

Banner Ads–Fast Facts[7]

- 4.8 trillion online banner ads were delivered in the United States in 2011.

- The average person online in the United States was served 19,000 banners in 2011.

- 31 percent of these were never seen.

- 54 percent of people don't click banner ads because they don't trust the ad.

- B2B marketers have had very limited success with Facebook banner ads.

If you're considering placing a banner ad, here are some tips:

- Study your industry's online trade sites; observe where your competitors' banner ads, if any, appear and how they're designed.

- As with PPC ads, less is more. Don't be cute. Keep the headline and body copy short, relevant, and to the point.

- As with PPC ads, focus on your offer, not your product. Remember that you have to be relevant to your prospects' needs.

- Tell prospects exactly what to do by including a "Download Now" button. Buttons encourage click-through.

- Use the offers from your Engagement Ladder, and have the banner ads click through to the corresponding Engagement Pages. Success from these campaigns can be measured, like PPC, by the Prospect Engagement Rate you generate (web form conversions divided by total Engagement Page hits).

Figure 12.4 shows a simple but effective banner ad.

Figure 12.4 Focus on the Offer, Not the Product

RETARGETING YOUR PROSPECTS

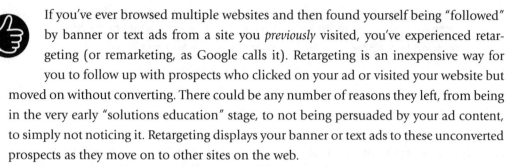

If you've ever browsed multiple websites and then found yourself being "followed" by banner or text ads from a site you *previously* visited, you've experienced retargeting (or remarketing, as Google calls it). Retargeting is an inexpensive way for you to follow up with prospects who clicked on your ad or visited your website but moved on without converting. There could be any number of reasons they left, from being in the very early "solutions education" stage, to not being persuaded by your ad content, to simply not noticing it. Retargeting displays your banner or text ads to these unconverted prospects as they move on to other sites on the web.

Retargeting works because it generally targets prospects who've shown an interest in your product or service category and who just didn't convert to an Engaged Prospect on your website for whatever reason. According to Joanna Lord at SEOmoz.com, consumers who were retargeted were found to be up to 70 percent more likely to complete a conversion than users who weren't.[8] There's no reason to believe B2B buyers would be much different.

There are two types of retargeting programs:

Site retargeting targets recent visitors to your website by dropping a cookie on your prospect's computer (it's completely legit, not to worry). From that point forward, as your prospect goes out across the Internet, the retargeting service will insert a banner or text ad for one of your offers on whatever website your best prospects are visiting. Some of the bigger players in the site retargeting space are AdRoll, Retargeter, and Fetchback.

Search retargeting targets web searchers who haven't yet visited your site but have been using keywords that match your ad campaign. Chango is one of the leaders in this space. How does search retargeting work? According to Chango, data is collected through a network of partner websites that cookie individuals arriving from search engines, making note of the keywords that sent them there. The advertising network that these websites are part of will then serve your retargeting ads when your keywords match the search keywords used. On its website, Chango explains that privacy isn't an issue because "all the data is collected anonymously and stored against a cookie ID, and we abide by all privacy rules and best practices, including those of the NAI and IAB."[9]

In all cases, you only pay if your prospect clicks on your ad, and you can control how much you're willing to spend when you get a better sense of the payback. In the meantime, your offers follow your prospects around the web providing you with a fantastic, no-cost awareness campaign. Importantly, to avoid having your prospects feel like they're being stalked, you can set frequency caps (the maximum number of times a prospect sees your ad), and you can decide to only retarget those prospects who've gone through a certain number of pages on your site (suggesting a certain interest level), rather than retargeting everyone who lands on, say, only your home page. You can also control what kind of websites your ads show up on using tools provided by the retargeting services. Google's Remarketing service is one of the easier retargeting services to use, it can be managed through your Google PPC account, and it gives you access to Google's entire advertising network.

GETTING VISIBLE WITH PR

PR, or Public Relations (meaning "unpaid" media coverage), is often at the top of many entrepreneurs' marketing wish lists. Who wouldn't want to get published on Forbes.com or cited by an editor or contributor in one of the leading trade journals? The problem is that pumping out a bunch of press releases about your product will do little to get anyone's notice. And yet, that's what PR is to legions of entrepreneurs (and businesspeople) around the world. They assume that their fascination for their own business is shared by others—when most often it isn't. As with everything we've discussed so far, success in PR is achieved by unswerving attention to what the editors/ writers/bloggers/journalists you're appealing to care about—that is, what is their pain, and how can you help them solve it?

Relationships with these gatekeepers are crucial to your getting airtime, and those relationships require time and trust to develop. In a nutshell, PR is most often not an area for do-it-yourselfers. So here's our recommendation: spend your resources on other marketing activities until you can afford to hire some qualified help. That help can be of the less expensive variety (a staffer who has a PR background and who can also be used for other marketing work like content creation) or the more expensive variety (hire a PR firm). A great book to ground you on the basics of PR is Steven Van Yoder's *Get Slightly Famous: Become a Celebrity in Your Field and Attract More Business with Less Effort.*

Many question the value of hiring a PR firm. After all, a decent PR firm will usually cost you a minimum of $5,000 per month. What do you get for that money? As one of our business associates demonstrated recently, used well, PR can provide very significant payback. With barely $20,000 in revenue, he managed to sell his fledgling software company to a Fortune 100 company for many millions of dollars, in large part because of PR. He targeted a set of companies he deemed to be high-potential buyers of his entire business. Then he hired a top-end PR firm with a boatload of contacts at those high-potential companies and among the influencers surrounding those companies. Before long, his story was known across these organizations, which led to a relatively quick acquisition. Of course, he first had to develop a product that served a very specific need that would appeal to the suitor companies, and he made sure his solution created a unique competitive advantage for those companies. But the fact that he's done the same kind of build-and-flip four times now, with PR as his key marketing tool, underscores the value of "unpaid media coverage" as an effective marketing strategy.

WIRE SERVICES

If you can't afford access to real PR help and you insist on getting your name out there, you have another option: the online wire services. If you have news or an announcement that you feel absolutely needs to be seen by the world, services like PRWeb, Business Wire, PR Newswire, and Marketwire will, for a fee, send your content to the major search engines and news outlets. As always, valued content (that is, valued by your Beast Prospects) travels the furthest. While you're unlikely to get many direct leads, it's possible to get some additional visibility this way because search engines tend to weigh these types of releases more heavily than some other search content (partly because of the source and, yes, partly because they're paid releases).

Of the four services mentioned above, PRWeb and Marketwire may be the best for budget conscious entrepreneurs. PRWeb says they can connect you to 30,000 bloggers and journalists, although who these bloggers and journalists are seems to be a well-kept secret. For roughly $200 (the cost of a one-off placement), it may be worthwhile to find out. Just make sure you link back to your website, and make sure your website and its contents are up to snuff, because while all these services are SEO optimized, it won't help your cause if your visitors can't find the path to your offers.

CAVE SCRATCHES
12
~ Focus PPC efforts on prospects' needs
~ Set a budget
~ Build high-value Engagement Pages
~ Content matches ad
~ Eliminate underperformers
~ Optimize keywords
~ Track results

NEXT UP

If the goal is to get found, you can do it through unpaid search (SEO); you can pay to get found with keyword-based, pay-per-click advertising; you can get found by retargeting unconverted prospects; and you can get found with online and offline PR. There's one more way to get found, and it brings us back to the idea of being *visible* and being *valuable* in order to be findable. The *valuable* part of that equation is the topic of Chapter 13.

Getting Found by Contribution

> **What you'll find in this chapter:**
> - Be helpful, be generous, get found
> - B2B and social media
> - Finding your influencers
> - Influencing your influencers
> - Contributing value
> - The 90-minute social media addict

You're already an innovator, a leader, an idea person, and an expert. Isn't it time to start promoting your ideas and expertise on a business blog or discussion forum or social network? It's certainly not bragging or chest-beating if you're helping people solve business problems and you're generous with your insights. That's why contributing to the social conversation—in a thoughtful, targeted, and consistently helpful way—can be one of the more effective ways to grow your influence and your business.

But—and there's always a *but*—social media won't work as a lead generation vehicle *unless* you complement it with a well-organized website filled with useful content backed by a clear value story and, specifically, a clear path to your offers to encourage conversions to Engaged Prospects. That's what the first three steps of *Feed the Startup Beast* were all about.

BECOMING PART OF THE CONVERSATION

For Outrageously Smart entrepreneurs like you, social media is not about following the herd or getting thousands of followers or boosting your ego with high Klout or Kred scores (influencer ratings). It's about learning and making connections and building your reputation as a go-to expert.

To get found, you must offer something valuable—your knowledge and insights and solutions—in exchange for the attention, interest, and engagement of your market—including some of the key influencers in your industry. It's about ensuring that these influencers (and their followers) are happy to cite you, quote you, and link to you because you're no longer a stranger; you've become a part of the conversation.

What conversation? The one that's ongoing between your *customers*, *prospects*, and *competitors* on blogs, discussion boards, Twitter feeds, LinkedIn groups, Google+ circles, and Facebook pages as well as on public and private social networks all over the globe. What's keeping the conversation going and driving it forward is the constant ebb and flow as business problems are unveiled and solutions are shared, as well as the ease with which people can observe and contribute (see Figure 13.1). You have solutions to share, so why not add your voice to the mix?

Figure 13.1 Technology Decision Makers Are Active in Social Media

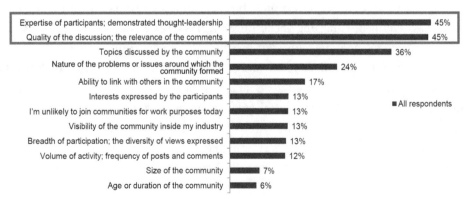

Quality interactions drive community participation

"Which factors most influence your decision to join or participate in community activity for work purposes?"

Expertise of participants; demonstrated thought-leadership	45%
Quality of the discussion; the relevance of the comments	45%
Topics discussed by the community	36%
Nature of the problems or issues around which the community formed	24%
Ability to link with others in the community	17%
Interests expressed by the participants	13%
I'm unlikely to join communities for work purposes today	13%
Visibility of the community inside my industry	13%
Breadth of participation; the diversity of views expressed	13%
Volume of activity; frequency of posts and comments	12%
Size of the community	7%
Age or duration of the community	6%

■ All respondents

Base: 1,001 US and European business technology decision-makers at companies with 100 or more employees
Source: Q1 2011 US And European B2B Social Technographics® Online Survey For Business Technology Buyers

Source: Forrester Research, Inc.[1] Graphic and data used with permission.

THE 80/20 SOCIAL MEDIA PLAN

So perhaps you're wondering how you'll find time to contribute to all these conversations? First, it's important to understand that conversations on social media are generally quite short because most people prefer to receive information and insights in short bursts. They're too busy to read or listen to extended lectures. Forrester Research predicts B2B marketers will move away from white papers and other forms of long content to more frequent and timely content vehicles like blog posts.[2]

Second, it's all about following the 80/20 rule. The Outrageously Smart social media plan is built on the belief that 20 percent of your efforts will be responsible for 80 percent of the results. Throughout *Feed the Startup Beast*, we've followed the 80/20 rule (Pareto Principle) because it works. However, as always, an effective social media plan takes patience and persistence because social credibility takes time to build. The B2B entrepreneur's 80/20 social media strategy is simply this:

- *Find* your industry's key influencers
- *Listen* in to the conversation
- *Contribute* value
- *Consider* your options
- Never *expect* anything in return

Pick your spots. You *don't* have to be part of every conversation or be on every social media channel. Karim, for example, had to be extremely targeted in his social media efforts because he was spending all of his energy getting his startup off the ground. His goal was to become a trusted resource to the hundreds of senior managers involved in pricing intelligence at the major retail chains. In order to do this, he:

1. Identified key IT bloggers and influencers among retail merchandising managers
2. Joined two forums and groups
3. Listened and learned
4. Wrote a compelling personal profile and company page on LinkedIn
5. Started small by contributing brief, useful comments, with links back to his website

Let's dig a little deeper and see how he began accomplishing his goal.

KARIM'S INFLUENCER STRATEGY

When Karim did a little research into the "social" world, he began to understand just how important a role influencers play in B2B social media. He came to realize that peer-to-peer conversations on professional social networking sites are of major importance to retail merchandising managers, with one study suggesting they're second only to live in-person events as a source of information.

Karim realized that for smaller companies like his that have little or no visibility, influencers (who often contribute to professional networking sites) could play a huge role in helping increase his profile and eventually drive traffic to his site if he were successful in engaging them. Being young and fairly new to the industry, his first task was to identify who the key influencers were and then to find their sites. Once again, he looked to his Engagement Template for help—particularly the answers to question 5 on the Target section of his Engagement Questionnaire (see Figure 13.2).

Influencers can include experts, consultants, analysts, journalists, advisors, associations, CTOs, CFOs, CXOs, VPs—in fact, really anyone within the customer organization in middle management or above. Karim's research revealed that a small group of influencers dominated his niche, including members of the Professional Pricing Society blog. Karim began to follow the blog, one of the most popular in his field, and the resource tab led him to a number of pricing bloggers and other key influencers in the pricing field. He also joined LinkedIn and subsequently joined two LinkedIn groups—the Professional Pricing Society group and the Pricing Strategies group.

For a while, Karim was only a listener. But over time, he began to add valuable comments and links and insights to the blogs and groups. He respectfully challenged a post by a key influencer and became a central figure in a lively discussion. Focusing mainly on a sub-speciality, competitive intelligence, he gradually built a reputation as an authority in that area, and people began posting links to the trends report from his Engagement Ladder that he had been referencing in his discussions. The quantity and the *quality* of the traffic to his website began to improve, and so did his conversions. In fact, his trends report was downloaded 42 times in three months, resulting in an Engagement Ladder supplemented with highly qualified prospects from the communities he participated in.

DON'T FORGET ABOUT YOUR PROFILE

In the rush to develop a social media presence, it can be easy to forget the basics. If you contribute to a social network on a regular basis, people will naturally want to check you

Figure 13.2 Engagement Questionnaire: Target

PART 1: THE TARGET

1. When it comes to decisions to purchase products/services/solutions such as ours, who is involved in the decision process?

Who do you need to target your marketing efforts to?

Who else is involved that needs to be addressed by you?

2. Who (title or role) has the final say in the purchase decision? Is there anyone else who influences the decision? Do the final *users* make or influence the decision?

3. How does the decision process work? How long does it usually take for a purchase decision to be made?

Confirmation.

4. What do you see your role being within that decision process?

Where can we find your decision team?

5. When you or your team are researching products/services/solutions such as ours, how would you rank each of the following information sources on a scale from 0 to 10, where 10 is "critically important" to your research:

   Personal referrals: _____
   User groups:_____
   Vendor sales rep: _____
   Vendor websites: _____
   Distributor reps: _____
   Online industy discussion forums: _____
   Other network groups:_____
   Industry blogs: _____
   LinkedIn:_____
   Twitter:_____
   Facebook: _____
   Other social media: _____
   Trade websites:_____
   Trade publications (print): _____
   Trade publications (online): _____
   Analysts: _____
   Analyst websites: _____
   Trade shows: _____

Probe for examples of each and rank as appropriate

6. *The following can be done without the customer's participation:*

   Add business demographics: industry/sector, company size (revenue and employees), number of locations, years in business, products/services sold.

Basic template for finding Beast Prospects

out. And the most common way they do so (after Googling you) is by looking at your social profile.

Whether you're on LinkedIn, Facebook, or Google+, you should spend the time to complete your profile and make it sing, so that it works harder to promote your image and expertise the right way. Get professional writing help if you need to, but get it right, because your profile is a key element in establishing paths back to your Beast Cave. LinkedIn and Google+ profiles are highly ranked by search engines, so when you update your profile, make sure you also insert links to your website and any articles and blog posts you've written.

LinkedIn has become a go-to networking site for many B2B entrepreneurs. Yet many of the profiles listed on the site are poorly written or simply boilerplate. Boilerplate means you're using the same language as everyone else, so how are you going to stand out from the crowd?

When you tell the world, "Jack is an innovative IT executive with a proven track record of success with over 20 years of experience working in the high tech and computer industry in Silicon Valley. Jack has held senior management roles in multinationals and managed global partnerships," what are you really saying? One thing you're saying with a profile like this is that you're not really putting yourself in your prospects' shoes. What are your prospects looking for? What do they need to know about you? A profile like this shouts out that you just wanted to make sure you had some kind of a LinkedIn "presence." Box checked. (Incidentally, this is an actual profile randomly pulled from the site. The name has been changed to protect the guilty party.)

So how do you make your profile compelling? First, stop thinking of it as a résumé, and start thinking of it as a *story*. Include the unexpected. Every entrepreneur has faced failure, and yet you wouldn't know it from most LinkedIn profiles. If it fits, include your struggles as part of your story, because struggle is real, and struggle *is* story. When you start to see your profile (and your life) as a story, people will instantly see you as more personal, more compelling, and more engaging. If you feel uncomfortable telling your story, then consider beginning your profile with a couple of thought-provoking questions. Figure 13.3 shows what Karim did.

Karim's language is simple, conversational, personal, and yet still professional. Notice the call to action at the end. People need to be given direction when they're online because they're easily distracted. Your profile offers you the chance to reveal the person behind the credentials. The goal is to help people understand *why* they should pay attention to what you have to say. By the way, make sure your company and employees have LinkedIn pages.

Figure 13.3 Karim's LinkedIn Profile

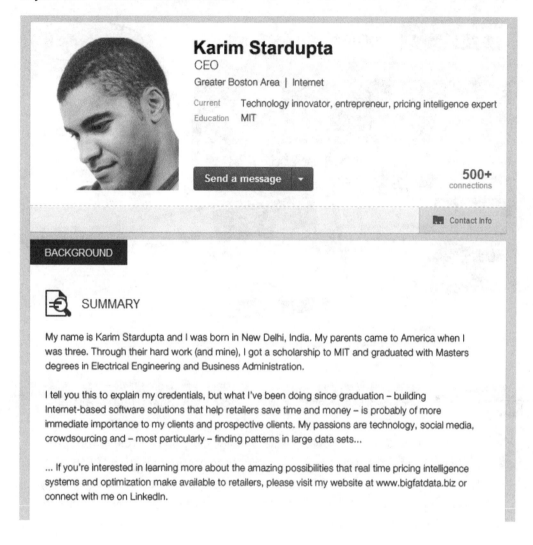

And whether you're on LinkedIn or Google+ or Facebook, it pays to have a company page (sometimes called a business page). Why not direct prospects to your website instead? Because it's not an either/or proposition. Having a company page allows your company to be "followed" at the click of a button, so prospects can keep track of your company's news and announcements. And what's more, company pages have a "recommendations" feature, so your Fans have an easy way to broadcast their satisfaction with your products and services. Karim's LinkedIn company page is shown in Figure 13.4.

Figure 13.4 BigFatData Inc. LinkedIn Company Page

 Social media works better for some sectors than others. IBM's 2012 Global CEO Study revealed that only 34 percent of CEOs in the industrial products sector think social media will play a significant role in the future. In contrast, education CEOs (77 percent), telecommunications CEOs (73 percent), and retail CEOs (72 percent) expect social media to be a key channel for customer engagement, while insurance CEOs (51 percent) and electronics CEOs (52 percent) were somewhat less enthusiastic.

CONSIDER YOUR OPTIONS

 If you're lucky enough to have the right staffing resources, you may be able to expand the 80/20 rule a bit and add to your social media presence with two more strategies: blogging and tweeting.

OPTION 1: THE 90-MINUTE BLOG

Thirty-nine percent of B2B marketers believe blog posts are their most valuable content asset, and 55 percent of B2B professionals turn to blogs for business information.[3] Starting your own blog isn't complicated, thanks to advances in WordPress and Blogger and other user-friendly content management systems. You can even choose a corporate-style design from a number of free, professional-looking templates, then make changes to give your blog a distinctive look and feel that matches your overall company branding. (Yes, there's some up-front time required to get your blog up and running, but it's a one-time-only investment.) The bigger issues are *finding the time* to post on a regular basis and *finding enough content* to post. Let's start with the time issue.

Finding the Time

There's never enough time to complete half of your to-do list, so where on earth will you find the time to blog? This is not an easy question to answer, which is why we suggest you follow the 90-minute rule or, more likely, engage a marketing assistant. This rule states that under no circumstances should you spend more than 90 minutes a week composing your blog posts, based on posting an average of once a week. If you're keeping current and you have a strong point of view on your industry, 90 minutes should give you plenty of time to get everything done. If you're really time-pressed, you can get away with posting twice a month, but keep in mind that you need to build momentum with your audience, and weekly momentum will work far harder for you than biweekly.

Finding the Content

If you're wondering what to write, now's the time to pull out all that Engagement Ladder content you created in Chapter 7. Not verbatim, mind you. Repurpose it by cutting and shaping it to fit the more conversational tone of your blog. Make sure you also place banner ads for your Engagement Ladder offers on your blog and have them point to the corresponding Engagement Pages. Once prospects are on your Engagement Ladder, you can nurture them toward a sale.

Here are two other content-creation tips:

1. Look at the news. Check out the most talked-about issues of the day or week, and then relate one or more of them to an issue that's facing your industry.
2. Another option is to look at the hot topics being discussed on your business forum or social media network. How do you quickly find questions that relate to your area of expertise? Go to your LinkedIn groups or Google+ circles and look at the most popular discussions and/or topics that seem to be resonating with members.

As appropriate, link your answers and contributions to the social conversation back to your blog where (based on the 90-minute rule) you'll have posted more in-depth analysis of the issue. Make sure your blog postings are well balanced and not product- or company-focused, because prospects find blogs in their quest to become more informed. Save the sales pitch for your website banner ads and Engagement Pages.

If you post and then do nothing until the next time you post, your blog will be deader than the proverbial doornail. To make the blogosphere aware that you've actually posted something that's (hopefully) worth reading, you need to make it findable by search engines, and you need to promote it online.

First, make sure your posts are keyword-optimized. This does *not* mean ladling your content with industry buzzwords, however. It means using words and phrases that your customers and prospects would likely use when searching for solutions to their pain. Use your PPC account for help in finding those words, or check out the keywords your competitors are using on their blogs and websites by observing their title tags (displayed in the browser tab at the top of each webpage). Revisit Chapter 12 for tips on how to use SEO to help make your blog as search-friendly as possible.

Links to your new blog posts can be emailed to customers and prospects, they can be tweeted (more on Twitter in a moment), they can be posted to relevant business forums, and they can feed your LinkedIn, Facebook, and Google+ updates. Don't forget to activate the subscribe feature on your blog so your clients and suppliers and influencers can follow you. And remember, everything should point back to your website or, more specifically, your Engagement Pages, because the end goal is always conversion of unEngaged Prospects to Engaged Prospects.

OPTION 2: BETWIXT AND BE-"TWEET"

Twitter is an odd little creature with its 140 character limit, but it can be a surprisingly useful relationship tool. "Twitter for B2B? Seriously?" The answer is yes. It's possible to create a direct line to hundreds or even thousands of your Beast Prospects, and have them share your thoughts and insights with their networks who, presumably, have interests that match their own (making those networks potential Beast Prospects for you). Twitter represents word-of-mouth on steroids with exponential sharing power. BigFatData, for example, tweets virtually every business day, sharing news, points of view, and useful links with its followers (see Figure 13.5).

So how do you establish yourself on Twitter? First, you need to build the right followers—those that match your Engagement Template. You do this on Twitter by using filters on tools like HootSuite or Pluggio to find individuals who rank highly against

Figure 13.5 BigFatData's Twitter Feed

certain keywords or hashtags. Then you follow them. Many will follow you back. Slowly, you'll build up a following of the right people. As you attract more of the right people, they'll introduce you to their networks, and more and more of their networks will begin following you. But to keep everyone following you, you have to provide them with remarkable value (again). You can do this by:

1. **Retweeting their tweets.** RTs (retweets) are the greatest currency on Twitter, and people generally value your effort to share their Tweets and will often take greater note of you as a result of it. But you must discriminate, sharing only that which you think your best prospects will value. And you should always try to add your 2 cents to give the retweet context, all in 140 characters. You should plan on five retweets for every original tweet you make.

2. **Tweet about your original content** where that content helps relieve your Beast Prospects' pain. You can tweet about each blog posting you make or about your Engagement Ladder offers. You can tweet news when you're at an event, you can ask questions about others' tweets, or you can share really useful content you find elsewhere on the web. Be careful with this last one, because everyone's doing it, and the value is limited. Try and dig for valuable content where few are looking.

3. **Tweet often.** You're going to get buried in the landslide of tweets that your followers receive, so don't be shy about repeating your tweets in different forms. Your goal is to get on your best prospects' Twitter lists. These are shortlists that users create of individuals they actually want to read/follow because the tweets from those individuals address some need they have.

But all of this can take a tremendous amount of time. Does it pay back? It often does in the most unexpected ways. In 2012, *Harvard Business Review* published an article on social media entitled "Tweet Me, Friend Me, Make Me Buy."[4] Authors Barbara Giamanco and Kent Gregoire tell the story of how Twitter helped connect a B2B sales rep with a CEO. Here's an excerpt:

> Not long ago a B2B rep for the virtual-meetings company PGi made the fastest sale of his career. One morning he contacted a CEO—someone who was no pushover, having had bad experiences with the type of product the rep sells. By late that afternoon he had a signed agreement. How did the rep pull off this feat? By using social media. Here's the way it worked. The rep is a Twitter user. Drawing on the TweetDeck feature, he had specified keywords so that he

would be alerted when they appeared in a tweet, whether from someone he "followed" or not.

On the day in question, a message containing the term "web conferencing" caught his eye. The point of the tweet was how poorly web conferencing works. "I clicked on the Twitter handle," the rep told us, "and noticed that it was a company account." He called the main number on the company's website and asked to speak to the person who handled Twitter. Moments later he was talking to the CEO, who, after marveling at the power of Twitter, described his frustration with the various web platforms he had used. "I told him all about GlobalMeet," the rep said, referring to a PGi conferencing service. "He checked out the website and said he wanted to try it, so I sent over the agreement and received it back within a few hours."

These kinds of scenarios don't play out every day, of course. And your sales rep needs to be equipped with a Twitter tool such as Hootsuite or TweetDeck to take advantage of these kinds of opportunities. Nevertheless, Twitter's raw lead generation potential cannot be ignored. Note this sentence: "[The rep] had specified keywords so that he would be alerted when they appeared in a tweet, *whether from someone he 'followed' or not."* Your prospects don't need to be followers to make a scenario like this happen for you.

But ultimately, Twitter feeds and blogs—and social media in general—are just another set of marketing channels—albeit, a very powerful set of marketing channels. But like all other marketing channels, they have to be fed and monitored and worked to be successful. Plus there's one big difference: *Social media success isn't bought, it's earned.* A significant commitment of time and effort is required if you want to increase your visibility and build your reputation as a thought leader and ultimately increase the flow of traffic and leads to your website. But once again, if you stick to the three *P*s—Patience, Persistence, and a Plan—you'll be rewarded.

Every industry is different, and so is every business. There is no one-size-fits-all "social media strategy." Out of necessity, this chapter has just scratched the surface. It's a good idea to learn as much as you can about this rapidly changing field before wading in. In that regard, two excellent social media books for B2B entrepreneurs are *Social Marketing to the Business Customer* by Paul Gillin and Eric Schwartzman and *Six Pixels of Separation* by Mitch Joel. Social media is still in its infancy, and new "territory" is constantly being opened up. In other words, it's still a bit of a Wild West. That said, don't shut the door on the opportunity to become part of the conversation, because as long as your goal is to help others solve their business issues, you'll find that they'll be willing to help you solve yours.

CAVE SCRATCHES

13

~ Add value to the conversation
~ Help, don't sell
~ Influencers strategy
~ Follow the 80/20 rule
~ Create a compelling profile
~ Blogging, tweeting optional

NEXT UP

Step 4 was all about attracting your Beast Prospects into your Beast Cave. You learned how to get found by search (SEO), by placement (PPC and banner ads), and by contribution (social media). Now it's time to venture outside the cave in pursuit of prospects. If you've targeted the right people with an intriguing offer that gets their attention and if you back it up with words they recognize (theirs), they're likely to respond to your overtures. How you make it all happen without breaking the bank is the focus of Step 5.

1: ASK
the right
question

2: LISTEN
to your best
customers

7: GROW!
measure your
success

Step Beast
Marketing
System

3: FOCUS
your resources

6: NURTURE
your engaged
prospects

5: PURSUE
your best prospects

4: ATTRACT
your best prospects

The secret to finding prospects

BEAST BRIEFING: INBOUND VS. OUTBOUND

Attracting your Beast Prospects (Step 4) is called *inbound marketing*. Pursuing your Beast Prospects (Step 5) is known as *outbound marketing*. There are those who believe that we are in a new age of marketing— that *outbound* marketing is old news, and that *inbound* marketing is all you need to be successful. The reasoning sounds good enough. It's argued that, because inbound marketing focuses primarily on prospects who are already looking to buy, it is far more efficient. Because the techniques and tools of inbound marketing are easily accessible, appear to cost little or nothing, and can be done mostly from the comfort of your desk, this argument is very appealing to many.

All we can say is, there's really nothing new under the hot, marketing sun. We've lived through and survived the dot-com euphoria when "nothing would be the same again." Turned out that everything was the same as always, only it happened much more quickly. The same is true today. There are no shortcuts. While social technologies have set inbound marketing on fire in a way that was never possible before, the same principles apply: *you must engage with value*. The added proviso is that *inbound marketing* today moves at the speed of light compared to its horse-and-buggy-paced predecessor, *word-of-mouth*.

And so, in our opinion, the best, most effective marketing continues to be equal parts inbound *and* outbound, *Attraction* and *Pursuit*. If you know and have identified who should be buying from you, for your Beast's sake, go out and pursue them right now. Wrap yourself around your Beast Prospects every way you can, inbound and outbound, and you'll usher more than your fair share of those prospects through your Cave, up your Ladder, down your funnel, and into the waiting belly of your ever-grateful Beast.

The Beast Prospect List

What you'll find in this chapter:

- Targeting your Beast Prospects
- Building a list
- Buying a list
- Testing and validating
- Placing in the Engagement Spreadsheet

"The best time to plant a tree is 20 years ago," says an old proverb. If you have aspirations of swinging in a hammock between two stately trees this afternoon, you'd better not be planting those trees this morning. The same is true of marketing your business. If you're hauling out your marketing instruction books (maybe even this one) now, because your sales have recently stalled, you're in for a bit of a rough ride. Why? Because effective marketing takes a long time to start producing the kinds of Sales-Ready Leads that will fill your Beast's belly. (Remember: Patience! Persistence!)

So the best time to start marketing is now, and hopefully now isn't your hour of need. But even if it is, now is always better than later or never. Besides, Lady Luck—your Beast's favorite benefactor—has been known to turn more than a few quick sales, hitting just the right prospect at just the right time (but don't bet your sales goals on her—she can be a heartbreaker).

Figure 14.1 Your Beast Cave

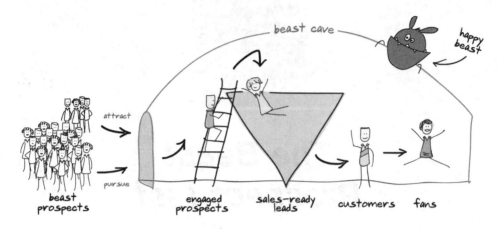

Now that you've made sure that your Beast Prospects can *find* you when they're researching what you're selling, let's get a second marketing front going that proactively reaches out to your Beast Prospects, grabs them by the collar, and pulls them into your Beast Cave (see Figure 14.1). Your goal in Chapter 14 is to build a list that contains the contact information of some or all of your Beast Prospects so that you can *find*, *pursue*, and *coax* as many of them as possible into your Beast Cave, up your Engagement Ladder, and down your sales funnel. As you can imagine, putting your best offers into the wrong hands will produce disappointing results. So you have to get your targeting right, above all else.

A RELATIONSHIP ROADMAP

The beauty of B2B, unlike B2C, is that the number of prospects who might buy your product or service is usually quite manageable—in the thousands rather than in the millions. For example, you can develop a targeted list of, say, the 1,000 Beast Prospects (representing 200 companies, at five prospects per company) you need to get to know in order to grow your business. Think about that. With your Beast Prospect List in hand, you'll have a roadmap pinpointing the exact relationships you need to build over the next 12 months.

The Engagement Template you built in Step 2 is once again the key. The more effort you put into building it, the more robust your list, and the more effective your pursuit tactics will be. To grow your business outrageously fast, your prospect list must be filled with diamonds, not gravel. To understand how this works, let's see how Karim, our software entrepreneur, was able to develop a winning targeting strategy on a shoestring budget.

KARIM'S TARGETING STRATEGY

As you'll recall, Karim's fledgling company, BigFatData, has only five customers, and his segmentation exercise suggested that his Beast Prospects were in the retail consumer electronics space. Through his investigations (including his customer interviews), he determined that consumer electronics, on its own, was too small a market. He realized that if he focused his efforts on both consumer electronics and mass merchandising retailers, the total market opportunity was around $300 million a year representing over 200 companies. With very little competition currently in these spaces, as well as a big, burning business pain that he has shown he can solve really well for these retailers, Karim reasoned that at least 10 percent of this potential market was sitting there, waiting for him to grab over the next few years. That would represent some pretty outrageously hairy growth for his small business.

The process Karim used to build his Beast Prospect List is shown in Figure 14.2.

First, Karim used his Engagement Template to build a list of likely Beast Prospect companies. Before building (and buying) his full list, he developed a smaller sample set and validated that sample set by researching each individual via the web and phone (he hired a marketing assistant) to confirm that:

1. They existed
2. Their title matched the Engagement Template target profile

The list looked good, so he went ahead and placed his test list into his Engagement Spreadsheet under the "Beast Prospects" tab (see Chapter 9 for a refresher). *A quick note*: If his sample list had proved inaccurate, he would have gone back and built a different list to test, possibly from a different list service, and then repeated the process. Karim also placed into his Engagement Spreadsheet any high-potential prospects he already

Figure 14.2 Building a Beast Prospect List

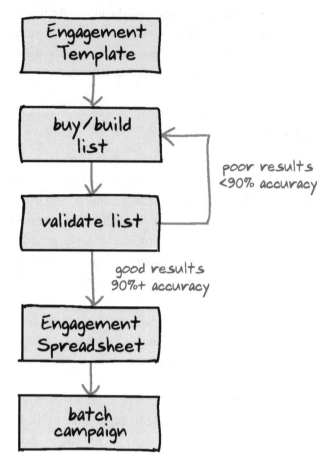

had in his "house list" (gathered from past inquiries, trade shows, references, marketing programs, and so on) that matched his Engagement Template.

You can build a list, rent a list, or buy a list. In this book, we'll consider only building and buying lists because the restrictions placed on rented lists (minimum order quantities, one-time use, etc.) tend to make them impractical. You want lists you can own and nurture over time with no restrictions. There are pros and cons to building versus buying, but time and resources you have available will generally inform the choice you make.

HOW KARIM BUILT HIS LIST

Now let's dig a little deeper and see how Karim developed his Beast Prospect List. In building his list, Karim identified appropriate prospect companies using his Engagement Template. He then researched those companies to see if he could find the names and contact information of the people he cared about.

Karim's Engagement Template Target Profile

1. Key Influencers: Senior retail merchandising managers (director, VP, senior VP, C-level), CEO. Secondary Influencers: IT managers, marketing managers, sourcing/procurement managers

2. U.S. retail chains with sales over $100 million

3. Consumer electronics and mass merchandise retailers

4. Sell via physical store *and* online

The main tools he used to research his list were the web, the phone, patience, and a little persistence. He began by looking in places where his and his prospects' interests aligned: industry associations, industry listings, and communities of interest on the web, as well as seminars and trade shows that listed the companies that attend their events. (Like Karim, you'll need to use your ingenuity and sleuthing skills.)

With a little digging, Karim found the "Top 500 Internet Retailers" directory online and bought it for $75, giving him quick access to a great starting test list of prospect companies and their senior personnel. His marketing assistant then visited each prospect company's website as well as networking sites such as LinkedIn to see if she could add the missing personnel that the directory didn't provide. Along the way, she gathered addresses, phone numbers, and email addresses for as many of these prospects as possible.

How many contacts do you need to gather per company? It depends. Buying decisions in companies most often involve a "buying team," which in some companies can comprise as many as 20 people. The more confident you are in your Engagement Template, the fewer people you need to target.

But, of course, you should test and validate your list to hedge your targeting bets. Karim identified five people per company who likely influenced the purchase decision. In a perfect world, he would reach out to them all, but to make best use of his limited resources, Karim started with one, because he felt his work on his Engagement Template was pretty thorough in identifying the key decision maker. He could then expand from there.

After his marketing assistant had gathered as many names and contact details as she could, she turned to the phone to complete the list. By calling the main reception of each prospect company on her list, she was able to fill out most of the missing names and validate the ones she didn't have. Many companies are hesitant to give out email addresses over the phone (although some do!), so to supplement the missing email addresses, the marketing assistant searched the web looking for any individual's email address from the same company, regardless of that person's role. (You'll often find at least one.)

Then, using the same format (e.g., firstname.lastname@company.com), she constructed the prospect email addresses she was missing. Her next trick was to go to a website set up by a programmer named James Shaw (http://www.coveryourasp.com/ValidateEmail .asp). Shaw's site validates email addresses, one at a time, for a small monetary contribution to his business (see Figure 14.3).

The marketing assistant used Shaw's tool to test the email addresses she had constructed and explore combinations of prospect names and company names that were valid when her initial constructions weren't.

So, are you allowed to build email lists this way? The CAN-SPAM Act, which has been in place since 2003, is very specific with regard to business-to-business emailing. The Act does not ban the sending of unsolicited email for business purposes—so there is no "opt-in" requirement. The only requirement is that the emails give the recipient a clear way to unsubscribe or opt out, and that this preference must be respected by the mailer. However, it is worth noting that new anti-spam legislation may be introduced that changes these guidelines. In Canada, for example, somewhat draconian legislation is on the books as we write, threatening to make B2B email very difficult to send without a *prior* opt-in from the receiver. A bit of an email catch-22, if you think it through.

Figure 14.3 James Shaw Email Validation

Email: test@test.com

Test SMTP

As we noted, Karim hired a marketing assistant to build his list. If you want to contract out the work, find a co-op student with good telephone skills (this may be challenging in an OMG LOL world), and you'll get your research done at very little cost. It takes a researcher about 20 hours at $15 per hour to confirm a list of 100 prospects, so you're looking at $300, or $3 per name. And if you can find government programs in your area that subsidize co-op students, you might get the work done at little or no cost to you.

The main drawback to building your own list (as opposed to buying it) is that this approach is usually slower and can be expensive if you have a large number of prospects and/or if you hire someone other than a co-op student to build it. That said, this approach often produces the highest quality results and, as mentioned earlier, if you develop your list in smaller "batches," the cost per batch can be quite manageable. Importantly, this approach can and should be applied from time to time to any list you buy or acquire to ensure list "hygiene," thereby creating more robust prospect lists.

BUYING YOUR LIST INSTEAD OF BUILDING IT

The world of buying lists has changed dramatically in the last several years (for the better). Not so long ago, Karim's best choice for buying lists would have been services that offer *compiled lists* such as InfoUSA, OneSource, USADATA, or AccuData America. These lists assemble data from a number of different sources, often including suppliers such as Dun & Bradstreet, and contain address, phone numbers, and email addresses (usually at an extra charge), as well as key "firmographics" such as annual sales and number of employees.

Depending on the volume of names bought, costs typically run from $0.20 to $0.65 per name. This is all well and good, but these list sources tend to fall down around job role or title selection. The titles you can usually select from are quite high-level and generic. As

Figure 14.4 InfoUSA Prospect Selection Screen[1]

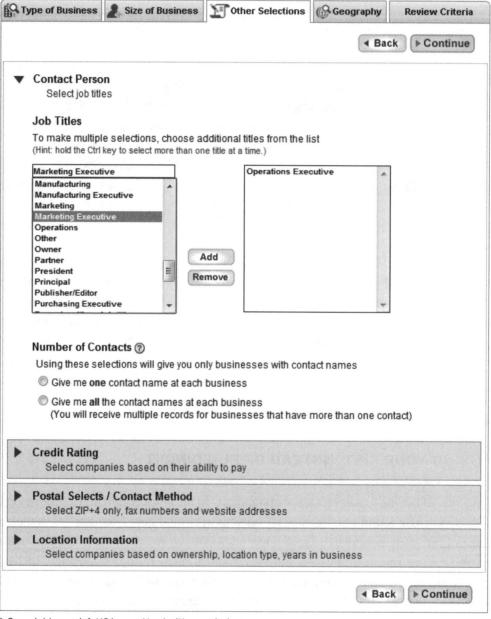

you can see in Figure 14.4, the closest Karim could get to "merchandising manager" was "operations executive" or "marketing executive."

If high-level titles are what you need, these list sources can provide good value and accurate data. Moreover, Karim could have gotten his CEO prospects for a reasonable price with these list services. However, since some of the most important decision-making roles from his Engagement Template included titles like "senior merchandising managers," using these higher level titles would reduce Karim's response rates to his programs among this group. One option would be to combine the *compiled list* with his earlier *researched list*. Or he could opt to explore brand new horizons—the world of *aggregated* or *crowd-sourced lists*.

USING AGGREGATED LISTS

Aggregated prospect lists such as those from NetProspex, Jigsaw.com (Data.com, if you use Salesforce.com), and Zoom Info have been contributed to by regular businesspeople on the web and then embellished by using technologies that comb the web for additional prospect information from sites such as LinkedIn. The list providers then cleanse the lists to reduce duplicates, ensure currency, and validate the information they contain. Karim could visit NetProspex's site, for instance, and contribute contact information for individuals he knows; in exchange, he would earn credits he could later use to purchase names of prospects he needs. Alternatively, he could purchase credits at fairly reasonable prices. This simple idea has resulted in databases containing tens of millions of business contacts with specific titles, phone numbers, and email addresses.

Our experience with aggregated lists has been excellent: *very* specific title searches, good response rates, low bounce rates, and low opt-out rates. No doubt, your experience will vary depending on whom you want to reach and how you go about doing it, but these lists are worth trying.

As mentioned, you can purchase names using earned credits or you can choose to pay between $0.65 and $2.00 per name (at the time of this writing), depending on the volume of names that you're purchasing. Aggregated lists are a very competitive business, so it's worth your while to call a list supplier and see what kind of deal you can get. Alternatively, you can really go to the source and use a service like Amazon's "Mechanical Turks" (www.mturk.com) where you can access over 500,000 workers from around the world who can be hired to do just about any kind of web-based work. It's possible, for instance, to outsource your list building to Amazon's service, and end up with a dependable prospect list within days that could cost you as little as $0.20 per prospect.

Using one of the aggregated list suppliers, Karim entered his Engagement Template profile information into the search fields of the prospect selection screen (see Figure 14.5). That search resulted in over 1,200 possible contacts that fit his needs. Karim selected 100 prospects more or less randomly and purchased them at a cost of $1.00 per lead because of the small quantity. He then set out to validate his sample list.

Figure 14.5 NetProspex Sales Prospector Screen

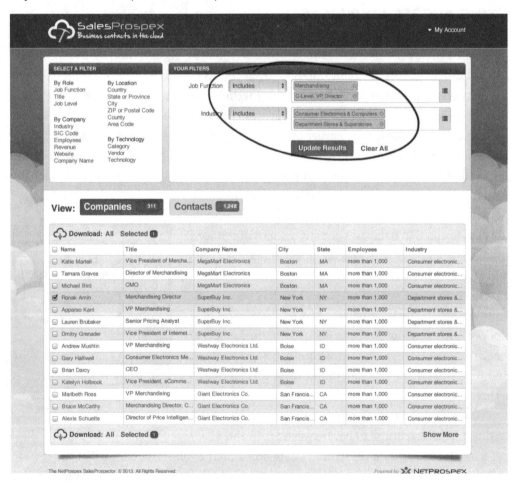

List validation ensures that those on the list are actually who they're supposed to be. To validate your list, you (or your intern) need to call each prospect company on your test list and verify names, titles, and contact information. If you find that 90 percent or more of your prospect data is accurate, you can use this list as your first batch of Beast Prospects and then proceed to purchase more prospects as you need them. If less than 90 percent make the cut, you might go back and test a different sample from the same list or, more likely, consider using a different list vendor. Because different lists have different strengths, a list vendor that works for Karim might not work for Paul, our chocolate entrepreneur. You need to find out for yourself.

Why did Karim build a test list of 100 prospects? Because a sample of 100 prospects on a population of 1,200 total prospects is considered statistically significant, plus or minus 10 percent, 95 percent of the time. That means any testing Karim does on the 100 prospects should be representative of the larger list of 1,200 prospects, should he choose to go back and develop a larger list from the same list source. You can calculate your own sample sizes by using the "sample size calculator" that has been set up for you at http://tools.FeedTheBeast.biz.

QR Code
Sample Size Calculator

Whichever list source you use, aggregated lists tend to be more accurate for larger rather than smaller companies. This makes sense since larger company information is more commonly available, and you would expect crowdsourced/aggregated lists to be more focused on the larger, more visible companies. If you have a very specific, lower-profile target group you want to reach, you may have to build your own researched list or use a combination of a purchased list and a researched list.

ONE MORE WAY TO "STRESS TEST" YOUR LIST

Another effective way to validate your prospect list until it cries "uncle" is to send out a simple email request to your prospects with the subject line "Your help . . .":

> Hi [first name],
>
> I was hoping you could refer me to the person within your company who would be most concerned with competitive price intelligence—especially as it relates to the growing challenge of price transparency among your customers.
>
> Our company, BigFatData, gives Global 500 retailers better visibility into competitive product and price activity. Our clients get complete visibility into competitors' product and pricing information, which helps them make smarter pricing decisions in challenging markets.
>
> We would like to explore whether we can bring the same benefits to your company.
>
> Many thanks in advance for your help.
>
> Best regards,
>
> Karim Stardupta
>
> CEO

This email should come from the most highly placed person in your company—meaning you, if you're the owner, or your CEO, if you're not. Using this technique, you can achieve remarkable reply rates (we've achieved over 40 percent response rates using this approach). Not only will you have a list of super-qualified prospect names, you'll be able to use an internal reference when later contacting this new referral (e.g., "Bill Smith referred me to you . . ."), which will further enhance your response rates. This one works like gangbusters.

A HOME FOR YOUR BEAST PROSPECT LIST

With his initial test list in hand, Karim proceeded to place the data within his Engagement Spreadsheet, which you were introduced to in Chapter 9. Karim organized the list he downloaded from the crowdsourced list supplier into the same column structure as his Engagement Spreadsheet, then he copied all the prospect data out of the crowdsource spreadsheet (except the first row that contained column headers) and pasted it into the first empty row of his Engagement Spreadsheet. He was ready to roll.

CAVE SCRATCHES

14

~ Target your prospects using your Engagement Template
~ Buy or build your list
~ Be creative
~ Crowdsourcing
~ Batch market to validate your list

NEXT UP

Now that you know where your Beast Prospects live (at least during the daytime), you want to make sure that whatever you put in front of them breaks through the clutter, engages them, and in the best of all worlds, intrigues them. Intrigue is one of the most underrated and underused marketing motivators out there. Turn the page, and let's start intriguing your Beast Prospects.

Step 5 PURSUE

CHAPTER 15

Pursuit and Breakthrough

What you'll find in this chapter:
- Think "different"
- Achieving Breakthrough with intrigue
- The elements of Breakthrough
- Return on Breakthrough

It's time to deal with a truth. This truth is, when you're *in pursuit* of new customers, the best value proposition and the most focused targeting and the most brilliant offer won't amount to a hill of beans unless you can find a way to break through and *grab your prospect's attention*. That's not easy when each day the average person is bombarded by a bajillion messages from all over, give or take.

Into this maelstrom goes your marketing campaign, hoping to be noticed. Some of our more deep-pocketed friends out there will spend a bajillion dollars to trump those bajillion competing messages. That's one way to break through, but when's the last time you had a bajillion dollars to spend?

If you haven't got the money, you need to be clever. Being clever is why you created an eight-rung Engagement Ladder, and it's how you're going to break through to your prospects right now. The nice thing about being clever is that it's not that common, and it doesn't have to cost very much. Clever means making your prospects smile and think

211

and maybe even marvel. Clever is about intriguing your prospects into your Beast Cave and saving the branding for once they're there. Above all, clever is appreciating the persuasion sequence that moves a prospect from curiosity to action.

The Game-Opening Persuasion Sequence
intrigue → breakthrough → value →
trust → consideration

The fastest way to *break through* to your prospects is to *intrigue* them. To engage your prospects, you need to offer *value*. To develop a relationship with your prospects, you have to create *trust*. If that trust takes root, you'll earn their *consideration* as a potential solution to their problem.

WHAT'S THE BIG PICTURE?

How does this whole idea of Pursuit—going out to proactively *find* your Beast Prospects—work? What's the big picture? For the next three chapters, here's the big picture (see Figure 15.1).

Figure 15.1 The Big Pursuit Picture

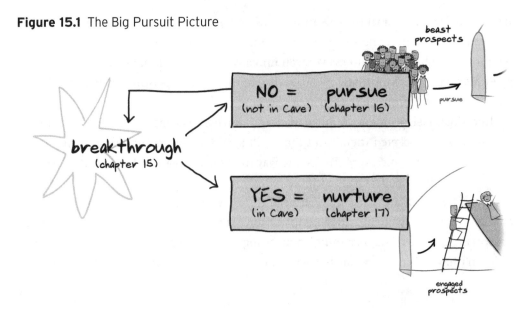

Your mission, should you choose to accept it, is to try and break through to the list of Beast Prospects you identified in the last chapter. We'll take you through some compelling ways to do that next. Of the Beast Prospects you try to break through to, many will happily step into your Cave and onto your Engagement Ladder. These you'll Nurture up your Ladder toward a sale, as we'll describe to you in Chapter 17. But others will choose not to engage with you, remaining outside your Cave (at least initially). These you'll recycle into an ongoing Pursuit Campaign, which you'll learn more about in Chapter 16. You'll continue this cycle—adding new Beast Prospects to your list and reworking existing, hesitant Beast Prospects— until you develop a constant flow of Beast Prospect traffic through your Cave. This is the surest way for you to achieve your sales goals. But, as we mentioned, it all starts with Breakthrough.

INTRIGUE

Breakthrough is about going big or going home. We want you to roll the dice on a big Breakthrough Campaign that will be a little more expensive than a typical email marketing campaign because you'll be sending this Breakthrough Campaign to a prospect only *once*. If it doesn't engage them, then you'll fall back to a more traditional email campaign to continue your Pursuit, in a more cost-effective manner (Chapter 16). But those it does engage will be intrigued, and money can't buy that kind of start to a relationship. Is it worth trying? You betcha. As you'll see, Breakthrough Campaigns can kick-start your marketing program like little else can (short of spending that bajillion dollars). Do Breakthrough Campaigns pay back? They do, as you'll see in Chapter 19.

You can choose to send your Breakthrough Campaign to anyone you like, but mostly you want to send it to those who haven't engaged with you yet—those who haven't entered your Beast Cave—regardless of how they got onto your Beast Prospect List.

So how do you do it? How do you entice the greatest possible number of Beast Prospects into your Beast Cave? We'd like to get back to the idea of *intrigue*. Intrigue is the key. To intrigue your prospects, you need to resist the usual, because everyone else is doing the usual. You need to start thinking in three dimensions. Don't worry, we're not going to ask that you become a creative genius. Our goal here is a much more practical one. We just want you to *think different*.

That's what Apple challenged us to do in their famous 1997 advertising campaign. While most people want to *be* different, few want to *think* differently because it takes effort, and it upsets the status quo. Not you, of course. You love seeing things differently. The simple fact that you've chosen to be an entrepreneur says that you're anything but status quo. Richard Branson had to think differently to get his startup off the ground. "We didn't have any money, so we had to come up with different ideas [. . .] be imaginative," he said when interviewed about the humble beginnings of Virgin.[1]

Now it's time to kick your own imagination into high gear, because this is your Breakthrough moment. You're going to intrigue your prospects by striving to create opening Breakthrough Campaigns that are a little unexpected, a little more noteworthy. If you do your job well, you'll hear Beast Prospects whispering throughout your Cave, "I think I like these guys." There's no better opening to a relationship.

START WITH THE UNEXPECTED

These days, email is one of the most popular ways to *pursue* prospects because it's inexpensive and measurable. There are other *pursuit* marketing channels you can use to reach out to your prospect in a B2B context, but their usage has diminished considerably because of high costs, lack of measurability, and, in some cases, unacceptable response rates:

MARKETING CHANNEL PERFORMANCE

Marketing Channel	Cost per Prospect	Value for Response	Value for Branding	Traditional Measurability
email	very low	very good	medium	very good
print	very high	poor	very good	poor
television	niche cable can be affordable, but production costs can be prohibitive	medium	very good	poor
radio	medium	good	medium	medium
trade shows & events	medium	good	medium	medium
outdoor & transit	very high	poor	high	poor
direct mail	high	very good	medium	very good

You might be surprised to learn that direct mail, last on our list, provides one of the biggest opportunities for intrigue. *Direct mail? The skinny kid on the beach who gets sand kicked in his face?* Yes indeed, that's the one. *The one with the high cost per prospect?* The same.

We're well aware of the perception of direct mail. Some call it snail mail and junk mail, while other, kinder folks accuse it of low response rates and high costs. As a result, most marketers today ignore it. It's not digital enough, they say. Perfect. Bear with us.

Trust us, it won't make your company look 1960s. Not when it's done right. We're fans of using direct mail for the first, critical outreach to your Beast Prospects. The absolute best way to break through to your prospects is to make use of the *physical* attributes of direct mail to surprise your prospects. Yes, there's still a deluge of paper and postcards coming through the mail, and much of it is discarded. Precious little of real value arrives in people's physical in-baskets these days (which by the way, are still sitting there, waiting). At the same time, thanks to *spam*, breaking through to brand new prospects electronically has become more of a challenge. This leaves a void. And like any good entrepreneur, it's a void *you're* going to fill.

ADD A THIRD DIMENSION

Now it's time to put your creative hat on. We're going to show you how to make the contents of your initial direct mail Breakthrough Campaign package as memorable and sharable as possible. We want you to start thinking about your messaging differently, so you can be perceived differently (while remaining totally professional). When your competitors are first contacting prospects, they're thinking email, which means they're thinking in two dimensions. We want you to start thinking in three.

Why? Because what's inside your Breakthrough package is a three-dimensional element designed to "surprise and delight" by appealing to your prospects' emotional side in a fun and relevant way. (We're going to show you some examples in a moment.) This component of your mailer should be tangible, touchable, sharable, inexpensive, and not easily destroyed. But along with your 3-D element, you need to include some reinforcing elements—usually a personalized letter or card that "completes" the puzzle:

The Elements of Breakthrough

- A bubble envelope or a box
- A mailing label
- Postage or courier fees
- A three-dimensional "mystery" piece
- A personalized letter or card that "completes" the puzzle

SOPHIE'S CHALLENGE

To see how these elements work together, let's look at some real-world examples, starting with Sophie, our home stager. She made excellent use of Breakthrough to get the attention of a notoriously busy and hard-to-reach target market—top real estate agents. This was her first contact, so most knew little or nothing about Sophie or her company. Sophie's challenge was to send something unique and professional that would (1) attract their curiosity, (2) not cost much money, and (3) be three-dimensional. You'll notice we didn't say that she had to send something that focused on her Beast Prospects' pain.

Remember, your objective on your first outreach is *Breakthrough*, not information or education. Without Breakthrough, all the smart thinking in the world will amount to nothing. If you have to err on the side of being "intriguing and fun" versus being "on strategy," lean toward the fun side. If you can combine fun and strategy in the same intriguing package, then your Breakthrough Campaign will be just that much stronger. That said, once you have your Beast Prospect inside your Cave, you should then reveal the relevant value *quickly* if you want to continue to engage your prospects.

Because real estate brokers are concerned with selling homes, it didn't take Sophie long to think of an intriguing angle: a simple house key. The key worked as a metaphor on a bunch of levels for agents, but she also wanted to think through how to tie the campaign back to the business pain she had uncovered in her Engagement Template: top agents were always looking for ways to do more, faster. The key to doing more, she reasoned, is quite obviously to clone yourself. From there, the idea grew.

She combined the house key with a very simple but somewhat mysterious letter (see Figure 15.2). Then she added a personalized URL—www.WhatIsTheKey.com?JoeAgent—to further promote the intrigue quotient.

Where do you get those cool URLs, and what's with the question mark followed by the name? URLs are easy and inexpensive to get. You can use any domain registration service (e.g., Yahoo Small Business, Tucows, GoDaddy, or Name.com) to test and buy various combinations of words to make up an intriguing URL for your Breakthrough Engagement Page. The question mark followed by your prospect's name is a device that allows you to know by name who is hitting your Engagement Page and, as a result, lets your Engagement Page personalize itself to your prospect. If you're using the basic version of the Engagement Engine (see Chapter 9), this personalization won't be available to you. If you opt to use the Beast Machine, it will. Alternatively, you can hire a web programmer who can achieve this for you. Regardless of whether you can make technical use of this "question mark/name string" or not, include it in your mail insert. It won't hurt anything (technically), and it creates more intrigue.

To encourage prospects to open her mailer, Sophie used a padded bubble envelope with what appeared to be a handwritten label affixed to it (see Figure 15.3). Sophie's open rate was higher than average, partly because padded envelopes give the impression that there's something of value inside. (Or else why bother with the bubble protection?)

So imagine for a moment that you're a real estate agent who received this package. Wouldn't you be curious? Don't you think you might go to the URL with your name in it? Do you think you might show this to other real estate agents in your office? Many would—and many did. We've had response rates as high as 72 percent with Breakthrough programs like this, with results being measured in a few days. The results are impressive compared to any marketing channel, by any measure. Further imagine if over half of your Beast Prospects first came to know you in this way. There's a very positive halo effect to making someone smile. Keep that in mind as we review the rest of the program.

One more idea to consider. If you're the fun or adventurous type, think about adding a sticker to the outside of your mailing envelope that says "REALLY, REALLY IMPORTANT." Most people get a kick out of it, and it promotes your new, best buddy: *intrigue*.

Figure 15.2 Sophie's Intriguing Letter

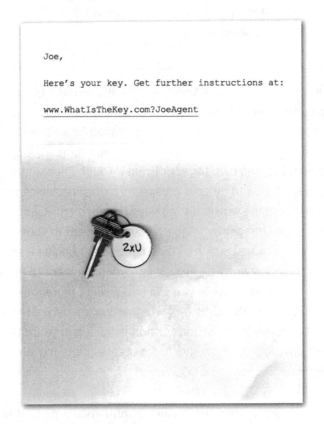

Figure 15.3 Sophie's Intriguing Envelope

When the agents entered the mysterious URL into their browsers, they were brought to Sophie's Breakthrough Engagement Page. There, they were presented with a quick transition from intrigue to value via a D-rung offer from Sophie's Engagement Ladder to encourage further involvement (see Figure 15.4).

To smooth the transition from intrigue to offer, Sophie decided to create a humorous video that featured some of her top agents (who kindly agreed to help) having a conversation with their clones about how darned efficient this whole cloning thing can be for a busy agent. Sophie's featured offer, "6 Ways to Clone Yourself," was taken from the D rung of her Engagement Ladder and played right into the agent's desire to do more, faster. To receive the "6 Ways to Clone Yourself" document, the agent had to fill in her web form, creating a value exchange: the agent's contact information (which Sophie already knew, so what she was really interested in was the agent's overt expression of interest) in exchange for the downloadable document. Lastly, in case the cloning document wasn't resonating with a given agent, Sophie included an Escape Hatch Offer with a more overt, albeit still humorous, pitch.

Figure 15.4 Sophie's Intriguing Engagement Page

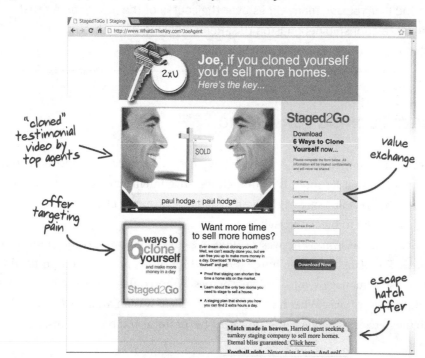

CALL OFF THE FRAUD SQUAD

Inevitably, some of your prospects may eye your Breakthrough mailer rather suspiciously. They may even wonder if it isn't some dastardly plot to defraud them of something or another. We had this happen once. A bank executive ran around collecting all the "suspicious looking packages" we sent her staff. Of course, once she opened the package and realized that it wasn't anything evil, she handed the packages back to the intended recipients, which only served to heighten the intrigue within that office. We couldn't have planned it better. Certainly, there'll be those who will be overly cautious and who might drop your package into the vertical file cabinet—but the response rates we've been experiencing suggests that this won't be a problem for you.

If you're struggling to come up with something clever, this is where you should spend some of your budget. Don't be too proud to get professional help. By hiring a creative agency or contractor, you improve the chances that your idea will be Breakthrough-worthy with viral (word-of-mouth) potential. While this could cost you several hundred or even thousands of dollars (depending on who you engage), this is a one-time investment that you'll be reusing many times over the course of the next year. A great opening relationship depends on this. Remember, no Breakthrough, no nothing.

KARIM GOES LOOKING FOR A HERO

Now let's see how Karim used intrigue to break down natural prospect resistance and build curiosity. You'll recall that Karim sells a competitive price intelligence solution to senior merchandising managers at some of the world's largest consumer electronics retailers—another tough audience to break through to.

Karim's idea came to him as he was reading over the value proposition portion of his Engagement Template. An image jumped out at him of his pricing solution turning mere merchandising managers into "pricing heroes" who could save their companies millions of dollars every year. What he needed, he decided, was an animated movie that had fun with the hero angle while communicating his promise and proof points, all in an entertaining fashion. He Googled "animated web video production" and came up with a list of companies who could produce what he was envisioning. His movie ended up costing him about $3,500 to produce and took four weeks to complete. He reasoned, quite rightly, that this movie could be used many times over in his marketing and sales. The cost of the video, therefore, could be spread out over a good 12-plus months of marketing activity.

His Breakthrough plan became:

1. Create a Breakthrough Campaign around the "hero" idea.
2. Have his animated video be the reward/transition on his Engagement Page.
3. Make the next step easy for his prospects to take. Feature a D-rung offer, "The Definitive Guide to Retail Price Intelligence," but repackage it a bit to match his "hero" campaign theme.

Figure 15.5 shows what his Breakthrough mailing looked like.

By the way, Karim used the same outer envelope approach as Sophie. Once again, do you think that this mailing might get your attention? Might you make a quick detour to the URL printed on the card? If you did, Figure 15.6 shows what you, and Karim's Beast Prospects, would see.

Karim also made use of an Escape Hatch Offer (see Figure 15.6). In his case, he was a little more straightforward in his call to action: "Not seeing what you need?" The phrase he used to title his Learning Hub, "Competitive Price Monitoring," was taken straight

Figure 15.5 Karim's Mysterious Mailer

Dan,

Here's your hero mask. For further instructions, go to:

WhatsTheMask.com?DanTucker

Figure 15.6 Karim's Hero Engagement Page

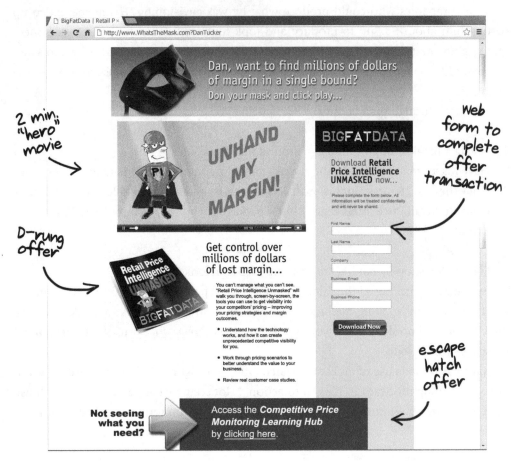

from his keyword work in Step 4. If that's the phrase his Beast Prospects are searching on, then it stands to reason that it will make his Learning Hub promise that much more appealing to his prospects.

If you're concerned that your outer envelope might be opened by a mailroom clerk before it gets to your prospect, which can happen in larger companies, you can add an extra layer of intrigue. Put the contents of your mailing into a manila inner envelope placed inside your outer envelope. Make sure you handwrite your prospect's name on the inner envelope (or use a handwriting font), and then seal the inner envelope. Nine times out of 10, this inner envelope will be delivered intact and unopened to your prospect's inbox, creating even more mystery: "How did this bulky, unaddressed envelope end up in my inbox? Is it internal mail?"

PAUL'S SPICY GROSS MARGIN

And what about Paul, our chocolatier with three market segments to pursue? He'd decided that his priority market for the new quarter was going to be private label programs for large department stores. The competitive advantage that he offers his private label Beast Prospects is "giving" the buyers their own professional buying team to guide their private label confectionery line—something the buyers can use to scale their limited resources and improve their ability to manage their gross margin. His Beast Prospects' greatest pain centered almost entirely around controlling gross margin. But knowing that wouldn't help him unless he broke through first.

Paul reviewed his notes from his Engagement Questionnaire Interviews, did a bit of research, and realized that exotic flavor combinations in chocolate, which were a serious worldwide trend, might do the Breakthrough trick. Rearing their questionable heads in the exotic flavor department were bacon bars, smoke and stout bars (as in, smoked salt and stout beer), and chocolate-covered insects. These last weren't finding a lot of traction in North America. But the others were.

Paul had recently introduced a line of exotic (but not too exotic) flavor combinations that he thought could be a great lead item for a private label program. Exotic flavors were interesting, and promoting them demonstrated an awareness and understanding of the market—critical if he wanted to impress his buyer prospects with the capabilities of the buying team he would be making available to them later on. One hot glue gun, a bunch of cards, and one dried, wrinkled vegetable later, Paul had what he needed (see Figure 15.7).

Gluing the hot pepper to the card gave Paul's mailing some heft. He then packed everything in a bubble envelope, much like his co-entrepreneurs Sophie and Karim.

On his Breakthrough Engagement Page (see Figure 15.8), Paul used a D-rung offer featuring his exotic flavors trend report. He felt it provided the kind of insight a buyer would appreciate while suggesting how exotic flavors and private label, combined, could create a good gross margin buffer. But, you'll notice, it doesn't sell Treadwater products directly. That comes later. First Paul wanted to get as many buyers as possible into his Beast Cave. To that end, you'll want to note Paul's Escape Hatch Offer. It bypasses the niceties and

Figure 15.7 Paul's Secret Weapon

Figure 15.8 Paul's Breakthrough Engagement Page

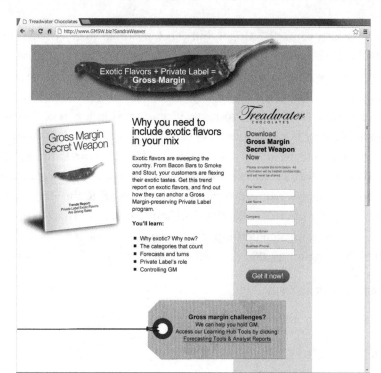

goes right to the promise of forecasting tools to help the challenged buyer better manage gross margin.

You may have noticed that two out of three of our entrepreneurs used video on their Engagement Pages. Video isn't a "gotta have," but video works well on the web, typically producing more engagement than comparable nonvideo approaches. Think about whether your product or service could be well represented by video. It's not cheap to produce, but you should be able to come up with a number of useful applications for the video (including a YouTube posting) that would amortize its cost across several marketing tactics in the next 12 to 18 months.

KARIM'S $440 BREAKTHROUGH CAMPAIGN

So you may be asking yourself, "Alright, but can I afford all this?" There's no question, direct mail will cost you more, but you get what you pay for. There's a reason why email response rates have become so anemic. Email costs very little, so everyone is doing it, so your prospects are inundated by it. You'll recall in Chapter 14 that Karim had identified a total of approximately 1,200 Beast Prospects, including all influencers, decision makers, and users: approximately five individuals per company across some 200 target companies. As you'll see in a moment, to hit his desired sales goal for the year, Karim started with the one, highest-potential Beast Prospect per company for an initial Beast Prospect List of 200 individuals. To mitigate his risk and maximize his outcome, Karim decided to send his Breakthrough Campaign out in smaller "batches," one per month. That would give him the chance to see how the campaign performed and then determine if he needed to continue his outreach to the remaining 1,000 prospects. So his initial distribution looked like this:

KARIM'S BATCH MARKETING

	Jan	Feb	Mar	Total
Beast Prospects	50	75	75	200

Here's how Karim's costs laid out for his Breakthrough Campaign:

KARIM'S BREAKTHROUGH CAMPAIGN COSTS

Element	Cost per Unit	Cost for First Batch of 50	Cost for 200 Mailings
Printed card (1-color digital printing, 12 pt card stock)	$0.45	$22.50	$90
3-D Intrigue item (mask)	$1.25	$62.50	$250
Bubble envelope	$0.40	$20	$80
Mailing label	$0.10	$5	$20
Assembly (including mail merge)*	$0.60	$30	$120
Postage (including delivery to post office)	$6.00	$300	$1,200
TOTALS	$8.80	$440	$1,760

* Karim chose to use a fulfillment house to handle his mailing. Use your favorite search engine to search on "fulfillment house" in your area. You'll find lots to choose from. They're a good value.

Since Karim is sending smaller mailing batches to his prospects, an interesting phenomenon occurs. He can actually afford to spend more per mailing because he's effectively amortizing the cost of his marketing program out over an extended period of time—kind of like a car loan. A $40,000 car might be cost prohibitive if you had to spend the money up front, but it might be quite affordable at $500 a month over a longer period.

This is a problem a lot of entrepreneurs face—struggling to budget a large sum of money up front to fund a marketing program. By sending your Breakthrough Campaigns out in batches (we call it "batch marketing"), you can actually spend a bit more per mailing and still make it affordable. Spending more per mailing allows you to up the *intrigue* quotient to help initial Breakthrough and engagement. You can also quite quickly measure the return on your investment, giving you confidence to continue your batch spending.

In Karim's case, he's starting with three batches. His first batch campaign would cost him $8.80 × 50 mailings = $440. Bear in mind that he could be sending out as many as 1,000 mailings over the course of the year *provided* he is seeing the return on investment (ROI) that justifies continuing. That would amount to an annual budget of $8,800—but once again, only if the results support the continued spending, and if he finds he needs the extra traffic flow through his Beast Cave. When you know who you're targeting, and they're a tightly defined group, it can be quite cost effective to reach out to them in a direct, physical way that most of your competitors aren't using.

SO DOES IT WORK?

If you're wondering about the rate of success of Breakthrough Campaigns in the real world, the following table shows four examples across different industries. As you can see, the average response rate to these Breakthrough programs was an impressive 46.4 percent. ("Response rate," in this case, means the prospect opened the Breakthrough package and went to the URL on the mailing.) In contrast, the 5 percent benchmark, which represents an "excellent" response rate for most any marketing channel (including email, by the way: a 25 percent open rate times a 25 percent click-through rate equals an overall 5 percent response rate), pales by comparison.

BREAKTHROUGH PROGRAM RESPONSE RATES (BY INDUSTRY)

Metric	Financial Services	Business Services	Tech Hardware	Internet Software	Programs Average	Benchmark	Index to Benchmark
Response rate	32.0%	57.6%	72.1%	24.0%	46.4%	5.0%	928

This is the kind of Breakthrough you're after. Response rates like these, if your target list is well constructed, will set you up for more conversions from unEngaged Prospects to Engaged Prospects and will build excellent momentum for your subsequent Nurture strategies, as we'll discuss in Step 6. However, it's easy to get caught up in response rate numbers. The truth is, the more important number is how many prospects you *convert* to Engaged Prospects—meaning that you get them into your Cave and onto your Engagement Ladder. If 100 percent of the prospects you send a Breakthrough Campaign to choose to respond, but none of them take you up on your offer, you'll have an amazing response rate you can brag about, but from a sales perspective, you'll be left holding a bag of rocks. So to make your life easier and to keep your focus on the one number that matters right now, this is the only number you'll be measuring in Chapters 15 and 16:

Prospect Engagement Rate (PER)
= Number of Engaged Prospects ÷ Annual Beast Prospects Targeted

And again, to keep your life simple, you'll set an *annual* PER target that, if achieved, will allow you to hit your annual revenue goal. You would expect, in that case, to have roughly achieved half your annual PER goal met by midyear. *Our intention is to have you keep your focus on your annual goal at all times.* It's too easy to get caught up in campaign-by-campaign results and to lose track of the bigger, more important goal of where you want to finish the year. See Figure 15.9 for a sneak preview of the reporting dashboard you'll be using in Chapter 19 to track your progress, demonstrating meeting a midyear goal.

KARIM'S PER

Let's look at how Karim's campaign is performing from a PER point of view. First, though, it'll be helpful to understand what Karim's annual revenue target is. Having worked through his plan, Karim felt confident that by using the 7-Step Beast Marketing System,

Figure 15.9 Beast PER Dashboard at Midyear

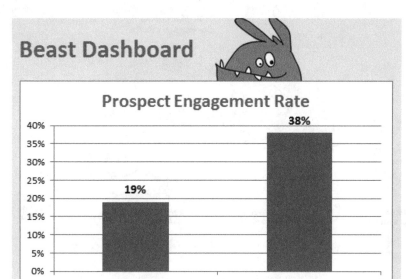

he'd be able to add five new customers in the next 12 months, almost doubling his annual revenue. The *annual* conversion rates that he would target are defined by the Beast Marketing System in Figure 15.10, and those conversion rates helped him determine his initial Beast Prospect sample size of 200 prospects in the first place.

Why these conversion rates? In our experience, these are the conversion rates that the 7-Step Beast Marketing System makes possible. These are aggressive numbers, in particular the first two, which are as much as three times higher than the norm. Use these as starting points, and adjust the numbers against your own experience. If you follow the 7 Steps contained in this book, there is every reason to believe that you can achieve them.

Figure 15.10 Karim's Target Annual Conversion Rates

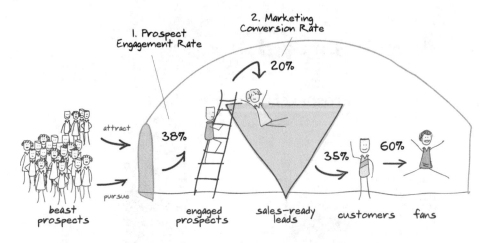

Using these rates, and working from the bottom to the top (see the following table), Karim was able to determine that if he wanted five new sales, he would need to start with 200 Beast Prospects out of his pool of 1,000 potentials. Keep in mind that at this point, the primary performance measure we're focused on is the PER:

KARIM'S GOALS FOR THE YEAR

	Annual %	Annual No.
Total addressable Beast Prospects		200
Prospect engagement rate	38%	76
Marketing conversion rate	20%	15
Sales conversion rate	35%	5

Karim's first set of batch Breakthrough Campaigns achieved the following results, measured on his annual goal:

KARIM'S BATCH MARKETING RESULTS

	Jan	Feb	Mar	Total
Beast Prospects	50	75	75	200
Engaged Prospects	2	4	11	17
Prospect engagement rate				8.5%

Using his Beast Dashboard, Karim can see that he's pretty much on track after the first three months since 25 percent (being one-quarter of the way through the year) of his 38 percent goal is 9.5 percent, and he's running at 8.5 percent (rounded up to 9 percent in Figure 15.11).

Remember that while Karim is in *pursuit* of new business with his Breakthrough Campaigns, at the same time he's *attracting* inbound prospects via his Attract campaigns. These inbound prospects will supplement the results that he's seeing in his marketing results table above (but which aren't represented in that table, to keep the discussion focused for now).

Figure 15.11 Karim's PER Results at Quarter's End

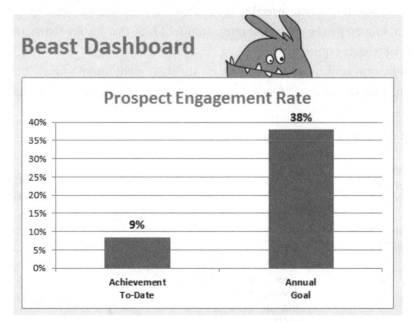

TROUBLESHOOTING

One last thing. While we've highlighted the shortfalls of tracking response rates, they're still fun to see, and they also provide a good diagnostic tool if your Prospect Engagement Rate isn't performing as expected. If your PER is underperforming, there are generally three possible reasons:

1. **Your list is off.** You've attracted the wrong people.
2. **Your offer is off.** You've attracted the right people, but the incentive to engage is too low.
3. **Your communication is off.** You've attracted the right people, the offer is good, but nobody gets it, *or* your Breakthrough creative isn't working as planned.

The first place you can go to get a look under the hood is your Engagement Page tool (e.g., Unbounce). The first test you want to perform is determining whether your Breakthrough creative is working as planned. Say by the second week of February, Karim wasn't satisfied by the progress of his Prospect Engagement Rate. By going to his Unbounce Engagement Page Dashboard (see Figure 15.12), he saw that 44 prospects of the 125 he had mailed to so far had actually hit his Engagement Page. That represents a 35 percent response rate, which is very respectable (your Breakthrough Campaigns should strive for a minimum of a 20 percent response rate). That told him that his Breakthrough creative seemed to be working quite well.

The 14 percent conversion rate you see on the dashboard doesn't figure into the PER calculation. PER calculates Engaged Prospects as a percentage of the *total* number of

Figure 15.12 Finding Your Response Rate

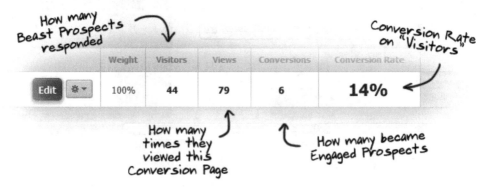

© Copyright Unbounce.com. Used with permission.

annual prospects you're targeting. Remember that *annual* viewpoint we're stressing. This conversion rate measures Engaged Prospects (or "Conversions" on this dashboard) as a percentage of visitors to this Engagement Page—useful, but different from PER and much more complicated to track in a meaningful way over a large number of campaigns over a longer period of time. PER gives you a quick, useful, manageable "shortcut" barometer to your performance. You'll see how easy it is to track your own PER in Chapter 19, when we discuss measurement in some depth.

So now Karim knows that a good number of the Beast Prospects he'd targeted had landed on his Breakthrough Engagement Page. Karim felt very confident in the work he had done on his Engagement Template, and he'd validated the accuracy of his Beast Prospect List a number of times in Chapter 14. That meant one of two things: either his offer wasn't converting, or the communication of his offer wasn't converting. For his next mailing in March, Karim decided to try repositioning his offer (the "Price Intelligence UNMASKED" document), tying it more closely to the pain his Beast Prospects felt rather than to the maybe-too-clever "unmasked" theme. Figure 15.13 shows what he ended up with.

Figure 15.13 Karim's Revised Offer

Problem solved. Karim's PER bounced up in March and put him pretty much on track for his quarterly goal. So much for judging a book by its cover.

CAVE SCRATCHES

15

≈ Think "different"
≈ Break through with 3-D intrigue
≈ Intrigue trumps strategy
≈ Breakthrough is affordable
≈ Success begins with measurable PER (Prospect Engagement Rates)

NEXT UP

So what about all the Beast Prospects who don't choose to enter your Beast Cave as a result of your Breakthrough Campaign? What do you do with them? You keep pursuing them, like a dog with a bone. Turn the page and let's find out how.

Step 5 | PURSUE

CHAPTER 16

Sophie Launches
Her Pursuit Campaign

What you'll find in this chapter:
- If at first you don't succeed, follow up
- Sophie's "personal training" program pays off
- Going live with a billboard and a recycled key
- The 80/20 Rule does it again

Are you a dog with a bone? Maybe a Beast with a bone? Either way, not letting go of that bone is the only way you're going to get enough Beast Prospects through your Beast Cave to feed your Beast the way you want it fed. To manage the work required to keep that Beast Prospect flow moving at a good clip, you're going to need a little automated help. Because when the work stops, so too does the flow. If the flow stops, good luck with that annual sales goal. So in this chapter, we're going to make it easier for you to feed the Beast in an automated sort of way.

PURSUING THEM TILL THEY CAVE

As you've seen, Breakthrough Campaigns are designed to provide a one-time "punch" to get the attention of the largest possible percentage of your Beast Prospect List and start a relationship with them. While you can expect unusually high Prospect Engagement Rates from your Breakthrough Campaigns, there'll still be a large-ish portion of your Beast Prospects who'll resist even your most creative attempts to woo them into your Beast Cave. In other words, even if as many as 60 percent step into your Cave, there's still 40 percent who don't. The reasons they resist include:

1. Their business pain, the one you address, isn't acute enough yet, or they're not even aware that it exists yet (often called latent pain).
2. You just didn't get their attention (they were away; they didn't see your package; your package got waylaid; your package got buried; or they're just no fun, and they threw your package in the garbage).
3. You're too late, and they've already started the buying process with someone else.
4. They're not on the decision team for your kind of solution (a "near-miss" from a targeting point of view).
5. They're completely the wrong target. Their business would never purchase the kind of solution you sell (e.g., selling ice to the Eskimos).

If you've built your Engagement Template carefully, the most likely cause of your prospects' lack of response would be one of the first three on the list above: they're just not ready yet, they missed it, or you're too late. Most often, there's not a lot you can do about being too late (although, if you do find out you're too late, giving it the old college try never hurts and has been known to win deals on occasion). For the first two, however, there is quite a bit more you can do. That is what Pursuit Campaigns are designed to address.

The Pursuit Cycle, seen in Figure 16.1, is intended to be a long-term process that continues to try and "break through" to your unEngaged Beast Prospects through a series of planned campaigns. These Pursuit Campaigns, though, are different and more cost-effective than the Breakthrough Campaigns of Chapter 15, acknowledging the long-term nature of the Pursuit exercise. Why is it a longer-term exercise? Because you're either waiting (1) for your prospects' business pain to go from "latent" to "I've got to do something about it"; (2) for their Decision Cycle need to match what you're offering them; or (3) for them to finally notice you. And as you work patiently to break through to these unEngaged Prospects, your goal remains to get them into your Beast Cave and onto your Engagement

Figure 16.1 The Pursuit Cycle

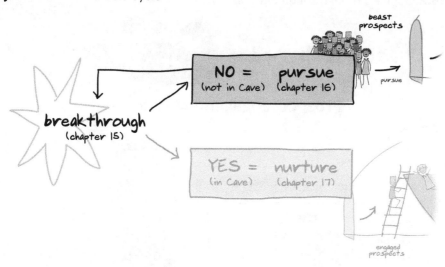

Ladder, where you can Nurture them up and into the eager hands of your sales team (or, your hands, if you're the sales team).

HOW SOPHIE MADE HER BREAKTHROUGH

The Breakthrough Campaign Sophie developed for her agent prospects in Chapter 15 (using a simple house key) achieved really encouraging engagement rates. Her prospects pretty much gobbled up the "cloning" concept and shared it around their offices. She could hear the laughing four blocks away. Sophie had started with a list of 362 of the top agents in town, and fully 12 percent of them (43 agents) downloaded her "6 Ways to Clone Yourself" document and became Engaged Prospects by the end of her third month out (see Figure 16.2). Those 43 agents would now be put into her Nurture Campaigns, which you'll read about in Chapter 17. Happily, three top agents from the Breakthrough Campaign had picked up the phone and called Sophie to have her come out and do a walk-through (which is basically a quote) for their homeowner clients. Of those, one had already turned into new business. Sophie's plan had only anticipated the first new agent in the second quarter, understanding that each top agent she added was worth about $90,000 in repeat business to her over the year. She was already ahead of her new business plan.

As Sophie reviewed her results on her dashboard, she could see that she was a third of the way to her annual PER target of 38 percent and yet only one-quarter of the way

Figure 16.2 Sophie's Breakthrough Success

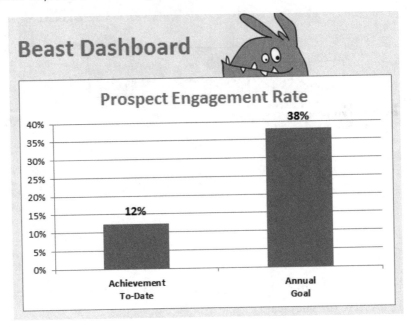

through the year. That put her ahead. But in spite of her strong results, Sophie was still looking at 319 agents who hadn't engaged with her yet, and she needed 11 more of them to sign up so she could hit her growth goals for the year (her goal for the year was 12 new top agents). The low-hanging fruit was now on the ground (of her Cave), and the tougher grind—to win the rest—was about to begin.

A MONTHLY PURSUIT

Following the same schedule as her Breakthrough Campaign, Sophie planned to send out Pursuit Campaign emails to her 319 unEngaged Prospects on a monthly basis (naturally, this number will change from month to month). To make sure that each of these 319 agents felt they were being dealt with on a personal level, Sophie needed a bit of a system to make it easier to personalize and keep track of the many changing relationships she would be juggling.

Sending out your email Pursuit Campaigns on a monthly basis serves several purposes. First, it ensures that you don't over- or underexpose yourself to your Beast Prospects. Once every four weeks is a good frequency and ensures that you're not forgotten, but don't become annoying. Second, running all of your campaigns (Breakthrough, Pursuit, and Nurture) in the first week of every month creates a consistent work flow for your business. You need to set yourself up to be able to manage this on an ongoing basis. A marketing assistant who comes in one week a month would be a great addition. Last, a monthly cycle makes for an easier and more predictable measurement period, with enough frequency to allow you to make midcourse corrections, if necessary, while you can still affect your annual outcome.

Sophie's system, also known as her Pursuit Plan, can be seen in Figure 16.3. Let's go through each step to see how it can work for you.

1. Sophie's List

Sophie wanted to create a list of all her unEngaged Prospects (her "P" prospects) so she could send a follow-up Pursuit Campaign to them. First, she went to her Engagement Spreadsheet and popped out a list of P prospects using her Beast Plug-In for Excel (see Figure 16.4 and Chapter 9). That produced a text file of P prospects ready for use with the email tool she was using. As you'll recall, P prospects are those she'd marketed to in the past (Sophie had sent them a "key" Breakthrough Campaign), but who hadn't taken her up on her offer yet.

2. Sophie's Offer

Because her campaign was going out to P prospects, Sophie wanted to use one of her D offers to try and hook them into her Cave and onto her Engagement Ladder. She decided to follow up her Breakthrough Campaign with an email version of the same, featuring the key and the cloning document.

Figure 16.3 Sophie's Pursuit Plan

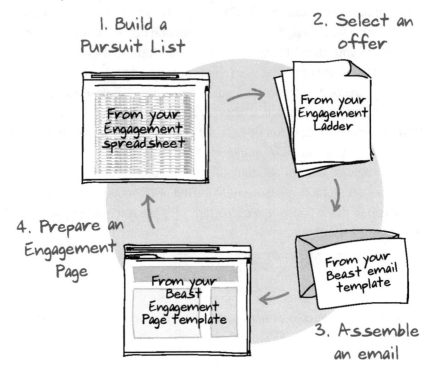

Figure 16.4 Sophie Creates Her List

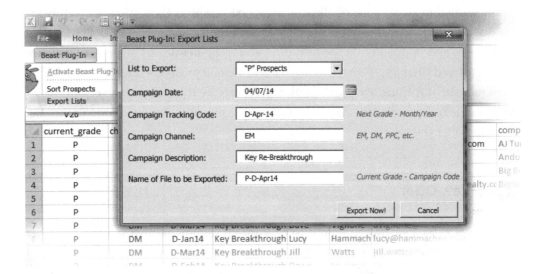

SOPHIE'S PARTIAL ENGAGEMENT LADDER

Touch	Offer	Lead Grade Goal	Decision Cycle Support
2nd	"Staging Works" (Before and after pictures, testimonials, and case studies an agent can offer to homeowner. Unbranded.)	D	Solution Education
1st	"6 Ways to Clone Yourself (and Make More Money in a Day)"		
Breakthrough	"Here's the key to cloning yourself . . ."	P	Awareness

Her rationale for repeating her Breakthrough creative was twofold. First, Sophie had gone to her campaign report (at Unbounce) and had seen that 210 of her 362 agent prospects (58 percent) had actually visited her Breakthrough Engagement Page (see Figure 16.5).

If she wanted her agent prospects to get to know her, this was a great start. She could also see that there must have been a lot of sharing of her direct mail Breakthrough Campaign, because there were on average 4.8 views of the Engagement Page per visitor (1012 ÷ 210). So, from what she could see, of her 319 unEngaged Prospects, 152 didn't go to her Engagement Page (362 – 210 = 152), while 167 went to the Engagement Page, but didn't request an offer (210 – 43 = 167).

Of that 167, some would not have been interested in the offer, some would have just deferred pursuing it, and some may have just been distracted before they could finish

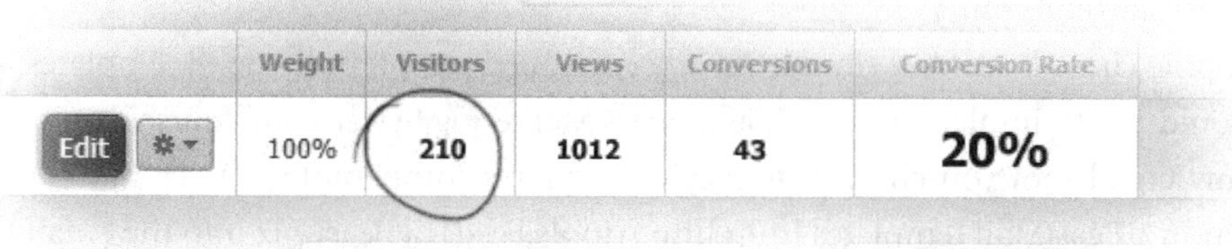

Figure 16.5 Sophie Reexamines Her Breakthrough Campaign Report

having a look. That told her that somewhere between 152 and 319 of her unEngaged Prospects either needed to be nudged or still needed to be broken through to. She felt an email version of the key campaign could do it. Sophie's second (but far lesser) reason for reusing the key concept was that it's always nice to try and amortize your development costs.

3. Sophie's Email

There are three reasons why Pursuit Campaigns make generous use of email:

1. Pursuit Campaigns are a long-term, ongoing commitment to the coaxing of unEngaged Prospects into your Beast Cave. Email is the most efficient and cost-effective way to do this.
2. Pursuit Campaigns are all about working the numbers (remember, marketing is math). High volume campaigns are needed, and email is ideally suited.
3. With a little creativity, email can be made to break through, despite generally flagging open and click-through rates.

To set up an effective email campaign, you'll need to look outside Outlook or Gmail or Yahoo! Mail. You need a tool that tracks your campaign's open rates and other performance indicators and helps to make sure that your emails are not flagged as spam. There are plenty of good email tools to choose from, including MailChimp, Constant Contact, Campaign Monitor, AWeber, ActiveCampaign, and Speak2Leads. Of them all, Campaign Monitor is our favorite for its ease of use, cost-effectiveness, and strong reporting. As a result, we selected Campaign Monitor to be the engine that drives BeastMail (see http://TheBeastMachine.com/).

Sophie chose BeastMail since it already contained our prebuilt email templates, which she could use to implement the 7-Step Beast Marketing System. Of course, you're free to use any email tool you choose, as they're all pretty comparable. What's more, you can import free BeastMail templates from http://tools.FeedTheBeast.biz into the email tool of your choosing and then apply everything that we'll be discussing here.

QR Code
Beast Email Templates

Sophie then needed to decide which *design* to use for her Pursuit Campaign emails, because three things affect your email response rates: subject line (for opens), email design, and message (for your click-throughs—i.e., how many prospects click on a link in your email). The table that follows gives a quick glimpse into the design options available. You'll see actual examples in the next chapter.

EMAIL DESIGN OPTIONS

Design Option	Description	Pros	Cons
Designed HTML	This is the most common kind of email. It makes use of banner images and formatted text. These email messages often look like mini web pages.	Virtually no limit to the design possibilities. Can be very intriguing when done well.	Costs more to develop (images, etc.) and may require a web developer. Has been done. Lots. Tends to be viewed as promotional email by all. Some prospects won't see the images contained in the email if their images are turned "off" in their email program.
Personal Text HTML	This is also an HTML email, but it is designed to look like a regular, personal email that you would receive from a coworker.	Done well, tends to get some of the best response rates. People respond well to personal email. Inexpensive to execute.	Stops working as well if you use it all the time with your prospect, unless a strong sense of relationship has developed.

(continued)

Design Option	Description	Pros	Cons
Billboard HTML	This is an HTML email as well, but it makes use of maybe one line of text and one very compelling image. It is uncommon (so far). You may never have seen one.	Gets higher response rates because of intrigue factor. Minimal text and images make it easier for prospect to review and respond.	Stops working as well if you use it for every mailing to your prospect (gets old). Some prospects won't see the images contained in the email if their images are turned "off" in their email program.

In general, mixing up the design approaches for your different campaigns works best because beyond changing up your subject line with each mailing, using different design approaches keeps your campaigns looking fresh to your prospects.

big, hairy tip

Many email readers today (i.e., the software or application your prospects will use to read your email) are set up so that images are turned off by default. This supposedly foils spammers (which it doesn't really, because they don't care—they're a bit of an indiscriminate bunch). At any rate, that means images in your HTML email may not be seen by some of your prospects. As a result, you need to be sure to design your email messages so they still sell, whether images are turned on or off. Make your words and your ALT tags count. If the words aren't selling, there's a good chance that your pictures won't help much anyway. Go back to your Engagement Template. Speak to your prospect's pain in plain words.

For her "house key" Pursuit Campaign, Sophie decided to use the billboard HTML email approach because its style most resembled the "house key" direct mailer that she had sent out in her direct mail Breakthrough Campaign, and familiarity is a big factor in any follow-up campaign. Sophie went into BeastMail and used the template there to assemble her email message (see Figure 16.6). The elements she needed to have ready before going to BeastMail included:

- Her Pursuit List, which she had already exported out of her Engagement Spreadsheet
- An image of the house key with the tag

Figure 16.6 Assembling Her Email in BeastMail

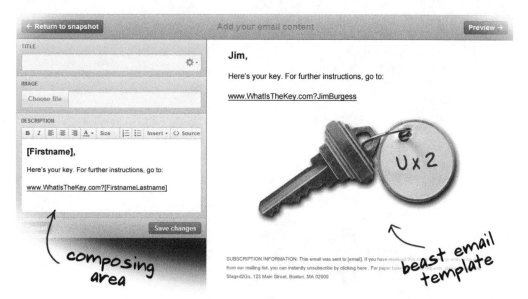

- Text for the ALT tag, which is what a prospect's email reader would display if her images were turned off
- An Escape Hatch Offer, if she wanted to use one

Sophie personalized her email, which BeastMail handles automatically for her. She also had to include an "unsubscribe" line at the bottom of her email so BeastMail would accept the email for delivery. For the ALT tag, Sophie used: "This is a picture of your key. You're just going to have to enable images if you want to see it :)" This would display in the prospect's email instead of the house-key image if the prospect had the images turned off in her email reader. Figure 16.7 shows what Sophie's billboard HTML email looked like. Sophie chose not to use an Escape Hatch Offer in this email because she felt that it would detract from the mystery and intrigue she was counting on. She did, however, keep the Escape Hatch Offer on her Pursuit Campaign Engagement Page (see Figure 16.8).

A few more notes on her email: Sophie kept the subject line very much in line with the "intrigue" creative, she personalized it, and she pulled the text from the body of the email. She felt it carried just enough mystery to prompt a look by her agent prospects. Sophie

Figure 16.7 Sophie's Billboard HTML Email

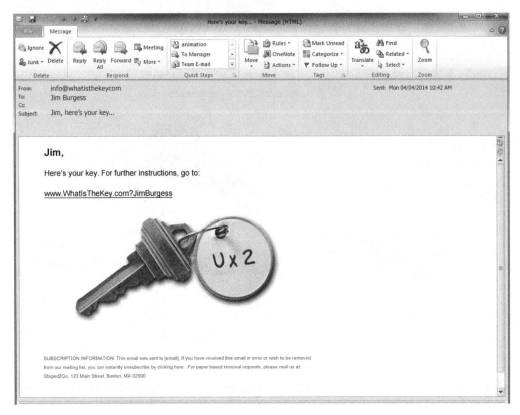

also chose to have her return email address be whatisthekey.com as opposed to her regular email address. There are mixed schools of thought on this. To pull off mailing from a different domain, you'll need your web guy to help you set it up, and you'll need him to further set up DomainKeys and authentication settings in BeastMail so whatisthekey.com doesn't trigger spam filters. Both tasks sound more complicated than they are. Web guys love this stuff.

Think about this for a moment. If Sophie had used her Staged2Go.com domain name on the return email address, it would have taken a bit of the mystery away from the mailing and would have, in our experience, affected the response rate. When it comes to intrigue, no branding is always better than even a little branding and far better than lots of branding. On the other hand, if the return email address wasn't recognizable *and* Sophie's creative looked a little unusual (which it did to encourage click-through), some

Figure 16.8 Sophie's Pursuit Campaign Engagement Page

recipients might view the email as spam and discard it before reading it. That said, the strong historical response rates we've recorded with this kind of approach suggest that more prospects are intrigued than frightened off.

4. Sophie's Engagement Page

For every campaign there is a dedicated Engagement Page. You want to be able to track conversions to Engaged Prospects for your Pursuit Campaigns, and as you've seen, Engagement

Pages are the best way to do that. In fact, if you were to use more than one marketing channel for the same campaign, say email and pay-per-click ads, you should think about having separate Engagement Pages for *each* channel, allowing you to measure performance by channel—which means you might be faced with multiple Engagement Pages *per* campaign. Before you panic, this too is easier than it sounds. Your Engagement Page tool makes it simple to "clone" Engagement Pages so you can knock off multiple copies in mere minutes. Of course, you'll need to download a campaign report for each Engagement Page you've set up, which represents more work, but that's what marketing assistants are for, right?

This discussion is quite apt for Sophie. She'd already developed a highly effective "house key" Engagement Page for her Breakthrough Campaign, so she was able to simply repurpose ("clone") that page (see Figure 16.8) since she was happy with how it had performed so far.

DOING IT ALL AGAIN

If you go back to Figure 16.3 for a moment, you'll notice Sophie's Pursuit Plan is a cycle that ends where it starts and vice versa. Pursuit Campaigns require that you keep at it, working the numbers until they produce the flow of traffic through your Beast Cave that you need to hit your goals. If you complete a D-rung campaign in April, for example, when May comes around, you'll need to make a new list of all those prospects who remained at a P grade and send them out another D-rung offer as your next Pursuit Campaign.

So, you may be asking yourself, "If I have only two D-rung offers, won't my target audience start suffering from offer-burnout?" Well, not necessarily. You can quite comfortably rotate your two D-rung offers across four months (which is four campaigns) by simply using *different subject lines* each time. Very often, the lack of response to an email message has more to do with your prospect not having even noticed your email in the first place.

If you're concerned that your prospects will start unsubscribing in droves if you start boring them with the same old offers, don't be. Generally, people unsubscribe when they're completely disinterested in what you have to offer, or if your email frequency has become unbearable. Your once-a-month campaign schedule is reasonable and shouldn't encourage many anger-related unsubscribes. On the other hand, if some of your prospects are genuinely disinterested in what you're offering, it's actually a good thing to know. If your unsubscribe numbers do become suspiciously high (over 1 percent per email campaign), you might want to review your Beast Prospect List quality.

Of course, the most important bellwether of when it's time to refresh your offer is when your campaign's *response* rates start consistently hitting unacceptable levels and aren't showing signs of perking up. Ongoing open rates under 10 percent are a typical warning sign. Your online Campaign Reports (produced by your Engagement Page tools) will show you the number of page hits and conversions you're getting. But another very useful tool to diagnose your email campaign's performance is the email report you'll find on your email service (see Figure 16.9).

The "clicked a link" measure in Figure 16.9 (19 people) should match the "visitors" number in your Unbounce Campaign Report for the Engagement Page belonging to this campaign. However, the "opened so far" or "open rate" number (17.53 percent) is unique to your email report and is a good leading indicator of how your campaign is performing. You'd like to see open rates above 15 percent, but open rates generally average around 20 percent in many B2B businesses. As mentioned above, an open rate below 10 percent is starting to show signs of wear-out. You might still be able to milk it for a few more rounds, but the kinds of response rates you'd really like to achieve (and should be able to if your Engagement Template and Beast Prospect List were well constructed) are north of 25 percent.

Figure 16.9 Your BeastMail Report

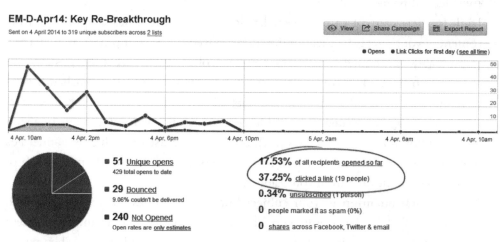

© Copyright CampaignMonitor.com. Used with permission.

HOW TO "STRETCH" YOUR CONTENT

If your response rate is still languishing after several revised subject lines and a few rotations of your D-rung offer, it might be time to switch things up a bit. Here are a few options that may help:

1. **The Escape Hatch.** Make sure there's an Escape Hatch at the bottom of every Engagement Page and most email messages you produce. The Escape Hatch should point back to the full range of content you've created and curated in your Learning Hub.
2. **Offer the next level up.** If your P prospects haven't budged in a few months, you might try sending them an offer from another rung of your Engagement Ladder and see what happens. It's important to note, however, that all P prospects should be treated the same—those you may have added a year ago and those you may have added yesterday. You can try to segment your P prospects into laggards and newbies, but your life will start getting complicated fast. Treating old and new the same isn't necessarily optimal, but it's very practical, and keeping things simple will almost always produce a better outcome in the long run (because it's easier to keep doing consistently!).
3. **Create new content.** You can always add new content to your Engagement Ladder. As we saw, this requires quite a resource commitment but will almost always return substantially more than your investment. If you feel your offers are tiring, you'll need to consider adding new content.
4. **Look for new content in unexpected places.** If you have a business blog and the content of your blog is focused on the social conversations your prospects are having (presumably concerning a problem you can solve), then each blog posting you produce can be used as content on your Engagement Ladder. Just finished a great posting? Use it as an offer one month to mix things up. There won't necessarily be an Engagement Page associated with the blog entry (although you could create one with a subscription form to your blog on it), but your blog itself can display banner ads offering your prospects an easy-to-follow Conversion Path to your Learning Hub or another high-value offer from your Ladder.
5. **Pay particular attention to your subject lines.** Subject lines are a subject all unto themselves. Much has been written on the importance of subject lines and the different approaches to use in writing them. Our advice is simple: less is more. When you're

developing your subject lines, get your Engagement Template and your Engagement Ladder out in front of you again. Then answer these three questions:

- What is this prospect's monetizable pain?
- How can this offer help to address that pain?
- What are the fewest words you could put into a subject line to convey how you can address your prospect's pain, as it relates to this offer?

You have only an instant to get your prospects' attention and draw them into your email, hopefully prompting a click-through.

6. **Keep your email really short.** Limit yourself to between five and ten lines of text, if you can swing it. It's safe to say that most people don't like reading big blocks of text. While you may feel that by telling your prospects everything there is to say about your service, you'll ensure that something gets their attention, you'll most often be wrong. Nothing will get their attention if they don't read your email in the first place. And they won't read it if it looks scary long.

7. **Keep your email really focused.** Two things should guide you here: your Engagement Template and your offer. Between those two inputs, you should be able to write a very short, very pointed reason why your prospects should click to find out more about your offer.

8. **Use the Beast Email templates.** The Beast Email templates follow best practices for encouraging the highest click-through rates possible on your email (click-through being the measure of one of your prospects actually clicking the link for the offer you've placed in your email).

CAVE SCRATCHES

16

~ Sophie launches her Pursuit Campaign

~ "What is the key?"

~ Sophie prepares her list, offer, assembles her email, prepares her Engagement Page

NEXT UP

Getting your prospects into your cave is a big challenge, and getting them there in substantial numbers, even more so. But once all of your hard work has gotten a bunch of prospects checking out your cave wall hangings, don't let them slip out again! It can take months to convert prospects to Engaged Prospects and as many more to convert them into Sales-Ready Leads. That's why it's so important to Nurture your Engaged Prospects. You need to provide them with useful offers from your Engagement Ladder so you can keep them enthralled with the wonders of your Beast Cave. How to Nurture your prospects throughout their Decision Cycle is what Chapter 17 is about.

Nurture, convert, and grow big

Paul Launches His Nurture Campaign

> ### What you'll find in this chapter:
> • The Nurture notion
> • Your marketing success rate
> • A Nurture Plan that paid Paul back
> • Keeping your influencers close

So here we are, standing on the bottom rung of a ladder within your Beast Cave. We're looking around at the wall hangings, the picture of Ma Beast hanging slightly askew over there, and at the ladder itself. The ladder looks good and sturdy, and as we examine it, we notice there appear to be attractive posters on the wall just behind each rung. We like what we see. This place feels like it can help us—the same feeling we get when we walk into a bookstore. And then, there you are, hand extended, welcoming us to your cave. Almost

Figure 17.1 When Nurture Calls

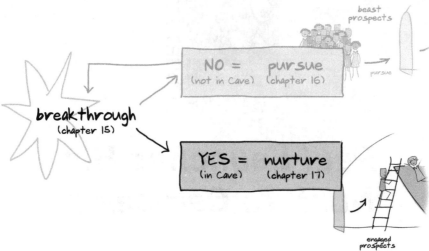

immediately, you start talking about the very business problems we have on our minds, offering us some fresh perspective on what we can do to ease our burden. You point up the ladder and to the posters on the wall behind it. The posters seem to promise something very helpful to us at this time, if only we'd climb up a bit and have a closer look. And so we do.

The Attraction, Breakthrough, and Pursuit Campaigns of the previous six chapters had one goal: to entice your Beast Prospects into your Beast Cave (see Figure 17.1). Now that they're in your Cave and engaged, your new goal is to "nurture" them up your Engagement Ladder and into the eager, capable, waiting hands of your sales team so they can be turned into customers and, eventually, Fans (see Figure 17.2).

Figure 17.2 A Prospect's Path Through Your Beast Cave

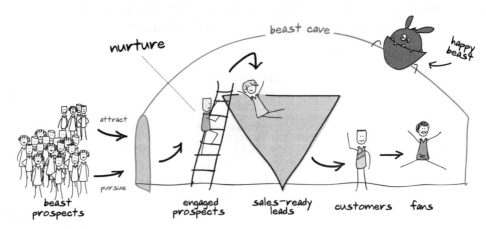

So how do you Nurture?

The simple idea behind Nurturing is that you want to add value to the Decision Cycle your Engaged Prospects are embarked on (see the following table).

YOUR PROSPECT'S DECISION CYCLE

	Prospect Thought Process	Decision Cycle Stage
	"I've got a problem."	1. Awareness
	"What's available to help me solve my problem?"	2. Solution education
	"Which solutions are credible and relevant?"	3. Vendor education
	"Which solutions are the best solutions for my needs?"	4. Vendor consideration
	"I choose . . ."	5. Vendor selection

Generally speaking, your prospects come to the realization that they've got a problem on their own (stage one in the above table). It's entirely possible that your Attraction and Pursuit Campaigns have helped to create awareness of the problem you solve, but in most cases prospects will take action because they're personally feeling discomfort (that is, a need) of some form.

So your ability to add value to your prospect's decision journey begins at "solution education" (stage two in the previous table) and runs through to "vendor selection," at which point your prospect had better be in your sales team's hands. And what is "adding value" exactly? Well, that brings us back to the Engagement Ladder you built earlier. Adding value, as you've seen, means giving your prospects the tools and information *they* need to help them better make *decisions* along each step of their journey. Remember, it's all about *them*.

Your Engagement Ladder is a kind of "early warning system," so that when a prospect reaches for a D-rung offer, it suggests that on the next campaign you send them, they may be ready for a C-rung offer. Each next-rung offer they take graduates them up to the next Prospect Grade (see Paul's Engagement Ladder below). Similarly, when you see your prospect starting to reach for one of your A-rung offers, you know it's time to graduate them to a Sales-Ready Lead, and off to sales they go. We'll explain more fully in a moment.

What about just calling your prospects when they step onto your Engagement Ladder? Actually calling a prospect when they hit, say, your C rung might be a good idea if you've got only one or two prospects wandering around your Cave. In that case, sure, . . . call them up and see if they want to have lunch. But here are two reasons it can be a problem:

1. You should have hundreds of prospects wandering through your Cave.
2. Most of your prospects don't want to talk to you yet.

It's hard to call hundreds of prospects with any kind of efficiency, and even harder if none of them want to speak with you. Nearly three-quarters of your Engaged Prospects just aren't sales-ready because they're still travelling through the education stages of their Decision Cycle, and they won't be rushed into a purchase.[1] It's called a "considered" purchase for a reason. The other 25 percent may or may not be tire kickers.

Trying to guess which small number of prospects may actually be ready for a sale pays diminishing returns—the payback doesn't generally support the effort. So instead, why not use a little automated help and Nurture *all* of your Engaged Prospects, so each feels like you're dealing with him or her personally, letting them self-identify where they are in their Decision Cycles. Over time, you'll produce far more Customers this way than any other, and you'll benefit from shorter sales cycles, higher close rates, smaller discounts, and larger deals.[2]

Why is active nurturing so important? Because even if a prospect has engaged with you, studies show she's likely to forget about you and your company within a month *if* she doesn't hear from you again. And by "hear," we don't mean a phone call requesting a meeting. It's too early for that.

PAUL, SO FAR

Let's jump onto our not-forgotten chocolate-maker's Engagement Ladder and see how he (that would be Paul) nurtured his private label retail buyers upward.

TREADWATER CHOCOLATES' ENGAGEMENT LADDER: PRIVATE LABEL

Touch	Offer	Prospect Grade Goal	Decision Cycle Support
8th	Custom market analysis and sample plan	A	Vendor selection
7th	Confectionery forecasting tool for private label		
6th	Treadwater private label sample kits	B	Vendor consideration
5th	Treadwater private label success stories		
4th	Treadwater private label program kit	C	Vendor education
3rd	"Private Label: The Treadwater Difference" (video)		
2nd	"Holding Margin with Private Label" (analyst study)	D	Solution education
1st	"Exotic Flavors Drive Sales" (trends report)		
Outside the Cave . . .			
Breakthrough	"GMSW (Gross Margin Secret Weapon)"	P	Awareness

First, we need to see what Paul's done and where he stands. In the first three months of the year, Paul sent out D-rung offers to 400 (unengaged) P prospects in a series of three Breakthrough Campaigns. Each month, some of those P prospects resisted his offer, remaining unengaged P prospects, and some took his offer, thereby appearing on his Engagement Ladder as Engaged Prospects. As soon as his Engaged Prospects showed up in his Cave, Paul started nurturing them the following month. That means his first Nurture Campaign launched in February. By April, here's what he'd accomplished (see Figure 17.3):

- Of his 65 Engaged Prospects, 39 had taken Paul up on his D-rung offers, which means they'd downloaded either the trend report or the analyst study from rung D of his Engagement Ladder that you saw in the previous table.
- Another 15 had requested either his private label kit or his video (rung C in the table). Three of these Engaged Prospects had come in through one of his Attraction Campaigns.
- Seven prospects selected one of his B-rung offers (sample kit or success stories). Two of these Engaged Prospects had come in through one of his Attraction Campaigns.
- Four prospects became Sales-Ready Leads. Of those, two had asked for meetings right away on the strength of his Breakthrough Campaign, and two had jumped onto his Ladder as C prospects in March and by April had downloaded everything Paul could throw at them. One of these March Engaged Prospects came in through Paul's Attraction Campaign.

Figure 17.3 Paul's Results After Four Months

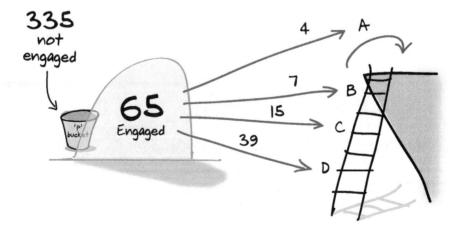

- The rest (335 unEngaged Prospects in all) didn't take Paul up on any of his offers. He put them in his P bucket, which he left outside the door of his Cave (don't laugh). Paul's P bucket contains all the Beast Prospects to whom he's already reached out but who haven't yet taken him up on one of his offers. These he continued to pursue through his monthly Pursuit Campaigns.
- The only other folks outside his Cave door were prospects he hadn't yet marketed to. These included prospects who were hovering near his door (lured to his website or Engagement Page by one of his Attraction Campaigns) and who were pondering whether to take him up on an offer and engage.

Paul had been using his Prospect Engagement Rate (PER) to track his Breakthrough and Pursuit Campaigns. But now Paul needed to track his progress using a second key metric: Marketing Conversion Rate (MCR). MCR measures how well your Nurture Campaigns are performing based on how many of your Engaged Prospects become Sales-Ready Leads. MCR ultimately defines the success of your overall marketing efforts at producing true Sales-Ready Leads on which the Beast might feed (refer back to Figure 17.2). MCR is calculated as:

Marketing Conversion Rate (MCR)
= Number of Sales-Ready Leads ÷ Number of Engaged Prospects

Thanks to his Nurture Campaign, Paul produced 4 Sales-Ready Leads out of a total of 65 Engaged Prospects. This put Paul's MCR to the end of April at a healthy 6 percent (see Figure 17.4).

Since four months is one-third of the year, and Paul's Marketing Conversion Rate is currently 6 percent, he's one-third of the way to his annual goal of 20 percent. In other words, Paul was right on track to make his year-end goal, which was to nurture and convert 13 of his 65 prospects into Sales-Ready Leads.

PAUL THE NURTURER

How did Paul do it? Let's have a look at the mechanics behind the curtain. Like Sophie before him in her Pursuit Campaigns, Paul decided to use email for his monthly Nurture Campaigns. Paul knew that email was especially useful at the Nurture stage because his prospects had all engaged with him at this point. As a result, his emails stood a better

Figure 17.4 Paul's MCR

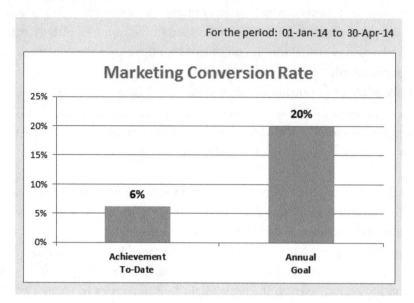

chance of being recognized when they arrived in his prospects' inboxes, which meant he could expect better than usual open and click-through rates. Paul's Nurture Campaign cycle looked like this (see Figure 17.5).

A quick note: When it comes to nurturing prospects, *consistency* is more important than *perfection*. You need to "touch" your prospects on a regular basis, even if each touch isn't perfect—just get it as close to perfect as you can, based on the groundwork you laid in Steps 1 to 3.

Figure 17.5 Paul's Nurture Plan

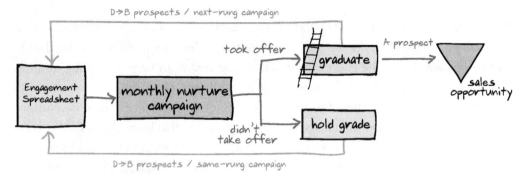

PAUL REVISITS HIS ESCAPE HATCHES

We discussed Escape Hatches in Chapter 8 in the context of the Learning Hub and in Chapters 15 and 16 when our entrepreneurs built their Breakthrough and Pursuit Campaigns. The purpose of the Escape Hatch is to give your prospects somewhere to go in case you've misidentified where they are in their purchase Decision Cycle. Until they start to reveal themselves to you, the odds of misidentification are pretty high.

Paul knew that if he sent a Nurture Campaign to prospects with a D-rung offer embedded in it (say, an industry white paper), but those prospects had already completed their Solution and Vendor Education and were now at the Vendor Consideration stage, he might miss his chance. Sure, getting the attention of late-stage prospects with a D-rung offer might still earn him consideration, but to improve his odds with advanced prospects, Paul realized he needed to create an Escape Hatch Offer. So his secondary offer was a demand forecasting calculator, a much more useful and timely offer for those prospects in the later stages of their Decision Cycle.

In general, Escape Hatch Offers should be placed at the bottom of every offer you present (and even at the bottom of your regular company email). What's more, your Escape Hatch Offer should go straight for the jugular. What jugular? The key, monetizable pain you uncovered in your Engagement Template. Knowing this, Paul included the following Escape Hatch Offer at the bottom of every email he sent and every Engagement Page he created: "Gross margin challenges? We can help you hold GM. Access our Learning Hub Tools by clicking: Forecasting Tools & Analyst Reports."

If Paul's message was "on the mark" for his Beast Prospects, it would resonate. Conversely, if he got his prospects' pain wrong in his Engagement Template, this Escape Hatch Offer wouldn't draw flies—incredible efficiency versus costly irrelevance. We'll see how he did in a moment.

PAUL'S NURTURE PLAN

As with Pursuit Campaigns, a plan and a little automation go a long way toward keeping the math gods happy (they're the gods who determine whether you make your Big, Hairy, Outrageous number at the end of the year). In that regard, to keep everything running smoothly, Paul realized he needed some help. After all, he had a business to run and staff to keep busy, and he didn't have the extra week a month it would take to keep his Nurture Program running smoothly and consistently over time. He also knew that if he'd chosen *not* to hire an assistant, over the long run "marketing" would have seen less and less of him than "chocolate" would, because Paul loved making chocolate and he viewed marketing as, at best, an acquired taste.

As we've said before, marketing is to growth what bookkeeping is to solvency. If you truly want to see outrageous growth, you'd do well to hire a marketing support person to run your Nurture Campaigns, much like you've probably hired a bookkeeper to tend to your books (or ought to have). Want to figure out the payback on a marketing assistant? Add $3,000 per month (benefits included) to the marketing ROI you'll calculate in Chapter 19. If you hit your numbers, a marketing assistant position is more than likely to pay for itself. And if you don't have assistance, do you think you could hit your numbers?

Paul's Nurture Plan (Figure 17.6) should look familiar to you. It's the same basic plan that Sophie used for her Pursuit Campaigns, except a little more ambitious. For each target group in his Engagement Spreadsheet (that is, his *D*s, *C*s, and *B*s), Paul's assistant ran a campaign cycle the first week of every month. That meant developing as many as three separate campaigns to three separate lists with three separate offers, emails, and Engagement Pages.

Actually, Paul's newly hired marketing assistant was able to make relatively short work of these tasks. She pulled the lists from Paul's Engagement Spreadsheet and used the offers Paul had already developed for his Engagement Ladder. That left building an email message and an Engagement Page for each offer (which she did once for each of the eight offers using Beast templates and then reused). Let's go through one of Paul's Nurture cycles.

Figure 17.6 Paul's Nurture Plan

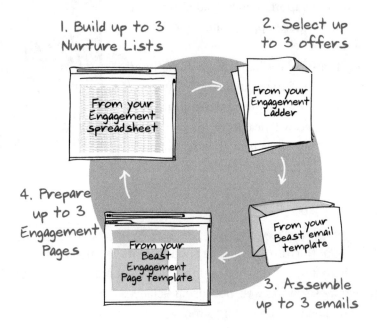

FOLLOWING PAUL'S NURTURE CYCLE

As mentioned, *consistency* is the key to a strong nurturing program. Paul needed to reach out to his prospects on a regular schedule that didn't overexpose them to Treadwater Chocolates (and encourage their opting out of Paul's mailings) and yet wasn't so infrequent that his prospects forgot who he was or else weren't thinking of him at the moment that they were ready to make a decision. Paul's nurturing calendar addressed that point.

To get the most impact for the least effort, his D, C, and B Nurture Campaigns all went out in the first week of every month. So Paul's calendar had one day a month marked off for nurturing, like this:

Whenever a prospect entered Paul's Beast Cave, he dropped them into the appropriately graded prospect bucket and sent them a grade-appropriate campaign on the next scheduled run.

A quick note: If a prospect happens to come in at the end of the month, and the next planned Nurturing Campaign is to go out the following week, just run it that way. Yes, the prospect will hear from you two weeks running but then will fall into a regular pattern of once a month.

One set of Nurture Campaigns should go out in the first week of every month, regardless of when your prospect last responded to you. Every four to five weeks works well, because it achieves a balance between not being annoying and not being forgotten.

To set up his monthly Nurture Campaign, Paul built his Beast Prospect List, added the details of the new campaign, selected the appropriate offers to match his prospects' lead grade, chose three HTML email designs, and prepared his Engagement Pages. Let's see how he did this in more detail.

1. Paul Built His List of Nurtured Prospects

You'll recall back in Figure 17.3, Paul's current count of Engaged Prospects who needed nurturing was:

D prospects = 39
C prospects = 15
B prospects = 7

For his next round of nurturing, he went into his Engagement Spreadsheet and exported a list for *each* of his three groups of prospects (see Figure 17.7).

As he made each list, the Beast Plug-In asked him to provide the details for the Nurture Campaign he was about to launch (see Figure 17.8).

Figure 17.7 Paul Exported a List from his Engagement Spreadsheet

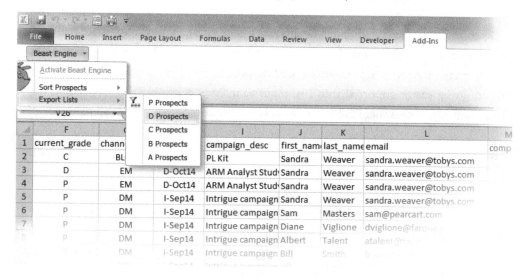

Figure 17.8 Paul Added New Campaign Details

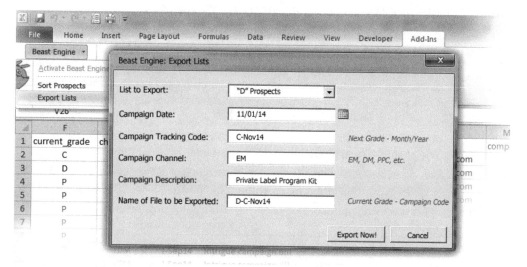

big, hairy tip

The campaign naming conventions used here are the same as those we introduced you to in Chapter 9. Paul could have exported these lists manually, but there's little point since the Beast Plug-In for Excel is free, and it saved Paul a world of work.

By submitting his new campaign details (see Figure 17.8), Paul accomplished two things: he (and his assistant) recorded the new campaign code in his Engagement Spreadsheet against every prospect it was going to, and he generated a properly formatted ".TXT" file that could be easily imported into his email tool. After repeating this exercise for each prospect group, Treadwater Chocolates now had three lists (D, C, and B) all ready to go.

2. Paul Then Selected the Appropriate Offers

For each of his three lists, Paul picked one offer from his Engagement Ladder to assign to each group. The process was pretty straightforward since he'd already prepared offers for each rung of his Engagement Ladder back in Chapter 7. Because he wanted to tempt each prospect to a rung above where they currently were, Paul offered his D prospects a C-rung offer (see the following table) and so on for each of his prospect groups:

PAUL'S OFFERS ARE MATCHED TO HIS PROSPECTS' GRADES

Prospect Grade	Description	Next Step
D prospect	A prospect who has stepped onto your Engagement Ladder, having taken you up on one of your D-rung offers.	Group D prospects and send them a C (vendor education) offer via email.
C prospect	A prospect who has taken you up on one of your C-rung offers.	Group C prospects and send them a B (vendor consideration) offer via email.
B prospect	A prospect who has taken you up on one of your B-rung offers.	Group B prospects and send them an A (vendor selection) offer via email.
A prospect	A prospect who has accepted one of your A-rung offers.	Transfer A prospects to your sales team for closing.

The next challenge Paul faced was the same that Sophie faced: he had only two offers per rung of his Engagement Ladder. What if this is the third Nurture Campaign to a D prospect who hasn't budged? Does he send them the same offer over and over again? Paul's solution was to alternate the two C offers he made every month until his D prospects either opted in or opted out. If they opted in, that means they responded to one of Paul's C offers and were now graduated to B status. If they opted out, it meant they chose to unsubscribe to Paul's mailing, they left the cave, and Paul could no longer market to them.

Chances are, some prospects will opt out of your mailings, but if so, they probably weren't a good fit to start with. It's not a perfect system, but given your limited resources, it's a smart approach that will produce a good return on the resources you invested into it.

3. Paul Chose Three Email Designs

Now that Paul had his list and offers ready to go, he needed to choose which HTML designs (introduced in Chapter 16) to apply to his emails. Paul decided on three designs, one for each of his prospect groups, as follows:

PAUL'S THREE-PRONGED APPROACH TO HIS NURTURE EMAIL CAMPAIGN

Group	What Paul will Send	Why
D prospects	Personal text HTML	These prospects have responded and are new to Paul's Engagement Ladder. He wants to welcome them in a personal manner, personally signed by him.
C prospects	Designed HTML	These prospects are firmly on the Engagement Ladder, and a well-designed HTML email will shake things up a bit.
B prospects	Personal text HTML	These prospects are becoming very engaged, and a personal email feels right once more, encouraging them to become A prospects (a.k.a. Sales-Ready Leads).

There's no hard and fast rule as to what style of email to use for what mailing. Look at the pros and cons of each email approach, the needs of your prospect group, and what they received last, and then make a call as to which approach would seem to be best for the current campaign. Paul knew that if his Engagement Template was on the mark in terms of identifying his Beast Prospects' true, monetizable business pain, then his campaigns will pretty much grab his prospects by the collar. If his Engagement Template was poorly defined somehow, his email approaches would get mediocre response rates at best and wouldn't resonate with his target market.

What you've just read in the preceding two sentences pretty much explains why most marketing campaigns generate average response rates. *Mediocre campaigns happen when the people responsible for those campaigns don't dig deeply enough into what makes their Beast Prospects tick.*

Paul didn't have to worry in that regard because his Engagement Template told him everything he needed to know about his Beast Prospects. As with Sophie in the previous chapter, Paul had several email tools to choose from, including MailChimp, Constant Contact, Campaign Monitor, AWeber, ActiveCampaign, and Speak2Leads. Paul chose BeastMail, a customized version of Campaign Monitor, since it already contained the prebuilt email templates he needed to implement the 7-Step Beast Marketing System. (But again, you're free to use any email tool you choose.) Take a look at the box that follows and you'll see the three pieces of creative Paul developed for his three prospect groups.

Figure 17.9 Paul's D Prospects Received a "Personal Text" Email

Nurture group:	D prospects (total of 39 prospects)
Email approach:	Personal text HTML
Offer:	Vendor education (C-rung offer): "Private Label: The Treadwater Difference" video
Subject line:	"Sandra, I wanted to introduce myself"
Rationale:	Sandra responded to Treadwater's last campaign and so is at least passingly familiar with the company. Paul wanted to extend a personal invitation to Sandra to learn more about how Treadwater can help her better meet her goals.
Note:	A stylized variation of the Escape Hatch Offer was used for this email.

Figure 17.10 Paul's C Prospects Received a "Designed" Email

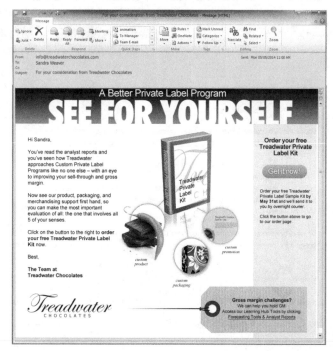

Nurture group: C prospects (total of 15 prospects)

Email approach: Designed HTML

Offer: Vendor consideration (B-rung offer): "Treadwater Private Label Sample Kit"

Subject line: "For your consideration from Treadwater Chocolates"

Rationale: Sandra had already downloaded the trends report and had seen the "Treadwater Story" video.

Now it was time for her to see the actual product for herself. Short of sending a sales rep in (which Paul would do gladly if she asked), Sandra was being given meaningful information to help her better evaluate Treadwater as a possible vendor. As a result, Paul's subject line now included the Treadwater name to reflect Sandra's growing relationship with the firm.

Figure 17.11 Paul's B Prospects Received a "Personal Text" Email

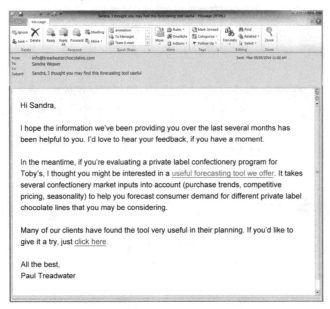

Nurture group:	B prospects (total of seven prospects)
Email approach:	Personal text HTML
Offer:	Decision support (A-rung offer): "Forecasting Tool"
Subject line:	"Sandra, I thought you might find this forecasting tool useful"
Rationale:	Based on Sandra's behaviors and Paul's knowledge that forecasting is a big challenge for retail buyers, this offer did a good job of identifying where Sandra was on her purchase Decision Cycle.
Note:	Because Sandra was quite advanced up Paul's Engagement Ladder, Paul didn't think it necessary to include an Escape Hatch Offer in this email.

4. Lastly, Paul Prepared His Engagement Pages

For every Nurture offer there must be a corresponding Engagement Page, so when a prospect clicked on an offer link in Paul's Nurture email, that prospect was delivered to an Engagement Page that presented the offer in all its splendor, and provided the prospect with a simple, one-click opportunity to access that offer (see Figure 17.12).

We discussed the development of Engagement Pages at length in Chapters 8, 15, and 16, so the goal to keep in mind here is that Paul wanted to convert or promote prospects up one rung on his Engagement Ladder by having them fill in the web form and then click the "Get it now!" button (see Figure 17.12). Once prospects did that, Paul knew they were converted because his Engagement Page tool (e.g., Unbounce) automatically assigned the "next-rung" *campaign tracking code* to the transaction. This code can be viewed in the Campaign Report download (see Figure 17.13).

For all of this to work, when Paul set up each Engagement Page, he assigned the following campaign tracking codes:

PAUL'S CAMPAIGN TRACKING CODES

Engagement Page	Current Grade	Earned Grade	Channel	Campaign Tracking Code	Campaign Description
C offer	D	C	EM	C-Oct14	Treadwater Difference Video
B offer	C	B	EM	B-Oct14	Private Label Sample Kit
A offer	B	A	EM	A-Oct14	Forecasting Tool

Figure 17.12 Paul's A-Offer Engagement Page

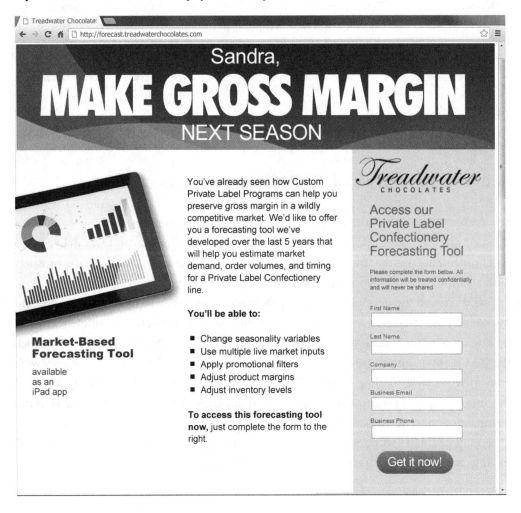

Figure 17.13 Campaign Report Download

You have 2 leads from your "D-Rung: ARM Analyst Study" page

Create CSV of Leads

	Date/Time Submitted	IP Address	Variant	Current grade	Channel	Campaign	Campaign desc	First name	Last name	Email
2	10/10/14 08:22 AM UTC	00.000.000.00	a	D	EM	C-Oct14	ARM Analyst Study	Sandra	Weaver	sandra.weaver@tobys.com
1	10/10/14 08:07 AM UTC	00.000.000.00	a	D	EM	C-Oct14	ARM Analyst Study	Jill	Watts	jill.watts@...

Here's a visual summary of the entire conversion tracking and reporting process beginning with building a list from the Engagement Spreadsheet (see Figure 17.14).

On Engagement Page web forms: Under the simplest version of the Beast Marketing System, a prospect will reach the Engagement Page, and the web form will be blank. That means if your prospect is a C grade and responds to your B offer, he'll be on the verge of filling out the same form for the third time. Frustrating for him, right? It may be, but keep in mind that the last time he filled out your form, it was a month ago. Besides, there are only four fields for him to complete. This is a minor inconvenience you'll be putting your prospects through to keep your system simple. If you decide to use your own web coder, the BeastMachine, or a marketing automation system, then you'll have the option of this web form being prepopulated with your prospects' personal information when your prospects reach your Engagement Page.

Figure 17.14 Tracking and Reporting a Conversion

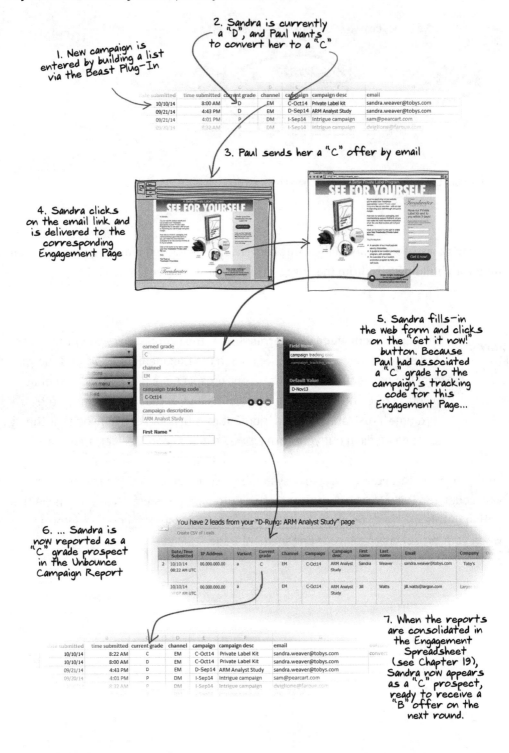

1. New campaign is entered by building a list via the Beast Plug-In

2. Sandra is currently a "D", and Paul wants to convert her to a "C"

3. Paul sends her a "C" offer by email

4. Sandra clicks on the email link and is delivered to the corresponding Engagement Page

5. Sandra fills-in the web form and clicks on the "Get it now!" button. Because Paul had associated a "C" grade to the campaign's tracking code for this Engagement Page...

6. ... Sandra is now reported as a "C" grade prospect in the Unbounce Campaign Report

7. When the reports are consolidated in the Engagement Spreadsheet (see Chapter 19), Sandra now appears as a "C" prospect, ready to receive a "B" offer on the next round.

big, hairy tip

On A/B testing: If you really want to lower your risk and improve the response rates to your Nurture Campaigns, you should test different versions of your email creative, different offers, and different Engagement Pages. Engagement Page tools like Unbounce make it very easy to do this from a results-measurement point of view (this is called A/B testing). Yes, there's a lot of work involved. To reduce the work, you could send your Nurture Campaigns out in smaller batches, with each batch being considered a "test." If the response or conversion rates are below what you expect, you can tweak one of the elements slightly before you send out the next batch. To preserve your sanity, we're going to suggest that you use the batch approach as your testing mechanism unless you feel you have sufficient resources to do full-blown A/B testing.

BEAST BRIEFING: NURTURING YOUR INFLUENCERS

There's another type of Nurture program you should consider. Remember the list of key influencers you developed in Chapter 13? These are individuals who have the ability to affect your sales success by virtue of the people they know or the people who follow them. This influencers list most often includes journalists, bloggers, high-profile industry leaders, analysts, and possibly even business partners.

The idea here is to set up a monthly outbound Nurture program to your list of key influencers that's very similar to the program you developed for your prospects in this chapter. The trick is that this Nurture program has to be entirely un-self-serving (at least initially). You're trying to build a relationship with these influencers by doing things for them and asking nothing in return. We call it the "Acts of Kindness" campaign, and the payback can be a little magical.

HERE'S WHAT YOU DO:
1. Take the top five key influencers on your list.
2. Research what's important to them, what motivates them. Remember that many people, in general, are motivated by recognition, referral, and reward.

3. Develop a mini Engagement Ladder for each, with up to eight ideas you can use to add value to their lives. These can be from the very simple to the more complex:
   - A note that informs them that you are a fan and admire their work.
   - A comment on some work that they have produced, sent to them via email or posted on the site where the work appeared.
   - A mention of them or their work in your blog. Let them know you referenced them.
   - Get a Twitter account and retweet their tweets. Retweeting is remarkably quick and easy to do, but make sure you add a useful comment because a retweet without adding value doesn't promote the conversation. Retweeting your influencers' tweets is generally valued because it extends the potential reach of their messages.
   - Send them articles, studies, or papers that are highly relevant to their work with a note that summarizes the article in a few lines and explains why you thought it might be of interest.
   - Nominate them for a relevant award or industry recognition and letting them know.
   - Send them ideas that you have that emerged from your understanding of their work. The ideas have to be completely non-self-serving. An example: Sophie, our staging entrepreneur, might send an influential real estate writer her thoughts on a story idea concerning affluent homeowners not having any art on their walls because they don't know what to look for or where to buy it, resulting in a disproportionate number of them having bare, white walls.
4. Launch your Acts of Kindness campaign to your influencers using a Breakthrough Campaign to create initial awareness.
5. Add one more key influencer to your list each month until you have a total of 20 key influencers, or whatever number you feel you can comfortably manage.
6. Seek out your key influencers at industry events and introduce yourself. Most will be pleased to actually meet you.

Remember that every touch you make to your key influencers has to be genuine, informed, and add value to their lives in some small way. How does an influencer Nurture program pay you back? You never know. Kindness has a strange way of paying people back. At the very least, after you've established your sincerity (which may take the better part of six months), you will be in a better position to make very small, easy-to-fulfill requests of your influencers. There's also the possibility that they'll write about you and/ or refer you and possibly even become a business acquaintance you can call on. The main ingredients to your success with your influencers are, as always, patience and persistence.

CAVE SCRATCHES

17

- Match content to prospects' Decision Cycle
- "P" buckets, Escape Hatches
- Paul's 3-part plan
- Right list, right offer
- Email tools
- Tracking the flow

NEXT UP

You're now ushering prospects through your Beast Cave and up your Engagement Ladder with frightening regularity. This is called "lead flow," and it represents the life blood of the Beast that is your business. To track it all and manage each successive Nurture Campaign (or hand-off to the sales team), you'll need to consolidate the results from your Engagement Page tool into your Engagement Spreadsheet, which we'll look at more closely in Chapter 19. Before we go there, however, we have one more stop to make. Your customers are prospects too who can represent many years of low-cost, repeat, and referral business for you—if you take care of them. Our next chapter looks at how you turn your customers into long-term Fans, bringing us back, in a sense, to where we started in Step 1.

Step 6 NURTURE

CHAPTER 18

Turning Customers into Fans

What you'll find in this chapter:

- The value of loving your customers
- The relationship bank account
- Customer Lifetime Value
- Retaining and upselling
- Putting customers to work

On average, how long do you keep your customers? A year? Three years? What would happen to your sales if you were to keep the average customer just *one* month longer than you currently do? You might be surprised to learn that it could represent an additional 5 to 10 percent growth for your business. And if you kept the average customer just six months longer than you currently do, it could represent as much as a 50 percent increase in sales for that year—*all without adding a single new customer*. On a rolling basis, this adds up to an awful lot of low-hanging fruit for you.

If you love your customers and work to make them Fans, there's a good chance they'll love you back with sales that make your quest for Big, Hairy, Outrageous Sales Growth that much easier to achieve. And the cost to do this? Minimal, compared to going out and finding new business. So whether you're a startup or an established business, turning those customers you work so hard to acquire into Fans (and keeping them for even a few months longer than the norm) will make your Beast a very efficient machine indeed.

fan

A STICKY BUSINESS

This book has been all about marketing leverage—doing the fewest marketing things possible to achieve the biggest possible sales effect—using finesse over brute force. Over-worked entrepreneurs, possibly more than most businesspeople, need to take advantage of marketing leverage. Turning your customers into Fans may be the best example of doing that yet.

As you know by now, Fans are your most loyal and enthusiastic customers. Fans, you'll recall, are capable of bringing in 2.6 times the revenue of "somewhat satisfied customers" and 14 times the revenue of "somewhat dissatisfied customers."[1] So fans have a double impact on your business: they're generally more profitable, and they stay with you longer than average (see Figure 18.1).

Business customers generally become Fans for the following reasons:

1. Your product or service satisfies a real need for them.
2. They feel they're getting fair value with you.
3. Your company is a pleasure to deal with.
4. There's a strong connection or relationship between your firms.

While the first three are beyond the scope of this book, making sure that your cus-tomers feel strongly connected to your firm is right in our wheelhouse. As you've seen, your job as a marketer is to initiate and nurture relationships so that you encourage an

Figure 18.1 Fan Impact on Lifetime Revenue

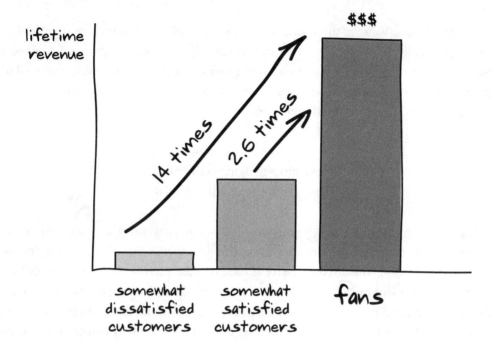

outcome that's beneficial to both parties. This is as true of your customers as it is of your prospects. We call it marketing follow-through—going beyond the closed sale, as we first discussed in Chapter 10. It's based on a concept introduced by Stephen Covey in *The 7 Habits of Highly Effective People*.

Covey saw relationships as "bank accounts" where "emotional units" are deposited and withdrawn. These emotional units are based on trust, and by making deposits through thoughtful or helpful actions, a store of trust is created. By creating a store of trust, relationships can better weather the inevitable ups and downs that they go through. However, if too many withdrawals are made and the emotional bank account reaches low or negative levels, relationships start breaking down.

One of the keys to retaining your customers and turning them into Fans is to ensure that your store of trust is kept high, providing some additional buffer around your product-value-service story. While a large store of trust is never a guarantee that a customer won't depart at some point (there can be many unrelated reasons for a departure), it does create a little more "stickiness" around your business so that being your customer is more desirable than not.

CUSTOMER LIFETIME VALUE (CLV)

Customer Lifetime Value is the measurable expression of everything we've discussed in this chapter so far. At its simplest, CLV can be roughly calculated as the total revenue a customer will generate over a two- to four-year period (or shorter or longer: you need to figure out what your *average* customer lifetime is). While there are far more complicated calculations for CLV, we're partial to this one:

$$\text{CLV} = \text{Year 1 gross margin}$$
$$+ \text{ (future years' gross margin} \times \text{a discount factor)}$$
$$+ \text{ (customer future upsell potential)}$$

Gross margin is used because if you make little or no gross margin on a group of customers, it doesn't matter how long they stick with you; there's a good chance they're not worth having around. The discount factor is used because future cash flow generally isn't as valuable as present cash flow and so is discounted. The amount you discount future cash flows, often called a "hurdle rate," depends on how much uncertainty you expect in the future. In Sophie's case below, she uses a discount rate of 15 percent (producing a *discount balance* of 0.85). In times of greater uncertainty, some companies will apply a hurdle rate of between 25 and 30 percent.

Sophie's CLV

Sophie calculated her CLV to be $154,980 based on these numbers:

($3,000 average selling price × 30 deals per year × 60% gross margin)

+ (the above × 2 more years of customer lifetime × a discount balance of 0.85)

+ (the line immediately above × 10% upsell)

= $154,980

This means every new top agent Sophie signs will be worth about $150,000 of *gross margin* to her over the next three years. Many companies choose to spend a maximum of 30 to 40 percent of their CLV on acquiring a new customer.[2] For Sophie that would represent an acceptable per customer acquisition budget of about $50,000. Put another way, it says Sophie would be willing to invest $50,000 to earn back $150,000 over three years. Because the approaches to marketing we've been discussing in the Beast Marketing System can be so finely tuned and run so cost-effectively, we're inclined to adjust the per acquisition budget to:

5 to 10 percent of LTV for more established companies
10 to 20 percent of LTV for startups

Once again, these are starting ranges that you'll have to validate for your own business situation. Since Sophie has been in business for over 10 years, she used a per customer acquisition budget of 8 percent, or about $12,000 per newly acquired customer. Because her goal was to add 12 new top agents this year, her annual marketing budget was extrapolated as $12,000 × 12 new agents = $144,000, including all the components that went into building her Beast Marketing System. That was the outside number for which a business case could be made. However, Sophie found that her new marketing system achieved her goals at about 55 percent of her upper budget limit—which, of course, made her very happy.

Sophie decided to invest some of that budget surplus into making deposits into the relationship bank accounts of her existing customer base, which improved her retention rates and long-term revenue yields.

SOPHIE'S ADVISORY PANEL

Over time, Sophie added and deleted service offerings from her home staging business. More recently, she discontinued decluttering and renovations as core services, preferring to have third parties handle those functions. While it did make her life easier from a management point of view, the risk was that it would make the lives of her agents a bit more complicated. That's why Sophie, fresh off her experience of building an Engagement Template with the help of her Very Best Customers, decided that she would again reach out to her key agents to get their opinions before making significant changes to her business.

Besides getting valuable input on which services her customers considered dispensable and indispensable, as well as suggestions on possible services she hadn't even thought of, Sophie reasoned that the simple act of asking her customers for their advice would serve to make them feel more involved in her business. So she sent out a personalized email campaign to all of her Very Best Customers (those she most wanted to retain and grow), asking them if they would be interested in joining Staged2Go's advisory board.

Their involvement would be limited to quarterly email surveys asking them for their thoughts on different directions she was considering for her business, and their time was respected, with a commitment of no more than 15 minutes a quarter. Every one of Sophie's Very Best Customers agreed to be on her advisory panel. And over time, she broadened the scope of the survey to include not only service queries but also to solicit agent input on sales support tools, email campaigns, and even truck signage.

Over 90 percent of her advisory panel consistently provided valuable (and free) counsel to her business, which allowed her to avoid unnecessary expenditures ("I never use those kinds of brochures"), made her service offerings far more relevant, and produced a level of engagement from her agents that money couldn't buy. All for a few hours of work every three months.

CONSTANT CONTACT

After her advisory panel was up and running, Sophie developed a "constant contact" campaign—a monthly communication to her Very Best Customers. Aware of her many failed attempts in the past to create monthly newsletters, Sophie this time followed the 80/20 Rule and created a very simple personal update email that she sent to each of her agents at the start of every month. Having seen how the personal text-based email messages she was sending out in her Pursuit and Nurture Campaigns were performing better than any other type of email, Sophie felt that this straightforward approach for her monthly update would have the best chance of success.

Her guiding themes for every update email were:

1. Staged2Go updates
2. Business ideas
3. Industry stories

She didn't try to include all three themes every month, and she intentionally kept the tone friendly and conversational. She also never tried to "sell" anything in her email, instead trying to always create an environment that might naturally produce queries. For example, the "updates" portion of her mailing let her communicate new service offerings or new furniture lines she was carrying, along with her rationale for adding them ("Your feedback suggested . . ."). In the "business ideas" portion she might share insights and tips. For instance, she let her Best Customers know that staging a main floor plus the master bedroom always resulted in quicker turns than a main floor staging alone (soft upselling the master bedroom staging).

And finally, the "industry stories" portion created an opportunity to discuss success stories or include ever-popular before-and-after pictures, adding testimonials to her communication. Everything she wrote always included links to her website or some other relevant website, allowing her customers to explore her topics further. It also let Sophie gauge the interest level of her audience by reviewing her email reporting to see who clicked on what links.

In fact, Sophie found that her simple, personalized update email was opened, on average, by 45 percent of her Very Best Customers, and of those, up to 50 percent clicked through on the links she provided.

Consistency is the key to success on these kinds of "constant contact" mailings. If you're thinking of doing one to your Very Best Customers, you might want to enlist the help of your marketing assistant to put this together and make sure it gets out the door every month.

ONE-QUESTION SURVEY

You'll recall that back in Step 1, Sophie sent a one-question survey to her entire customer base to discover her Beast Potential score and help her identify her Best Customers. When she reviewed it later, she realized that her Beast Potential score was a terrific barometer of her company's health and so she decided to meaasure it on an ongoing basis. In addition to keeping a check on the color of her Beast, it further engaged her customers and helped solicit their input on her business while strengthening their relationship with Staged2Go, which, of course, created more deposits in her relationship bank account.

Sophie sends out her one-question survey to all of her customers once every six months to keep track of her Beast Potential score and to note any trend changes. As a result, Sophie has a very simple early warning system that tells her whether her business is on the right track and whether she's positioning the company to maximize long-term revenue by continuing to meet her Fans' expectations.

When you receive feedback from your customers, you need to do three things: (1) acknowledge their feedback; (2) explain to them what action (or not) you'll be taking as a result of their feedback; and (3) follow up with them to let them know what actions were taken and what outcomes resulted from their feedback. Failure to respond in this fashion can result in serious withdrawals from your relationship bank account. Nobody likes to be ignored when they've made an effort to help.

REFERRAL CAMPAIGNS

The interesting thing about the one-question survey is that it actually asks your customers whether they'd be willing to recommend you to their colleagues or associates. Sophie noted this and decided that if her customers tell her they're willing to refer her, then by gum, she'd take them up on their offer.

Her firm had not had any success with points-based referral programs in the past, so Sophie chose instead to take a very simple approach to her referral program. After vetting it with her customer advisory panel, Sophie started following up every biannual, one-question survey with a personalized email to every customer who answered the "referral" question with a 9 or 10 out of 10. Here's what she sent (see Figure 18.2).

Sophie's referral campaign started generating referrals immediately, with almost 20 percent of those she mailed providing an average of two referrals each. And the best news of all: the referrals were mostly to agents who matched her Best Customer profile. It may be your experience that most referral programs don't seem to work quite this well. The secret to Sophie's referral campaign was that it piggybacked on a satisfaction survey (the one-question survey), and it zeroed in on the customers who cared about her success the most.

Figure 18.2 Sophie's Referral Campaign Email

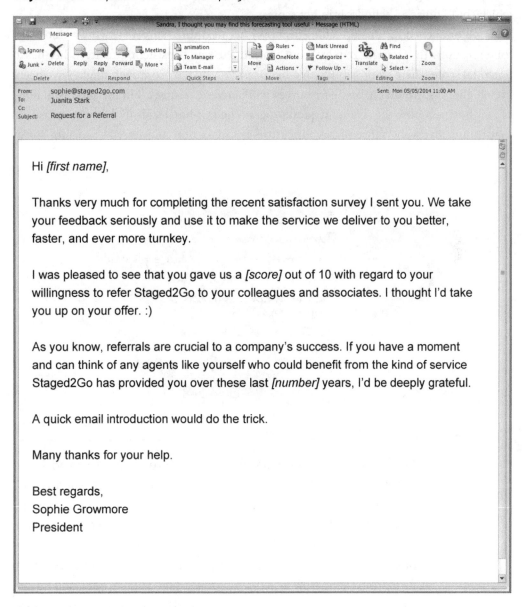

Besides, her advisory panel felt somewhat obligated to refer her. They were "involved" in the concept in the first place.

Sophie's advisory panel had indicated that they didn't think that asking for a referral would handicap her future Beast Potential scores (as in: "if I give Sophie a lower score, she won't bother me for a referral"). In fact, they suggested that knowing a referral request might be coming would probably serve to keep the respondents' answers more honest, which could cause a slight *decay* in her scores.

Sophie watched for this possible effect over her next three surveys (each of which she followed up with a referral request), but instead she saw consistent growth in her Beast Potential score. There's a possibility that her Beast Potential score growth might have been even higher if she didn't follow each survey with a referral request, but the successful flow of new business from the referral request program helped her decide that, by the measures that count, it was the most successful customer satisfaction and referral program she'd ever run.

CAVE SCRATCHES
~ Turn customers into Fans
~ Customer Lifetime Value explained
~ Creating an Advisory Panel
~ Stay in constant contact with Fans
~ Referral campaigns

NEXT UP

By running four very simple customer Nurture programs—an advisory panel, a "constant contact" program, her one-question survey, and the referral program—Sophie helped to substantially increase both the engagement of her agents and the stickiness of her company among her most important customers. That, of course, put her in a strong position to retain her customers longer and to enjoy higher revenue yield from them. Now let's have a look at how Sophie, Paul, and Karim tracked the overall success of their marketing campaigns so they could continue to do more of what worked and less of what didn't.

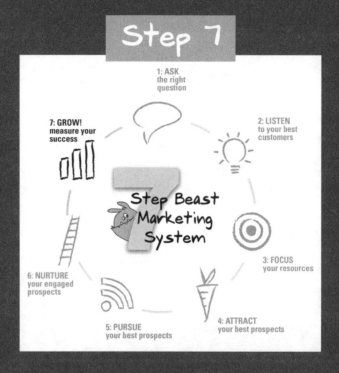

Step 7

1: ASK
the right
question

2: LISTEN
to your best
customers

7: GROW!
measure your
success

7 Step Beast
Marketing
System

3: FOCUS
your resources

6: NURTURE
your engaged
prospects

5: PURSUE
your best prospects

4: ATTRACT
your best prospects

Measure your growth and track your success

Step 7 GROW!

CHAPTER 19

Unleashing Your Beast

What you'll find in this chapter:
- Preparing your Beast Dashboard
- Conversion measures that matter
- Financial measures that matter
- Potentially double your conversion rates
- Troubleshooting

There seems to be an awful lot of traffic running through your Beast Cave. One would think that you must be doing quite well. But are you? And, more to the point, at the rate the traffic is flowing through your Beast Cave, will you:

- End the year where you want to from a revenue point of view?
- Do so at a return that's better than leaving your money in the bank?

Unleashing your Beast really depends on being able to predict the answers to these two questions early in your measurement cycle (most often a year) and being able to do something about their outcome before it's too late. Put another way: "If you can't measure something, you can't understand it. If you can't understand it, you can't control it. If you can't control it, you can't improve it."[1]

To achieve the Big, Hairy, Outrageous Sales Growth we've been promising, you need to track your progress on an ongoing basis so you can stop doing what's not working and double down on what is working. There's no faster path to growth.

THE FOUR CONVERSION RATES THAT MATTER

Let's bring back our Beast Cave drawing one more time (see Figure 19.1). What you see in this diagram are the four essential conversion rates that you need to track as your prospects make their journey through your Cave from prospect to customer and, finally, to Fan.

We first defined these measures in Chapter 10, but here's a reminder:

1. **Prospect Engagement Rate (PER)** measures the percentage of your Beast Prospects who've engaged with you by filling out a web form for one of your offers. They're identified, and they're on your Engagement Ladder. Over the year, you should convert 38 percent of your Beast Prospects to Engaged Prospects. (Beast Prospects are those you defined and selected in the "Target" portion of your Engagement Template.)
2. **Marketing Conversion Rate (MCR)** measures the percentage of Engaged Prospects on your Ladder who've become Sales-Ready Leads because they've expressed a level of interest that's best handled by a sales rep. Over the year, you should convert 20 percent of your Engaged Prospects to Sales-Ready Leads.
3. **Sales Conversion Rate (SCR)** measures the percentage of Sales-Ready Prospects who've been converted into customers by your sales team. Over the year, you should convert 35 percent of your Sales-Ready Leads to customers.
4. **Fan Conversion Rate (FCR)** measures the percentage of customers who've been converted into Fans through your efforts to Nurture them. Over the year, you should be able to convert 60 percent of your customers to Fans.

There's a world of measures you can track, of course, but if you can keep these four numbers in your sights, you'll be in a strong position to fill your Beast's belly exactly as you planned to. Let's examine each so you can understand why we think they're important, where to find them, and how to use them. But first, you need to set up your Beast Dashboard.

Figure 19.1 Conversion Rates (Annualized)

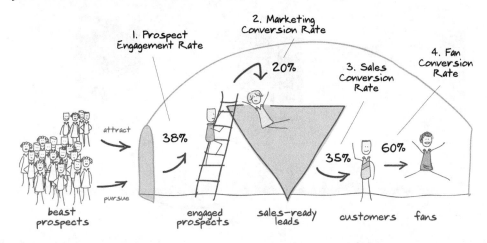

About one day a month of administrative work will be required to ensure your measurements are accurate and meaningful. You shouldn't be the one doing this administrative work. You probably won't like it, and no doubt you have a thousand other jobs that need doing. Gathering and updating conversion results on your Engagement Spreadsheet is a perfect job for your ubiquitous marketing assistant. Just a tip.

TRACK YOUR SUCCESS

Your Beast Dashboard tracks the progress and the results of your marketing campaigns against the four essential conversion rates. You'll find your Beast Dashboard under the "Beast Dashboard" tab of your Engagement Spreadsheet (see Figure 19.2). If you download the starter Engagement Spreadsheet from http://tools.FeedTheBeast.biz, it'll all be preloaded and preformatted for you.

QR Code
Engagement Spreadsheet

Figure 19.2 Beast Dashboard Tab

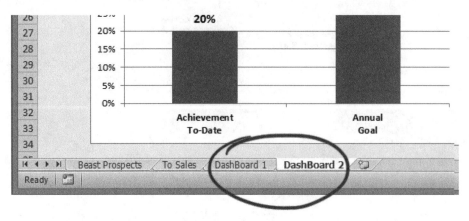

For your Beast Dashboard to do what you want it to do, there's a monthly routine that you'll need to follow to bring all the prospect conversion data from your Engagement Pages into your Engagement Spreadsheet. Once all of your prospect conversion data has been consolidated into one place, you'll be able to see exactly what's working for you and what isn't. Where do you find all this prospect conversion data? You've been using it in earlier chapters. It comes from the Campaign Report that you downloaded from each of your Engagement Pages after every campaign from Unbounce.com (see Figure 19.3).

Figure 19.3 Prospect Conversion Data

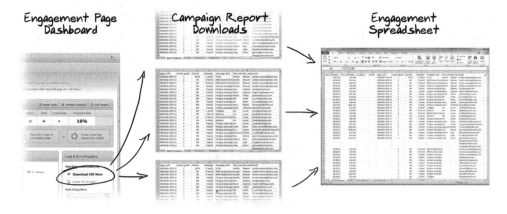

BE PATIENT

When you run your monthly marketing campaigns, you'll likely be tempted to go to your Engagement Page Dashboard (e.g., Unbounce.com) to see how you did (see Figure 19.4). Don't rush things. Let a week pass before you inspect your results. That one week ensures that most of your results will have been recorded for that campaign. Naturally, email results come in faster than direct mail results, but we've found that for virtually every Beastly campaign you run, you'll have 95 percent of the results you need after a week.

Figure 19.4 Engagement Page Dashboard

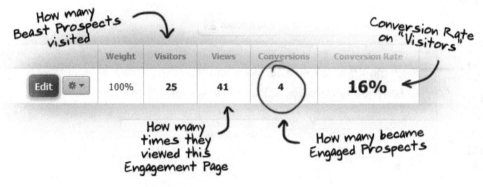

A week after your monthly campaign has run, go to your Engagement Page Dashboard and download your Campaign Report for that month's campaign.

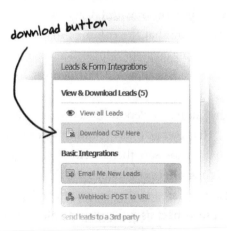

You'll end up with one or more CSV Campaign Report spreadsheets on your computer (CSV stands for "comma separated variable"). When you open them, you'll find that a CSV file is just a spreadsheet file by another name. Keep in mind that each campaign you run could have multiple Engagement Pages associated with it. These pages would be identical except for their slightly different tracking codes. (As you saw in Chapter 8, it's easy to set these up for a campaign.)

Having different Engagement Pages lets you track the performance of each of your marketing channels (for instance, having one page each for direct mail, email, PPC, SEO, and/or other Attract programs) as well as test different creative approaches and offers so you can determine which approach produces the best results and which you should discontinue.

big, hairy tip

Each month, make sure to download the results from each of the Engagement Pages you set up for that month's campaign.

COLLECTING AND SORTING YOUR RESULTS

Your next step is to open each CSV Campaign Report spreadsheet you downloaded from your Engagement Page Dashboard, and then copy and paste the contents of the file (except the first row) into the next empty row of your Engagement Spreadsheet (see Figure 19.5).

It's critical that you make sure that the columns match up between all of your conversion spreadsheets and the Engagement Spreadsheet you're pasting them into. If you followed the Engagement Spreadsheet set-up instructions in Chapter 9, you shouldn't have any problems.

All the details of each Campaign Report spreadsheet will be preserved within your Engagement Spreadsheet. That means that if Sandra Weaver (a D prospect) found your blog, clicked on the banner ad she saw there, went to the associated Engagement Page, and decided to take the C-rung offer presented, she (1) would have been captured in the Campaign Report spreadsheet related to that Engagement Page; and (2) would now show up in your Engagement Spreadsheet as a C prospect, along with the relevant campaign tracking code.

Figure 19.5 Collecting the Results on Your Engagement Spreadsheet

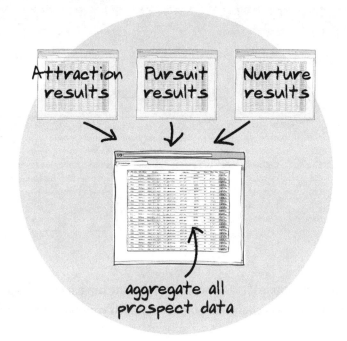

As you've seen, the campaign tracking code will tell you what campaign and channel she came in through (see Figure 19.6 for a reminder). Then, when you organize your Engagement Spreadsheet by using the sort option on the Beast Plug-In, you'd see Sandra's complete marketing history with your company, with her most current interaction ("PL Kit") and prospect grade ("C") at the top.

SO HOW ARE *YOU* DOING?

Now that you've updated your Engagement Spreadsheet, you're ready to go back to your Beast Dashboard tab (as opposed to the Engagement Dashboard) to see your overall progress against your annual goals (see Figure 19.8). Once you've updated your Engagement Spreadsheet with your Campaign Reports, the dashboard will automatically run the calculations to tell you the status of the four conversion rates we identified above. You'll notice there are actually two dashboard tabs on your spreadsheet.

Figure 19.6 Sorting Your Engagement Spreadsheet

	F				I	J	K	L	M
1	current_grade	channel	campaign	campaign_desc	first_name	last_name	email		comp
2	C	BLOG	C-Nov14	PL Kit	Sandra	Weaver	sandra.weaver@tobys.com		
3	D	EM	D-Oct14	ARM Analyst Study	Sandra	Weaver	sandra.weaver@tobys.com		
4	P	EM	D-Oct14	ARM Analyst Study	Sandra	Weaver	sandra.weaver@tobys.com		
5	P	DM	I-Sep14	Intrigue campaign	Sandra	Weaver	sandra.weaver@tobys.com		
6	P	DM	I-Sep14	Intrigue campaign	Sam	Masters	sam@pearcart.com		
7	P	DM	I-Sep14	Intrigue campaign	Diane	Viglione	dviglione@farque		
	P	DM	I-Sep14	Intrigue campaign	Albert	Talent	atalent@		
		DM	I-Sep14	Intrigue campaign	Bill	Smith			

Beast Plug-In menu:
- Activate Beast Plug-In
- Sort Prospects ▶ Sort by Prospect / Sort by Channel / Sort by Campaign / Sort by Grade
- Export Lists ▶

Think of Beast Dashboard 1 as your number crunching page. It gives you all the detailed analysis and lets you change the inputs to match your business requirements (see Figure 19.7).

Think of Beast Dashboard 2 as your big picture page. It graphically summarizes and displays your key conversion metrics and shows you at a glance how well you're currently performing against the annual goals you set (see Figure 19.8).

Figure 19.7 Beast Dashboard 1 Inputs

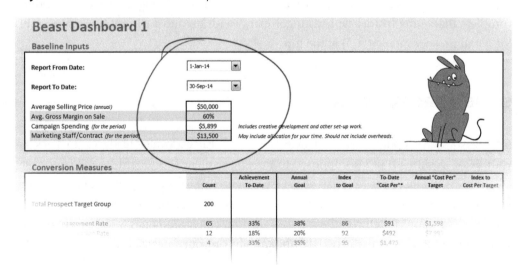

Beast Dashboard 1

Baseline Inputs

Report From Date:	1-Jan-14
Report To Date:	30-Sep-14
Average Selling Price *(annual)*	$50,000
Avg. Gross Margin on Sale	60%
Campaign Spending *(for the period)*	$5,899	Includes creative development and other set-up work.
Marketing Staff/Contract *(for the period)*	$13,500	May include allocation for your time. Should not include overheads.

Conversion Measures

	Count	Achievement To-Date	Annual Goal	Index to Goal	To-Date "Cost Per"*	Annual "Cost Per" Target	Index to Cost Per Target
Total Prospect Target Group	200						
Engagement Rate	65	33%	38%	86	$91	$1,598	
Rate	12	18%	20%	92	$492	$2,99	
	4	33%	35%	95	$1,475		

Figure 19.8 Beast Dashboard 2 Inputs

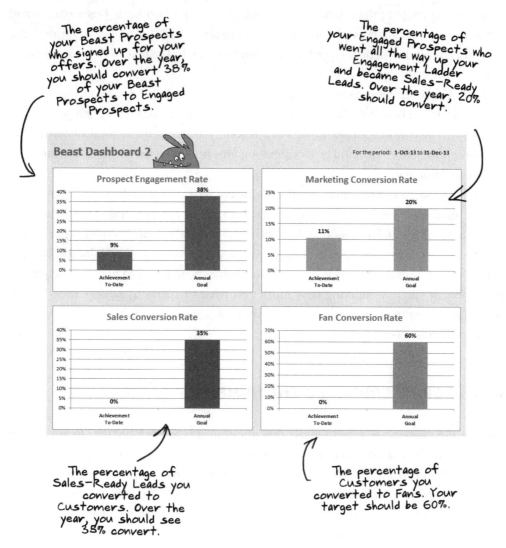

The percentage of your Beast Prospects who signed up for your offers. Over the year, you should convert 38% of your Beast Prospects to Engaged Prospects.

The percentage of your Engaged Prospects who went all the way up your Engagement Ladder and became Sales-Ready Leads. Over the year, 20% should convert.

The percentage of Sales-Ready Leads you converted to Customers. Over the year, you should see 35% convert.

The percentage of Customers you converted to Fans. Your target should be 60%.

For each of the four metrics you see on Beast Dashboard 2, you'll be comparing your "achievement to date" on the left to your "annual goal" on the right. Seasonality and other weightings notwithstanding, by midyear, you'd like to see the left bar somewhere around half the height of the right bar. If you're lagging behind, you'll want to investigate the cause. By year-end, you'd ideally like to see the bars about even. If your business is seasonal, or if your sales are expected to weigh toward one end of the year or the other, you'll have to adjust your performance benchmarking accordingly.

The annual goals for each of these measures are set by you in Beast Dashboard 1, as is the date range of the report. At any time, you can go into Beast Dashboard 1 and adjust your annual goals as you see fit.[2] The default goals you see on Beast Dashboard 2 represent the kind of performance that can result in *near 100 percent year-over-year revenue growth.*

Is this kind of growth actually possible by following the 7-Step Beast Marketing System? Absolutely. If you take the 7 Steps to heart and do the work, Big, Hairy, Outrageous Sales Growth will be within your reach. We've consistently achieved these kinds of conversion rates over hundreds of demand generation programs in the last decade by following these very same guidelines.

Are you guaranteed to experience these kinds of results? We wish we could say "yes," but the answer is "no." Nothing is guaranteed, in life or in marketing. Many factors go into determining your success, including such fundamental building blocks as the quality of the salespeople you hire and whether your product or service is actually meeting the market's need. (Remember, your one-question survey is designed to help you determine this.) Now, if you're wondering how much you need to spend to achieve these results and what kind of return you can expect on your investment, let's turn to our three entre-preneurs for answers.

WHEN SOPHIE CRUNCHED THE NUMBERS

Early in the process, we asked Sophie this question: If you had $20,000 to spend and you could invest it in marketing your company, would you? Her answer was: "I would if I were confident that my $20,000 would return more than leaving it in a savings account." Like every entrepreneur, Sophie wants to get the best return on her money possible. She started her business because, at least in part, she believed that the Beast she created could provide her with greater financial reward than she was ever likely to get by investing her money elsewhere. And for Sophie, one of the greatest appeals of the 7-Step Beast Marketing System was its thoroughly systematic approach to lowering marketing risk.

True to her word, in the first quarter of year 1, Sophie decided to invest almost $20,000 in marketing to the top 362 agents in her market. Her average sale per agent ran around $3,000, but she knew that top agents were good for between 20 and 40 stagings per year. What's more, her working relationships with top agents usually lasted an average of three years. Let's follow along as Sophie tracked the results of her marketing programs through the first quarter of the year.

Sophie's Financial Dashboard, which she found by scrolling further down on Beast Dashboard 1, looks like this (see Figure 19.9).

Sophie's return on her marketing investment (ROMI) is currently sitting at *minus* 91 percent. That's because she's spent $19,900 so far this year, and that investment has returned only one sale for $3,000 (at 60 percent gross margin, in case you're checking the math). But this was a temporary situation. First off, that calculation didn't account for that initial sale having an expected annual value of $90,000 ($3,000 × 30 stagings), nor did it yet measure other sales that were still developing and that would come in from that initial $19,900 spend. There's always a lag in sales as prospects tarry through your Cave.

Secondly, the $19,900 included an up-front investment in her Engagement Ladder content, her web "cloning" movie, and other elements that went toward bringing in her goal of 12 new top agents by year-end. These costs were amortized out over the year as her marketing spending normalized through the remainder of the year. Sophie knew her ROMI would improve significantly by midyear.

The Cave lag-effect was also seen in Sophie's Cost per Customer measure. Both her cost per Engaged Prospect and her cost per Sales-Ready Lead were very much in line with her goals, but her Cost per Customer in the first quarter was very high at $19,900, since the full marketing spend was allocated to just one customer. Her marketing programs were performing well, pulling prospects through her Beast Cave and up the ladder toward

Figure 19.9 Sophie Looks at Her Financials

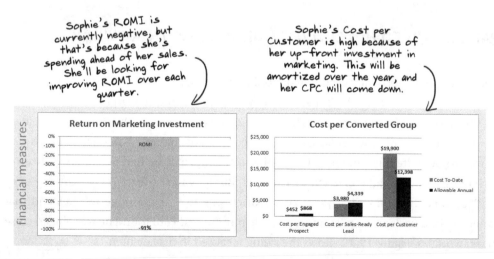

Figure 19.10 Sophie's Financial Beast Dashboard 1

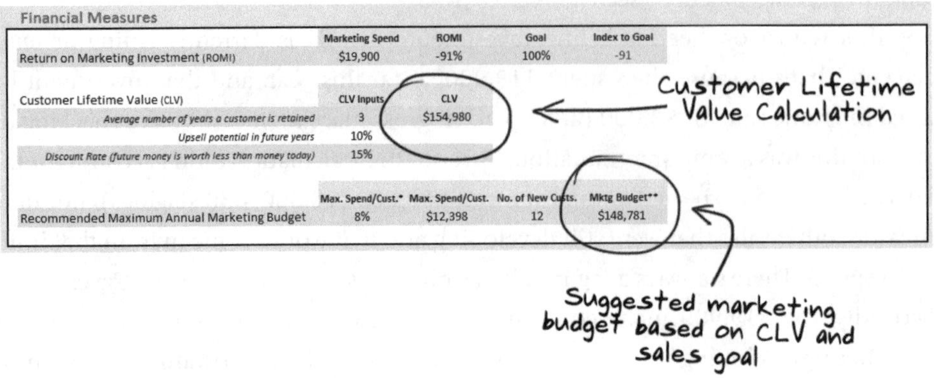

conversion. Yes, final conversions (from Sales-Ready Lead to customer) lagged behind her two other indicators, but she knew they would normalize shortly.

You'll notice Sophie's Financial Beast Dashboard 1 in Figure 19.10 suggests that her marketing budget for the year should be around $150,000, yet her first quarter spending of $19,900 was more in line with an annual budget of under $80,000. Why? Based on her early results, Sophie was confident she could acquire 12 new agents over the course of the year on the smaller budget. And those 12 would translate into over $1 million in incremental gross sales for Staged2Go—representing 110 percent year-over-year sales growth.

PAUL DOUBLED HIS CONVERSION RATE–WITH A TWEAK

When Paul, our chocolate entrepreneur, looked at his Beast Dashboard 2 in April, he was satisfied with his PER and MCR because they were both on or ahead of plan (see Figure 19.11). However, Paul was watching his Sales Conversion Rate closely. His plan had called for one sale in April, and so far he had none. Three of the four Sales-Ready Leads had proven to be quite high quality, but in spite of the fact that he had personally called on each of them, none had converted to a sale yet. But they were frustratingly close.

Paul knew that he had a good chance of closing two of the three in May, and that would get him back on plan. Fast forward one month, and Paul found he was able to close those two sales. Figure 19.12 shows the swing it caused in his key metrics.

Figure 19.11 Paul's Beast Dashboard 2 in April

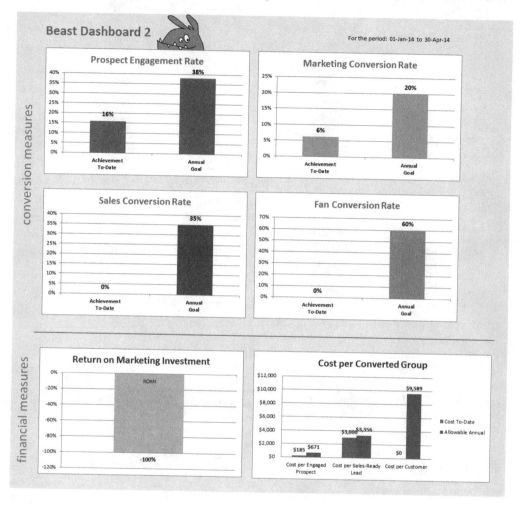

By closing the two sales, the return on his marketing investment went significantly positive in spite of new marketing spending in the month. His MCR and SCR numbers popped way above mere respectability, and his costs per converted group all sat nicely below his maximum allowance. While Paul's April SCR number had him a little concerned, the fact that he had been able to do "what if" scenarios with his Beast Dashboard made him feel like he was in more control than he had ever been before in his quest to find 10 new private label customers by year-end. At an average selling price of $60,000 each, 10 new customers would more than double the private label portion of his business.

Figure 19.12 Paul's Beast Dashboard 2 in May

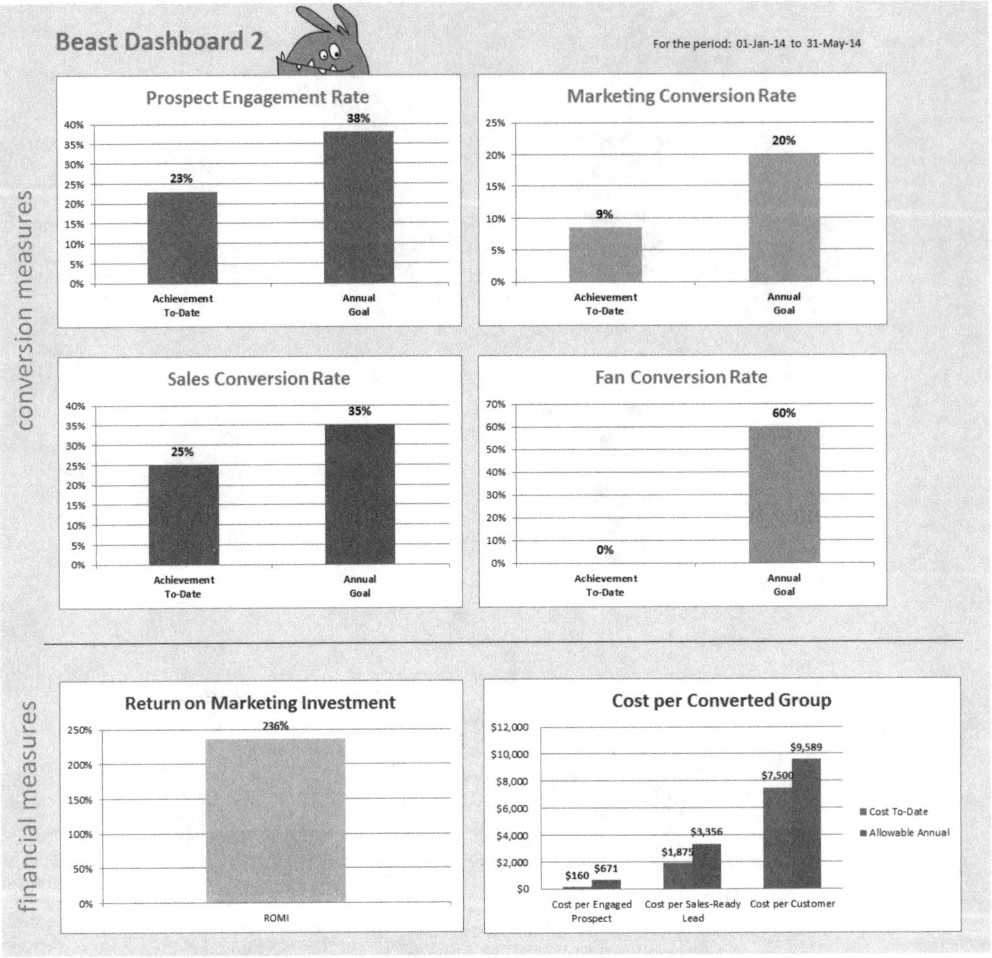

He'd already closed two sales, and he had just eight more to go. As he left the office for home that day in May, Paul found that his step had just a little more bounce in it.

BIGFATDATA WAS GROWING FAST, BUT KARIM NEEDED HELP

Karim, our software entrepreneur, had diligently run a series of Attraction, Pursuit, and Nurture Campaigns to his target group of 200 Beast Prospects. By the end of September, he was seeing very encouraging results on his Beast Dashboard 2 (see Figure 19.13).

Figure 19.13 Karim's Beast Dashboard 2

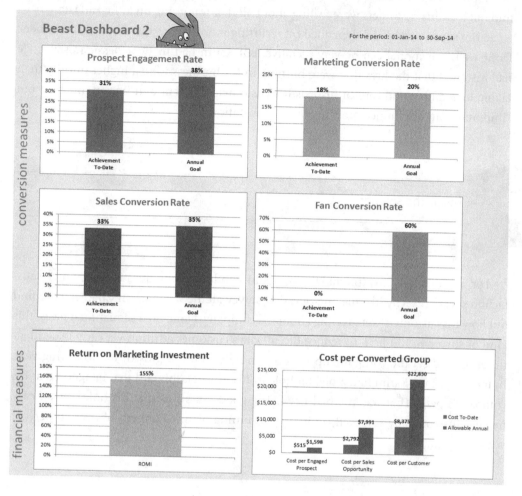

Following the 7-Step Beast Marketing System, he'd been making a substantial return on his marketing investment, having already secured four of his targeted five new customers in the consumer electronics space this year. What was even more impressive, he'd been achieving his goals at a substantially lower cost per converted group (Engaged Prospects, Sales-Ready Leads, and Customers) than his business model had projected (at least partly because he was able to do all his web work in-house). At an average selling price of $50,000, Karim was well on his way to a sizable increase in his business this year.

The only spoiler to be seen on Karim's Beast Dashboard? It was now September, and he hadn't converted any customers to Fans. The reality is that Karim has resembled something closer to a headless chicken these last nine months, running around managing product development, customer support, marketing, and sales. As a result, he didn't have time to find out how his customers were feeling about all that was going on at BigFatData.

Karim's business model depended on recurring monthly revenue from his customers. Done well, this model can be very lucrative. But Karim had made a classic mistake. He had assumed that the fires that were burning in his business were a higher priority than taking incredibly good care of his existing customers. "Urgent and important" beat out "important but not immediately urgent." The solution?

marketing assistant

This is the solution.

For a very small investment, Karim could conduct a one-question customer satisfaction survey (exactly like his one-question survey all the way back in Chapter 1) to find out how his customers were feeling about his company. Done on a semiannual basis, this kind of survey would help to reduce BigFatData's customer attrition via early issue identification and set the company up for even more significant growth the following year. In the meantime, Karim had a big, fat hole in his Beast Dashboard that he ignored at his company's peril. That was the bad news. The good news was that his hole was an easy fix, and his company was well on its way to hitting planned growth of over 70 percent year-over-year.

CAVE SCRATCHES

19

~ 4 key conversion metrics

~ Downloading and sorting your results

~ Beast Dashboards

~ Sophie, Paul, and Karim crunch the numbers, tweak ... and grow

NEXT UP

Congratulations! You've just completed one full cycle of the 7-Step Beast Marketing System. What's next? Get ready to do it all again, except more and more, faster and faster, bigger and bigger. Outrageously bigger.

Maintaining Outrageous Growth

When we began this book, we asked you to think of the 7-Step cycle as your marketing flywheel, because each step you complete causes the wheel to rotate with increasing speed, energy, and momentum. Well, we've come full circle. Quite literally. And now it's up to you to continue the momentum—to go back to the beginning and keep involving your customers in your business, keep focusing your strategy, and keep ushering a rich flow of Engaged Prospects through your Beast Cave.

What isn't on the wheel but underpins every step of it is patience and persistence. "What makes a great entrepreneur? Tenacity," says Brad Feld, one of the world's leading venture capitalists and entrepreneur's entrepreneur. It's the not-so-hidden secret to Big, Hairy, Outrageous Sales Growth. Along with these, of course:

1. Ask your Fans for help
2. Listen closely to their answers
3. Focus your resources
4. Attract your Beast Prospects
5. Pursue your Beast Prospects
6. Nurture your Cave guests
7. Grow your Beast

Ah. The 7 Steps. They may be simple, but they're not easy. But of course, nothing worthwhile ever is. Out of these 7 Steps you'll have forged a marketing system that lets you

do more with less and, in doing so, build an unbeatable Beast that is your business. "But I'm an entrepreneur, not a marketer," you say. "Why should I learn these marketing techniques?" Because marketing isn't *part* of your business; it *is* your business.

Here's to the round pegs in the square holes—the entrepreneurs who dare to think big and scale big. Those who want to change the world and are happy to take others along for the ride. Are you ready for your 15 years of fame? Then get ready to stop reading and start doing. "Say what you need to say, then leave," says Seth Godin. We're taking his advice.

Thank you, and goodbye.

Oh. And good luck!

Notes

Chapter 1

1. Howard Ploman, "Net Promoter Score—The Search for the Magic Pill," InfoQuest International, 2008.
2. James Allen, Frederick F. Reichheld, and Barney Hamilton, "The Three 'Ds' of Customer Experience," HBS Working Knowledge archives, #5075. Excerpted from "Tuning In to the Voice of Your Customer," *Harvard Management Update*, vol. 10, no. 10, October 2005. See http://hbswk.hbs.edu/archive/5075.html.
3. Frederick F. Reichheld, "Learning from Customer Defections," *Harvard Business Review*, March 1996. See http://hbr.org/1996/03/learning-from-customer-defections/ar/1.
4. Frederick F. Reichheld, "The One Number You Need to Grow," *Harvard Business Review*, December 2003. See http://hbr.org/2003/12/the-one-number-you-need-to-grow/ar/1. The Beast Potential score is based on the Net Promoter Score, developed and tested across 14,000 companies by Frederick Reichheld in 2003. For more information on the Net Promoter Score and its application to B2B companies, please visit www.satmetrix .com.

Chapter 2

1. Paul M. Dholakia and Vicki G. Morewitz, "How Surveys Influence Customers," *Harvard Business Review*, May 2002. See http://hbr.org/2002/05/how-surveys-influence -customers/ar/1.
2. Jacques Bughin, Jonathan Doogan, and Ole Jørgen Vetvik, "A New Way to Measure Word-of-Mouth Marketing," *McKinsey Quarterly*, April 2010. See http://www.mckinseyquarterly .com/A_new_way_to_measure_word-of-mouth_marketing_2567.
3. "Building Effective Landing Pages: Get More Conversions with Lower Bids in Your Online Marketing Campaigns," Marketo.com. See http://docs.cdn.marketo.com/building-effective-landing-pages.pdf?mkt.

Chapter 3

1. Paul Hague, "A Practical Guide to Improving Customer Satisfaction," B2B International, January 2011. See http://www.b2binternational.com/assets/whitepapers/pdf/improving _customer_satisfaction.pdf.
2. Adam Ramshaw, "Net Promoter Score Success Stories and Case Studies," Genroe.com. See http://www.genroe.com/blog/net-promoter-score-success-stories-and-case-studies/984 for useful NPS case studies.
3. This chart was assembled by the authors from publicly available information.

Chapter 4

1. CSO Insights, "2012 Sales Performance Optimization survey." See http://www .csoinsights.com/.

Chapter 5

1. Johannes Bussman, Gregor Harter, Evan Hirsh, *Strategy + Business Magazine* (p. 5), Booz & Company, Inc., 2006. Originally published as "Results-Driven Marketing," Johannes Bussman, Gregor Harter, Evan Hirsh. See http://www.strategy-business.com/ media/file/enews-01-31-06.pdf. The authors were quoting Mike Fritsch from a report entitled "Customer ROI: The New Science of Profitable Customer Relationships," Booz Allen Hamilton, 2005.
2. Content from this section drawn from: Bob Stone, Ron Jacobs, *Successful Direct Marketing Methods*, 8th ed., McGraw-Hill, 2008.

Chapter 7

1. Corporate Executive Board survey of more than 1,400 B2B customers. See http:// www.executiveboard.com/exbd/sales-service/the-end-of-solution-sales/index.page. Also featured in *Harvard Business Review*: "The End of Solution Sales," article by Brent Adamson, Matthew Dixon, and Nicholas Toman, *Harvard Business Review*, July–August 2012. See http://hbr.org/2012/07/the-end-of-solution-sales/ar/1.
2. "2012 Buyersphere Report: The Annual Survey of Changing B2B Buyer Behavior," BaseOne. See http://www.baseone.co.uk/beyond/2012/07/the-great-b2b-social-media-collapse.html.
3. Christine Crandell, "Influencing Your Buyer," Forbes.com, June 26, 2011. See http:// www.forbes.com/sites/christinecrandell/2011/06/26/influencing-your-buyer/.

4. "B2B Content Marketing: 2013 Benchmarks, Budgets, and Trends—North America," p. 17, Content Marketing Institute and Marketing Profs. See http://contentmarketinginstitute .com/wp-content/uploads/2012/11/b2bresearch2013cmi-121023151728-phpapp01-1 .pdf.

Chapter 9

1. Kristin Zhivago, "How to Become Indispensable to Your CEO," MarketingSherpa Special Report, 2008. See http://www.revenuejournal.com/blog/marketers-how-become -indispensable.

Chapter 10

1. "How measurement Can Align Marketing and Sales," MathMarketing.com. See http:// www.mathmarketing.com/how-measurement-can-align-marketing-and-sales.
2. The 30-20-10 Rule is a simplified version of the "Rule of 45" and some work done by the Advertising Research Foundation, which have proven to be good directional indicators over time, where B2B response is concerned. Russell M. Kern, *S.U.R.E.-Fire Direct Response Marketing* (New York: McGraw-Hill, 2001), 149–150; and Bob Stone, *Successful Direct Marketing Methods* (New York: McGraw-Hill, 2008), 201–202.

Chapter 11

1. "comScore Explicit Core Search Share Report, October 2012 vs. September 2012," comScore notes that "Explicit Core Search" excludes contextually driven searches that do not reflect specific user intent to interact with the search results. See http://www.comscore.com/Insights/ Press_Releases/2012/11/comScore_Releases_October_2012_U.S._Search_Engine_Rankings.
2. "Title Tag Best Practices," Seomoz.com, Learn SEO - Resources tab. See http://www. seomoz.org/learn-seo/title-tag.
3. Haydn Shaughnessy, "Who are the top 20 influencers in big data?" Forbes.com. Feb. 3, 2012. See http://www.forbes.com/sites/haydnshaughnessy/2012/02/03/who-are-the-top -20-influencers-in-big-data/.

Chapter 12

1. Google Analytics help page: Traffic Sources Report. See http://support.google.com/ analytics/bin/answer.py?hl=en&answer=1247841.
2. "The Future of Paid Search—Google, Bing, & Beyond," Kissmetrics blog, August 2011. See http://blog.kissmetrics.com/future-of-paid-search/.

3. "2012 B2B Marketing Benchmark Report," p. 9, Optify.net website, see http://www .optify.net/wp-content/uploads/2013/01/Optify-2012-B2B-Marketing-Benchmark -Report.pdf.

4. "Find Keyword Bids for First Page Ad Position," Google AdWords help page, 2012, Google Inc. See http://support.google.com/adwords/bin/answer.py?hl=en&answer=2472712.

5. Source for Hubspot: *Introductory Guide to Paid Search*, Hubspot.com, see http://offers. hubspot.com/marketing-ebook/introductory-guide-to-paid-search; and source for Geddes: Brad Geddes, *Advanced Google AdWords*, 2nd ed. (Indianapolis, Sybex/John Wiley & Sons, 2012).

6. "comScore Introduces Validated Campaign Essentials™ (vCE), a Holistic Measurement Solution That Validates Advertising Impressions and Audiences Reached with Digital Advertising Campaigns," comScore.com press release, January 18, 2012. See http://www.comscore.com/Insights/Press_Releases/2012/1/comScore_Introduces _Validated_Campaign_Essentials.

7. "2012 U.S. Digital Future in Focus," comScore.com white paper, February 9, 2012. See http://www.comscore.com/Insights/Presentations_and_Whitepapers/2012/2012_US _Digital_Future_in_Focus.

8. Joanna Lord, "Leveraging Retargeting for SEO Success," SEOmoz.com slideshare presentation, October 2011. See http://www.slideshare.net/JoannaLord/leveraging-the -power-of-retargeting-for-seo.

9. "Search Retargeting—How It Works," Chango.com website. See http://www.chango .com/solutions/search-retargeting/how-it-works/.

Chapter 13

1. Forrester Research, Inc., "The Who and How of Influencing Customers' IT Decisions," August 2011. See http://www.forrester.com/The+Who+And+How+Of+Influencing+ Customers+IT+Decisions/-/E-WEB8093.

2. Forrester Research, Inc., "B2B Marketing Trends and Predictions," February 2012. See http://www.forrester.com/home#/B2B+Marketing+Trends+And+Predictions+For+ 2012/fulltext/-/E-RES60343.

3. Grande Guide #12, "The Grande Guide to B2B Blogging," Eloqua Grande Guides. See http://www.eloqua.com/grande/grande_guide_to_B2B_Blogging.html.

4. Barbara Giamanco and Kent Gregoire, "Tweet Me, Friend Me, Make Me Buy," *Harvard Business Review*, July–August 2012. See http://hbr.org/2012/07/tweet-me -friend-me-make-me-buy/ar/1.

Chapter 14

1. InfoUSA.com. Screenshot by permission.

Chapter 15

1. "Be brave and think differently, Richard Branson tells entrepreneurs at GEC 2012," Smarta, March 13, 2012. See http://www.smarta.com/blog/2012/3/be-brave-and-think -differently-richard-branson-tells-entrepreneurs-at-gec-2012.

Chapter 17

1. David Kirkpatrick, "Email Marketing: The Importance of Lead Nurturing in the Complex B2B Sale," Marketing Sherpa blog, January 19, 2012. See http://sherpablog .marketingsherpa.com/email-marketing/b2b-lead-nurturing-importance/.
2. Lori Wizdo, "The Lead-Nurturing Payoff for the Tech Industry," Forrester Research Inc., 2011.

Chapter 18

1. Howard Ploman, "Net Promoter Score—The Search for the Magic Pill," InfoQuest International, 2008.
2. Bob Stone, *Successful Direct Marketing Methods* (New York: McGraw-Hill, 2008), p. 533.

Chapter 19

1. H. James Harrington, Glen D. Hoffherr, and Robert P. Reid, *Area Activity Analysis: Aligning Work Activities and Measurements to Enhance Business Performance* (New York: McGraw-Hill, 1999), p. 40.
2. There are many sources to determine benchmark conversion numbers. One of the most insightful reviews of conversion rates we've come across is from marketing automation vendor Marketo and may be viewed at http://www.marketo.com/b2b-marketing-resources/best-practices/the-definitive-guide-to-marketing-metrics-and-marketing-analytics.php.

Index

About the Authors

 **Drew Williams** is a serial marketing entrepreneur who sold one of his creations, an internet software company, to a Boston firm for eight figures. For over 30 years, he has successfully marketed everything from television to high-tech to financial services to chocolate, as head of marketing for a $10 billion company, a $100 million company, a $10 million company, and a bunch of $1 million companies. He has also been an award-winning advertising copywriter, working for and with some of the largest advertising agencies in the world. *Feed the Startup Beast* is the culmination of his experience and passion in building and marketing startups. He is currently managing partner at nuRevenue Partners (nuRevenue.com). Drew and his family live in Toronto, Canada.

 **Jonathan Verney** is an entrepreneur in his own right, having founded and sold his interest in a leading Toronto-based communications agency in the 1990s. In addition to *Feed the Startup Beast*, he has coauthored two books with Patricia Lovett-Reid, chief financial commentator for CTV News, Canada's largest private television network. A strong, insightful writer, Jonathan is currently president of The Corporate Storyteller Inc. (CorporateStoryteller.ca), a story-driven communications agency. His passion is helping businesses articulate their vision and their story.